A BRIEF GUIDE TO

OZ

PAUL SIMPSON

ROBINSON

RUNNING PRESS
PHILADELPHIA · LONDON

Constable & Robinson Ltd
55–56 Russell Square
London WC1B 4HP
www.constablerobinson.com

First published in the UK by Robinson,
an imprint of Constable & Robinson Ltd, 2013

A copy of the British Library Cataloguing in
Publication data is available from the British Library

ISBN 978-1-47210-988-0 (paperback)
ISBN 978-1-47211-036-7 (ebook)

1 3 5 7 9 10 8 6 4 2

First published in the United States in 2014 by Running Press Book Publishers,
A Member of the Perseus Books Group

Books published by Running Press are available at special discounts for bulk purchases
in the United States by corporations, institutions, and other organizations. For more
information, please contact the Special Markets Department at the Perseus Books
Group, 2300 Chestnut Street, Suite 200, Philadelphia, PA 19103, or call (800) 810-4145,
ext. 5, or email special.markets@perseusbooks.com.

US ISBN 978-0-7624-5239-2
US Library of Congress Control Number: 2013942504

9 8 7 6 5 4 3 2 1
Digit on the right indicates the number of this printing

Running Press Book Publishers
2300 Chestnut Street
Philadelphia, PA 19103-4371

Visit us on the web!
www.runningpress.com

Typeset by TW Typesetting, Plymouth, Devon

Printed and bound in the UK

This book is gratefully dedicated to Alison Dewdney, Jackie Cannon, Janet Brailey, Linda Jones, Maeve Larkin, Laura Billings, Tamsie Flood-Murphy, Frances Novis, David Purcell, Sheila Peart and Angela O'Hara – Sophie's guides along St Wilfrid's Yellow Brick Road for the past seven years.

'I have learned to regard fame as a will-o-the-wisp,
which when caught, is not worth the possession;
but to please a child is a sweet and lovely thing
that warms one's heart and brings its own reward.'
– L. Frank Baum

CONTENTS

INTRODUCTION: TRAVELLING DOWN THE YELLOW BRICK ROAD

There are no doubt millions of people who, if you were to ask them what they can recall about *The Wizard of Oz*, would mention Judy Garland and the Yellow Brick Road, the Scarecrow, the Tin Man, the Cowardly Lion and the Wizard himself. They'd probably quote the Witch's line about getting Dorothy 'and her little dog too' and almost certainly cackle in a mad manner. Ask about the creator of Oz, and some might recognize the name 'L. Frank Baum', particularly if it was given to them among a list of possibilities. In Britain or Canada, they may recall the reality TV show that searched for a Dorothy for a new stage production. But ask them about Ozma or Billina; the Hungry Tiger or Tik-Tok; the Nome King or the Deadly Desert, and chances are high that you'll just get a blank stare.

That indicates both how much the 1939 MGM musical version of *The Wizard of Oz* has become part of our psyches over the last seventy-five years – it's regularly voted as one of the top, if not *the* top, film of all time – and how little its origins are known. Lyman Frank Baum didn't just write one tale about Oz; he penned fourteen novels, and a collection of short stories. After his death, other writers continued the saga, and there are forty tales in all which are regarded as the official history of Oz. Amazing as it seems now, Dorothy Gale and the Cowardly Lion don't even appear in the first sequel (although on the rare occasions that story has been translated to the screen, at the very least Dorothy has usually been incorporated).

There's not just been one Oz film either: while *The Wizard of Oz* is celebrating its 75th birthday in 2014, preparations are underway for a sequel to Disney's prequel, *Oz the Great and Powerful*. But even the 1939 movie was merely another in a long line of live-action versions of the children's story: legendary names from Hollywood history, including Hal Roach, Harold Lloyd and Oliver Hardy (shortly before he teamed up with Stan Laurel), all appeared in stories set in Oz – although it's fair to say that some of these deviated quite considerably from Baum's vision.

There have been plenty of other films between 1939 and 2013: Disney brought a darker vision of Oz to the screen in the much-maligned *Return to Oz* and Michael Jackson jived his way to see *The Wiz*. There have been television adaptations featuring Shirley Temple and the Muppets. It's been a favoured choice by animators, with a major Japanese anime series in the mid-1980s adapting four of Baum's early Oz books.

And Oz has been ripe for reinvention. *Alice in Wonderland* director Tim Burton worked on an update entitled *Lost in Oz*, and a pilot episode with the same title was made a couple of years later. (Sadly neither developed into a series.) In 2007, the American Sci-Fi Channel was behind *Tin Man*, a complete reworking of the story that achieved stellar ratings for the channel. At the time of writing, Warner Bros. Television are looking at a series that will infuse the Oz universe with the spirit of the *Game of Thrones* TV show – a much bleaker and less innocent world than L. Frank Baum could ever have imagined.

This *Brief Guide to Oz* isn't a history of the land of Oz: if you want to see how all the pieces fit together within the chronology of the land, then the website The Royal Timeline of Oz (http://timelineuniverse.net/Oz/OzMap.htm) is highly recommended. There you'll find all the official and unofficial stories melded into one – moderately consistent – whole.

This book is a guide to the many different visions of Oz. Starting with a look at the lives of the two main Royal Historians of Oz – L. Frank Baum and his successor Ruth Plumly Thompson, who actually wrote more official Oz stories than its creator – we then examine the so-called 'Famous Forty', the tales that laid down the rules of Oz.

From there we look at Oz on screen: its roots in the silent era, including the trio of films produced by Baum himself, and the long journey that the MGM musical took to the screen. After a good look at the Judy Garland movie, we examine Disney's attempts to bring Oz to the screen which culminated in *Return to Oz*, and more recently *Oz the Great and Powerful*. There's also a detailed discussion of the many small-screen versions based directly on Baum's story, and a perusal of the radio and audio editions of the books and films, as well as the comic book adaptations.

The 1939 film was brought to the stage in a production that has been performed around the world on thousands of occasions over the last seventy-five years, but there have been many other theatrical versions that have gone off to see the Wizard. Baum himself tried to capitalize on his creation and only managed to make himself nearly bankrupt in the process; others have invested more wisely, and we look at the 1970s phenomenon *The Wiz*, as well as the latest Oz stage success, *Wicked*.

This leads neatly into our final section, which charts the many different ways in which Oz has been reimagined – from the horrors of Christopher Golden and James A. Moore's *Bloodstained Oz* to the later adventures of an emotionally damaged Dorothy Gale in Alan Moore's controversial series *Lost Girls*; from the sci-fi madness of *The Wonderful Galaxy of Oz* to Stephen King, Robert Heinlein and Philip José Farmer's various recreations of the Oz world in their fiction; and the many continuation stories, created by fans to fill in the gaps in the history of their favourite Wonderful World, as well as the Russian reworking of the tales by Alexander Volkov and Sergei Sukhinov, which spun off completely new versions of Oz history.

L. Frank Baum wrote in his introduction to *The Lost Princess of Oz* in 1917: 'I believe that dreams – day dreams, you know, with your eyes wide open and your brain machinery whizzing – are likely to lead to the betterment of the world.' Prepare to have your eyes opened and your brains set to whiz as we enter the *Marvelous Land of Oz*...

Paul Simpson
August 2013

AUTHOR'S NOTE

L. Frank Baum wasn't meticulous about continuity from book to book, and the spelling of the names of some of the characters – particularly Tik-Tok – varies considerably. In the text, I have used the spelling indicated in the book, film or play being discussed. Similarly, the second book is usually referred to as *The Marvelous Land of Oz*, using the American spelling; that has also been retained throughout.

I. OZ AND ITS CREATORS

I

L. FRANK BAUM BEFORE OZ

For several generations of children, the tales of the land of Oz have provided a fantastical escape from the mundane banality of their everyday lives. For their creator, they were perhaps the logical culmination of being a thwarted storyteller for many years; through them his imagination was allowed to roam free.

Lyman Frank Baum was born in Chittenango, New York, on 15 May 1856, the seventh child of Benjamin Ward Baum, a barrel-maker, and Cynthia Stanton, the daughter of a well-to-do farmer, who had eloped together when they were twenty-one. Prior to Frank's birth, his father, an astute businessman, had built his own barrel factory, and in 1859, Benjamin invested in the oilfields that had been discovered near Titusville, Pennsylvania. The proceeds from this allowed him to buy a large house in Syracuse, New York. When Frank was ten, his father added a country estate named Rose Lawn, a few miles north of the city, as well as Spring Farm, eighty acres of dairy land next door. Although as a child Frank regarded Rose Lawn as a paradise, it was here that he first encountered scarecrows, which 'seemed to my childish imagination as just about to wave their arms, straighten up and stalk across the field on their long legs', and caused him recurrent nightmares.

Frank was named after his uncle Lyman, but made it clear early on that he disliked the name – as early as the 1860 census, his name is given as 'Frankie'. He wasn't a particularly healthy child: he had heart problems as a youngster, but by the time he was twelve, he was fit enough to be sent to Peekskill Military Academy, after receiving home schooling until then. He disliked the academy intensely during the two years he spent there, and after suffering a heart attack while being disciplined for looking out of the window instead of concentrating on his school work, his parents agreed to bring him home – at least, that's the version given in Frank's son's biography of him, which did resort to guesswork in places.

Reading was one of Frank's pleasures, and he devoured the works of Dickens, Thackeray and Shakespeare. The production of the books also fascinated him: when he was fourteen, he visited a printing shop in Syracuse, and became engrossed in the process. His father bought him a small printing press of his own, and Frank, helped by his younger brother Harry, began to produce his own monthly paper, the *Rose Lawn Home Journal*, which debuted in October 1870. It featured various fictional and factual pieces, as well as poetry by his sister Mary Louise.

It wasn't the only magazine Frank produced: his interest in philately led to *The Stamp Collector* as well as a *Complete Stamp Dealer's Directory*, and he and Harry teamed up with Thomas G. Alvord Jr, the son of the lieutenant governor, to create a short-lived monthly literary journal, *The Empire*. After a year spent at the Syracuse Classical School in 1873, Frank's education was deemed complete.

A pattern began to emerge early on in Frank's business life, when he was duped by the manager of a Shakespearean troupe. His love of theatrics meant that he spent a lot of time watching the various travelling companies who visited Syracuse, but none of them would allow him to join them, until one manager agreed, as long as he brought along with him 'a complete set of costumes for all the starring roles he might be called upon to take'. Over his father's misgivings, Frank ordered thousands of dollars' worth of fine costumes, and became part of the troupe – using the pseudonym of George Brooks, since his father was concerned about potential damage to the family name by being associated with the stage. Within a few days, however, all his costumes had been borrowed by his unscrupulous fellows; a few weeks later, Frank returned home empty-handed, after only playing a few small walk-on parts.

Soon after this, Frank jumped on board the developing interest in breeding fancy poultry. B.W. Baum and Sons – comprising Benjamin, Frank and Harry – was formed to raise Hamburg chickens, and Frank was instrumental in setting up the Empire State Poultry Association in late 1878, as well as the trade journal *The Poultry Record* in March 1880. Chickens would remain one of Frank's passions, with his lengthy article on Hamburgs for another trade magazine, *The Poultry World*, reprinted as *The Book of the Hamburgs* in 1886; one of the key characters in the Oz saga is the self-obsessed chicken, Billina, who first appears in the third story, *Ozma of Oz*.

After spending the next few months working at his brother-in-law's store in Syracuse, and setting up the chicken business, Frank returned to his real love, since he still very much wanted to be an actor. Using the name Louis F. Baum, he appeared in the hit play *The Banker's Daughter*, at the Union Square Theatre in New York from 30 November 1878, which ran for a hundred nights. He supplemented his income with articles for New York papers, and he then worked on the *Bradford Era* newspaper for a year. In 1880, his father promoted him to manager of a small chain of theatres that he owned in the oilfields towns; quite quickly, Frank deduced that it made more sense to create his own company of players than try to get bigger companies to visit the small towns. After some attempts to bring Shakespeare to the masses, which didn't go down so well with the audiences of oil workers, Frank began writing his own shows.

The Maid of Arran was by far the most popular of these, which Frank adapted from a popular novel, *A Princess of Thule*, by William Black. Its tale of a painter who tries to introduce an unsophisticated woman to London society was heavily rewritten, relocating the story to Ireland and incorporating numerous extra twists. Frank toured with the play for some months, visiting Toronto, Chicago and New York before returning in triumph to Syracuse in February 1883.

By this stage, Frank was a married man. He had been introduced to Maud Gage, the room-mate of his cousin Josephine, at a party over the Christmas holidays of 1881, with the words, 'Frank, I want you to know Maud Gage. I'm sure you will love her.' Frank graciously replied, 'Consider yourself loved, Miss Gage,' to which Maud replied, 'Thank you, Mr Baum. That's a promise. Please see that you live up to it.'

Maud was the daughter of the women's suffrage campaigner Matilda Joselyn Gage, who would become a heavy influence on Frank's writing, particularly her belief in theosophy, which claimed to provide a rational basis for faith in a spiritual world, by incorporating the 'essential truths' of religion and science without making distinctions based on race, religion, class or gender. Frank courted Maud across the summer of 1882, but when she agreed to marry him, her mother was not happy at the prospect of her being 'a darned fool' by marrying an actor and dropping out of college.

Maud was as strong-willed as her mother, and made it clear that she was wedding Frank whether her mother liked it or not; Matilda backed down and agreed they could marry at her home. This they did on 9 November 1882, and their first child, Frank Junior, was born on 4 December 1883 at their new home in Syracuse.

Maud's will exerted itself at home: in the late nineteenth century it was expected that a wife would be compliant with her husband's wishes. Not so in the Baum household: Maud was the disciplinarian with their children, and made it clear that her wishes were paramount. The family regularly recalled the incident of the Bismarcks (jam-filled doughnuts) which Frank had brought home one day without being asked; when challenged why, Frank protested that he liked the meals Maud provided for him, but also liked Bismarcks for breakfasts. Maud wasn't happy. She proceeded to serve the doughnuts to him every day despite their going stale, since she wasn't prepared to see food go to waste. She eventually let him off 'this time if you will promise never again to buy any food unless I ask you to get it'.

In July 1883, Frank became proprietor of a store for lubricating oil, which helped to keep the family solvent when the theatrical business suffered a major downturn: Frank's uncle John, who had acted as business manager, fell ill, and a bookkeeper was hired, who promptly mismanaged the business, then vanished. A fire that destroyed one of Frank's theatres, along with the costumes, scenery and props for *The Maid of Arran*, was the last straw; Frank had to sell everything connected to the theatres, including the rights to *The Maid*. It wasn't the last time that he would have to give up important rights as a result of his desire to be a theatrical impresario.

It wasn't the only catastrophe to hit the Baums over the next few years. In 1884, Frank's older brother, Benjamin William, invented a new lubricant oil, Castorine, and

Frank became superintendent of the company set up to manufacture and distribute it. However, Benjamin died in February 1886, and the clerk left in charge of the company by Frank's uncle Adam gambled away most of the capital, leaving Frank in spring 1888 with little option but to sell the company to which he had devoted many hours on the road. His father had died a year earlier, after being injured in a horse and buggy accident in 1885 from which he never fully recovered; his fortune had been whittled away, and he had been forced to sell Spring Farm. Maud nearly died in childbirth with their second son, Robert Stanton, on 1 February 1886, and took two years to recover.

It was clear that it was time to head somewhere new to start afresh. Maud's sister Helen and her husband Charles Gage had moved to the frontier town of Aberdeen, South Dakota in 1887. Three of her siblings were already there, and in September 1888, Frank, Maud and their sons joined them. Frank became the proprietor and owner of Baum's Bazaar, which sold 'a magnificent and complete assortment' of items, ranging from 'Bohemian and Native Glass Ware' to 'Gunther's Celebrated Chicago Candles'. What Frank couldn't have anticipated was the downturn in the local economy following a drought; desirable as his stock was, he wasn't selling essentials and the Northwestern National Bank of Aberdeen foreclosed on their mortgage on 1 January 1890. (It was bought by his sister-in-law, Helen, who managed to run it successfully for twelve years by selling practical items that were needed by the inhabitants of a frontier town.) Matters hadn't been helped by the loss of a shipment of goods in Lake Huron in December 1888, by Frank's sponsorship of the Aberdeen Baseball Club, which lost money because of the team's remote location, and by the increase in his outgoings caused by the birth of his third son, Harry Neal, on 17 December 1889.

Undeterred, Frank returned to journalism, buying the *Dakota Pioneer*, a weekly paper whose owner was anxious to sell, and renaming it the *Aberdeen Saturday Pioneer.* He was not just the editor, but also in charge of subscriptions, advertising and writing much of the content. He was also able to use the printing press to handle outside commissions, which helped to maintain the cash flow.

Frank owned the paper for around fifteen months, during which time he wrote editorials on many subjects dear to his heart, including women's suffrage. In April 1890, he became the secretary of the Equal Suffrage Club in Aberdeen, and he used his position on the paper to try to advance the cause, while downplaying, where necessary, the various rifts that grew between the assorted participants. He maintained this stance throughout the summer: a vote to strike the word 'male' from the state constitution on the issue was set for November. However, once that had been defeated, he simply noted that '[t]he defeat of Equal Suffrage will stand as a lasting reproach to the state of South Dakota'. He also regularly wrote about his interest in theosophy.

One regular feature was written by Frank, but appeared under the byline of 'Our Landlady', one Mrs Bilkins, the owner of a boarding house who had trenchant opinions on many matters. Although she seemed to share many of Frank's core beliefs, she arrived at them through a much less considered route, and could express them more forcibly, for instance noting on the economic woes that 'If only every man would say "I will do suthin'" instead o' sayin' "why don't somebody else do suthin'?" times would change mighty quick.' She also had a common interest with Frank in potential inventions for the future, something which Baum expanded upon in his novel *The Master Key* in 1901.

The elections in November 1890 saw defeat for nearly every cause that Frank had supported and he seemed to lose interest thereafter. A month later, he wrote two editorials, which have become the subject of some notoriety in recent years. In them, he apparently suggested that 'our only safety depends upon the total extirmination [*sic*] of the Indians' following the death of the Lakota Sioux holy man Sitting Bull and the massacre at Wounded Knee. Although his descendants would apologize for these texts in 2006, it seems more likely that Frank was using reverse psychology: such a callous disregard for life doesn't match his other attitudes, or reflect other pieces that he wrote about the Native Americans.

At the start of 1891, advertising sales continued to dwindle with a further economic downturn, and fewer copies were being sold. By February, the *Pioneer* was down to eight pages, after experimenting with larger formats, and Frank himself had to withdraw for a large part from writing while undergoing successful treatment for a tumour under his tongue.

With a fourth child, Kenneth Gage, arriving in March 1891, it was once again clear to the Baums that Frank would need to seek better paid and more reliable employ. This he found in Chicago; at the start of April, the *Aberdeen Daily News* reported that Frank was now working on one of the leading dailies in the Windy City, and that he had closed down the *Pioneer*. Although he didn't actually find a job until the start of May – he was turned down by eight of the papers before the *Chicago Evening Post* took him on – it was time to put his writing experience to good use.

Or so Frank thought. When he realized that the *Post* was paying him $80 a calendar month, rather than the $20 a week he had been expecting (leaving him with a shortfall of $6, a sizeable sum each month), he once again, at the age of thirty-five, had to find a new career.

Within six months of arriving in Chicago, Frank was working as a china buyer for a large department store, after quickly reading up on the subject at the library so he could bluff his way through the interview. He soon swapped this for a role as a travelling salesman, at which he turned out to be excellent, even if the arduous nature of the job was not conducive to his health. Not only was he responsible for sales in central and southern Illinois, Iowa and Missouri, which meant spending many hours on the railroads, but he had to pack and unpack hundreds of pieces of china and glassware at each stop ready to impress the buyers. By 1894, he was already being advised to find something less strenuous – but he was not able to risk losing the regular payments for a further three years by resigning from the job, during which time he was the firm's leading salesman, and the Baums were able to move to a larger home, buy a dog, and hire a Swedish maid.

Although Frank was often away on business, when he was at home his priority was his family, and he ensured that holidays such as the Fourth of July and Christmas were celebrated properly. For the latter, he would place the tree in front of closed curtains, and talk to the family from behind the curtains – a forerunner of the Wizard's actions in Oz.

Frank continued to try to find lucrative 'sidelines' which would help to alleviate the pressure on the family's finances: he promoted new 'nut locks' (a sort of wing nut) for a time, but the most financially rewarding continued to be his writing. Although he tried to sell verses and stories, most were rejected by publishers (Frank noted them all in a book he called his 'Record of Failure'), although there were some notable successes, including a third-prize-winning contribution to a piece on 'Chicago's International Exposition, AD 2090', which appeared in 1896 and suggested that by 2090, Ireland would be an independent republic, England would have a female president, and people would communicate over long distance, using thought transference.

However, when he combined his two jobs, he hit on a winning formula: he had always been interested in the art of window dressing, and came up with a trade journal that would pass on the tricks of the trade. *The Show Window:*

A Journal of Practical Window Training for the Merchant and the Professional made its debut on 1 November 1897, and Frank was quick to resign from his sales job to concentrate on its future. It was a smart move: the magazine was a success, and the income from it allowed the Baums to move even further upmarket, to a house on Humboldt Park Boulevard on the North-West Side of Chicago. By the turn of the century, Frank had been able to reprint material from the magazine into a book entitled *The Art of Decorating Dry Goods Windows and Interiors.*

However, in October 1900, Frank announced that he was stepping down from the editorship. What had been a sideline was about to become a major source of income. 'The generous reception . . . of my books for children, during the past two years, has resulted in such constant demands upon my time that I find it necessary to devote my entire attention, hereafter, to this class of work.' A month earlier, *The Wizard of Oz* had been published. It wasn't Frank's first book for children, but it was the one that ensured his legacy.

2
INTO OZ

L. Frank Baum's first published fiction had nothing to do with the Emerald City or the adventures of Dorothy and her friends. Thanks to the influence of his mother-in-law, who heard him telling stories to his children and their friends, Frank wrote books of fairy tales entitled *Adventures in Phunnyland* and *Tales of Mother Goose*, both of which he copyrighted in 1896 and started sending around publishers the following year.

Tales of Mother Goose was snapped up by Chancey L. Williams, the owner of Way & Williams publishers, to whom Frank was introduced in June 1897 by Opie Read, another member of the Chicago Press Club to which Frank belonged. It was printed under the title *Mother Goose in Prose*, illustrated with fourteen black and white drawings by Maxwell Parrish. In it, Frank retold the well-known nursery stories in a new way, providing backstories for the characters that explained how they arrived in the fantastical situations in the rhymes. Its modest success encouraged the publishers to consider following it up with *Adventures in Phunnyland*, but unfortunately they went bust before they could print it.

Although he was pleased by the reaction to his children's stories, Frank's main focus had to be on *The Show Window* during 1897 and 1898. He did find time to collect his various pieces of verse in *By the Candelabra's Glare*, a self-published book which he gave to his friends and family. This was illustrated by three artists including William Wallace Denslow, a very successful designer of book covers and posters, who had also been introduced to Frank by Opie Read. Denslow and Frank became good friends, and started work on a 'sequel' to *Mother Goose*, which was based on the notion that Mother Goose had joined a Woman's Club, leaving her husband at home to amuse the children. *Father Goose* was a true collaboration between Frank and Denslow – each was inspired by the other's work, with Frank sometimes rewriting his poems completely once he saw Denslow's illustrations, which were consciously restricted to a yellow, red, grey and black colour palette.

Father Goose was completed by early 1899, and copyrighted by the pair jointly. It was published in September by George M. Hill, who insisted that the two creators should cover a large proportion of the printing costs. It was far more successful than either Frank or Denslow could have anticipated: over 75,000 copies were sold before the end of 1899. Twenty-six of the verses were set to music by Alberta N. Hall, and published as *The Songs of Father Goose, for the Home, School and Nursery* in June 1900. Frank worked with two other artists, Harry Kennedy and Charles Costello, on a couple of other books of verse – *The Army Alphabet* and *The Navy Alphabet* – which appeared in the spring and summer of 1900, but since these lacked Denslow's distinctive drawings, they were not so well received. *Adventures in Phunnyland* – a set of four-teen stories set in a magical valley – finally saw print in October 1900 under the title *A New Wonderland*; the comparison in the title with Lewis Carroll's famous work led one reviewer to note that 'Mr Baum is not Carroll, indeed, but he is Baum, and Baum is a very satisfactory personage in himself'.

However, the book that Frank considered to be 'the best thing I ever have written' (as noted in a letter to his brother Harry) was the one on which he pinned most of his hopes. *The Wonderful Wizard of Oz* didn't pop into his head fully formed: his tales of ''I'he Emerald City' (the title by which the first Oz book was known throughout its writing) had been percolating for some years, but he sat down in the spring of 1899 with Denslow and began charting the story of Dorothy's journey from Kansas to Oz, and her travails there. George M. Hill agreed to publish it on the same shared-cost basis as 'Father Goose', but wanted to wait until he knew how well that had done before printing 'The Emerald City'. He also requested a different title, and for a time the book was known as 'From Kansas to Fairyland'. By January 1900, Hill was confident that a further Baum/Denslow book would be a hit, and paid the pair $500 each as an advance on royalties for the book that was now known as 'The Land of Oz'. In early March, the final title was agreed, and *The Wonderful Wizard of Oz* was sent to press. Over 37,000 copies of the book were sold between its official publication date in September 1900 and Christmas 1901.

Like many fantasy authors, Frank couldn't always identify exactly where his inspiration had come from, and when he was later asked where the name Oz derived from, he claimed that he had been in the middle of telling a story about Dorothy, the Scarecrow and the Tin Woodman to a group of children and they had asked where the stories were located. He looked around the room and saw a filing cabinet labelled O–Z and simply adopted the letters. He could even specifically date the tale to 7 May 1898, since a newspaper headline in the room referenced Admiral Dewey's victory in Manila. (Dalek creator Terry Nation similarly maintained for years that he had found the name for his monsters from the title of a telephone directory.) However, given Frank's predilection for giving his countries two-letter names (Ev, Mo, Ix), chances are that Oz was simply a mellifluous combination plucked from thin air.

The Wonderful Wizard of Oz wasn't intended as the start of a series of adventures, and Frank moved on to a new set of characters in his next book, *Dot and Tot of Merryland*, which was aimed at a younger audience. This too was illustrated by Denslow, but was not as popular as their previous collaborations. Frank tried to update fairy tales in his *American Fairy Tales*, which included such delights as a trio of bandits arriving in contemporary Chicago (with the little girl who finds them suggesting they could become politicians!), and 'The Dummy That Lived' about a wax dummy who gains consciousness but not acceptance. *American Fairy Tales* was initially published in 1901, and then reprinted, with extra stories and some tidying-up of the originals, in 1908.

Frank's other book from 1901 was a science-fiction tale, entitled *The Master Key: An Electrical Fairy Tale, Founded upon the Mysteries of Electricity and the Optimism of its Devotees*. It was dedicated to Frank's son Robert, who was one of the devotees referred to in the title. The lead character, Rob Joslyn, somehow touches the Master Key of Electricity and summons the Demon of Electricity, who promises that there are far wider and better uses for electrical power than even Thomas Edison could dream of. The Demon grants Rob nine gifts, spread three per week for three weeks. The first ones are pills that provide food for an entire day, a stun tube, and a transporter resembling a watch that uses electromagnetic currents to move Rob wherever he pleases. After Rob has some adventures with these, he is then given a missile-repelling garment, a small flat box that will show him everything happening everywhere (essentially an iPad!), and the Character Marker, which will show people's true natures. Again, Rob goes adventuring, and realizes that his gifts could be exploited by unscrupulous scientists or businessmen. However, when the Demon offers the first of his final trio of presents, an Electro-Magnetic Restorer that will bring back the dead if their blood is still warm, Rob refuses it and returns all his gifts, saying he's not wise enough to use them – nor is the rest of Mankind. *The Master Key* was a success, and Frank regretted not leaving the ending open enough to allow for a sequel.

The following year Frank focused on another mythical icon in *The Life and Adventures of Santa Claus* that was perhaps a little too twee in its approach to the character. The book's publication was delayed when the George M. Hill Company went into bankruptcy in February 1902; Bowen-Merrill, who had commissioned and published *The Master Key*, bought the plates and the rights to Baum's work from the receiver and published *Santa Claus*, as well as their own edition of *The Wonderful Wizard of Oz*, under the rather misleading title *The New Wizard of Oz*. They also printed a revised version of *A New Wonderland* as *The Magical Monarch of Mo and His People*.

One reason for the change of title for the first Oz novel was the popularity of the musical version of *The Wizard of Oz* that had opened at the Grand Opera House in Chicago on 16 June 1902. Frank and Denslow had worked on this with composer Paul Tietjens and during the process (discussed in detail in part three), the story had deviated dramatically from the original, concentrating far more on the characters of the Scarecrow and the Tin Woodman, as well as new characters such as Sir Dashemoff Daily, and

Imogen the Cow (a replacement for Toto). It was a major success: 185,000 people saw it in the fourteen weeks it played in Chicago, and it travelled around North America for eight years, spending two seasons in the Majestic Theatre in New York along the way. Frank and Tietjens made between $90,000 and $100,000 each from the royalties.

Frank and Denslow fell out over the question of royalties: Denslow felt that because he had a half-share in the copyright of the original book, and that the costumes used in the show were based on his designs, he should receive a larger share of the royalties from the show. Denslow tried to create his own Oz adventures – *Pictures from the Wonderful Wizard of Oz*, with a story by Thomas H. Russell; *Denslow's Scarecrow and the Tin-Man*; and a short-lived comic page about the two characters. None of these had the staying power of Frank's tales.

However, Frank had to take some time away from writing in 1902, following an attack of Bell's palsy, which paralyses the muscles of the face for a time. On doctor's advice, he performed manual work in the new cottage that he had been able to buy at Macatawa Park overlooking Black Lake (now Lake Macatawa). During 1902 and 1903, Frank wrote much less than normal: *The Enchanted Island of Yew* was his only original book published during 1903. However, he was also working on a new comic opera, *King Jonah XIII*, with Nathaniel D. Mann; a musical comedy *Montezuma* with popular novelist Emerson Hough; as well as developing his own new Oz extravaganza, *The Woggle-Bug*.

It wasn't that he was actively avoiding writing a new story of Oz, simply that he felt that the tale was told. However, when Frank K. Reilly and Sumner C. Britton, two former employees of Hill Publishing, started up their own publishing house, he suggested a sequel that he entitled 'His Majesty the Scarecrow'. After some discussion this became *The Marvelous Land of Oz* (often simply known as *The Land of Oz*), subtitled 'Being an Account of the Further Adventures of the Scarecrow and the Tin Woodman and Also the Strange Experiences of the Highly Magnified Woggle-Bug, Jack Pumpkinhead, the Animated Saw-Horse and the Gump'. Set entirely within Oz, it introduced the key figures of Princess Ozma, who would go on to feature heavily within the series, as well as Jack Pumpkinhead and the Woggle-Bug, whose name popped into Frank's head when he was asked the name of a sand crab by a little girl at the beach. The Woggle-Bug proved to be one of the most popular characters in the Oz series, perhaps because he gave Frank – and his successors – the opportunity to engage in puns. *The Marvelous Land of Oz* seems to have been written with one eye on a stage production – its central idea of a girl dressed as a boy, and the all-female army of its antagonist, General Jinjur, were eminently suited.

A new artist was hired to provide drawings for the sequel. John R. Neill, who had been working as a newspaper illustrator, was never allowed to share the copyright in the Oz books, but did receive royalties from his second book onwards, and spent around a month working on each one.

The Marvelous Land of Oz was published on 5 July 1904, with Reilly & Britton ensuring that they received maximum publicity. A series of short stories by Frank, illustrated by Walt McDougall, appeared in various newspapers under the title 'Queer Visitors from the Marvelous Land of Oz', featuring the Tin Woodman, Jack Pumpkinhead, the Scarecrow, the Woggle-Bug, the Saw-Horse and the Gump having various misadventures around America. When the twenty-six stories were concluded, Reilly & Britton produced *The Woggle-Bug Book*, illustrated by Ike Morgan, which saw the Bug falling in love with a dress that he sees in a shop window, and following it from woman to woman.

Frank had hoped to create a second stage play based on the book, again built around the Tin Woodman and the Scarecrow, but Fred Stone and David Montgomery declined to be involved, worried about being typecast in the roles. Frank removed them from the story, and rebuilt it around Jack Pumpkinhead and the Woggle-Bug. Chicago producer Henry Raeder agreed to put on the show 'in a first-class manner' by 1 July 1905, assuming that Frank delivered the libretto by 1 March, and made any revisions that were 'deemed advisable'. If all went well – and with *The Wizard of Oz* still packing houses, there was no reason to think it wouldn't – Raeder would mount further musicals in subsequent years. However, Raeder wasn't able to get financial backing, so the contract was annulled, but the show still went ahead, opening on 18 June 1905. It was panned by the critics as 'a shabby and dull repetition of a cheapened *Wizard of Oz*', and closed on 13 July.

While he was working on the script, Frank was also producing other stories. *Queen Zixi of Ix, or The Story of the Magic Cloak* was originally serialized in *St Nicholas* magazine from November 1904 onwards, and then published in hardcover in October 1905. *Animal Fairy Tales* initially saw print in the women's magazine *Delineator* between January and September 1905. And Frank's first novel for adults, an adventure thriller, *The Fate of the Crown*, was appearing in the *Philadelphian North American*, under the title *The Emperor's Spy*. It was apparently written by 'Schuyler Staunton', a name Frank borrowed from one of his maternal uncles, as was its sequel *Daughters of Destiny* – both novels were published by Reilly & Britton with no reference to Frank's involvement.

They weren't the only pseudonymous books Frank wrote. Reilly & Britton wanted to capitalize on the popularity of fiction aimed at teenagers – what today is described as the YA (young adult) market – and commissioned Frank to write various books both for that market and also for younger children. Frank did not want to risk ruining the Oz stories' reputation by association, so requested that these appeared under a pen name. They appeared as *Twinkle Tales*, six stories by Laura Bancroft for small children; *Annabel* by Suzanne Metcalf; *Aunt Jane's Nieces* – the first of a long-running series 'on the style of the Louisa M. Alcott stories, but not so good' – by Edith Van Dyne; and *Sam Steele's Adventures on Land & Sea* by Captain Hugh Fitzgerald, aimed at adolescent boys. They also ordered material for what became *Father Goose's Year Book*.

This spawned a period of massive productivity for Frank. The Van Dyne stories for adolescent girls were very popular, with ten *Aunt Jane's Nieces* tales eventually appearing: two books featuring *The Flying Girl*, and four mystery stories starring Mary Louise. Captain Hugh Fitzgerald penned a further Sam Steele adventure, but neither sold particularly well; they were reprinted in 1908 as *The Boy Fortune Hunters* by Floyd Akers, and for some reason sold much better, leading to four more sequels between then and 1911. 'Laura Bancroft' also wrote *Policeman Bluejay*, one of Frank's more intriguing works, which wraps a discussion about religion, heaven and the nature of evil in a story for small children. (Towards the end of his life, Frank suggested reprinting this as an Oz tale but his publishers refused; it was, though, finally ascribed to him in 1917.)

While working on these, Frank and Maud took a trip around the Mediterranean in the early part of 1906, and later that year, Frank also produced *John Dough and the Cherub*. This tale about the adventures of an animated doughboy was serialized in various newspapers before appearing in print but didn't inspire the same sort of interest as his other work.

He was also returning to Oz. When he and Maud came back from their travels to Egypt and Sicily, a trip that also inspired his adult novel *The Last Egyptian: A Romance of the Nile* (published anonymously in 1908), Frank signed a contract to write *Ozma of Oz* by 1 December 1906, and to provide two further books in 1909 and 1911. The subtitle of *Ozma of Oz* mentions all the key participants including new characters: the Yellow Hen, Tiktok, the Hungry Tiger, 'Besides Other Good People Too Numerous to Mention'. Dorothy has grown up in the years between *The Wizard of Oz* and this adventure, making her a more attractive heroine to the readers of Frank's other books. The second book, *Dorothy and the Wizard in Oz*, which appeared in 1908, was not as well received by audiences, particularly given its harsh treatment of some of the characters. It did, however, get something of a push into the public eye through Frank's latest foray into the theatre – one that would cost him dearly.

3

THE ROAD TO HOLLYWOOD

Frank Baum never lost his love of the theatre, and it came as no surprise to those who knew him that he also embraced the new medium of moving pictures. In 1908, he came up with the idea of *Fairylogue and Radio-Plays*, which he intended as a combination of the two forms. The *Chicago Tribune* described it as 'a travelogue that takes you to Oz instead of China . . . A radio play is a fairylogue with an orchestra on the left-hand side of the stage.'

Fairylogue and Radio-Plays was a two-hour long extravaganza, which brought together live actors performing excerpts from Frank's books, slides and short films. The 'radio-plays' of the title were actually short films, hand coloured by the Duval Frères, in a process which Frank claimed was invented by Parisian Michel Radio, thus justifying the use of the word 'radio', which is more likely to have been chosen because it sounded modern! Unfortunately the costs involved were prohibitive, and although the show was popular with those who saw it, it devastated Frank's finances, to the extent that the family had to sell their beloved cottage in Macatawa in 1909, and move to rented accommodation in Los Angeles. Eventually, on 1 August 1910, Frank had to sign over the rights and royalties on all his books published by Bobbs-Merill – *The Wizard of Oz* and nine others – to his major creditor, Harrison Rountree.

While Frank continued to produce more novels, including three further Oz adventures, the family settled in Los Angeles, and in 1910, Maud purchased a corner lot in the quiet suburb of Hollywood. A house was constructed at 1749 Cherokee Avenue, a block north of Hollywood Boulevard, which Frank named Ozcot. However financial worries continued to plague them: the loss of the royalties from *The Wizard of Oz*, and the decline in sales of the later books in the series meant that the Baums were constantly fending off creditors. On 3 June 1911, Frank filed for bankruptcy.

This curtailed Frank's lifestyle to an extent, but he was still able to play golf and be an active member of the Los Angeles Athletic Club, as well as part of the Lofty and Exalted Order of Uplifters, one of the inner groups of its members. He was able to 'pay' his dues by using his talents, writing shows for them, and keeping them amused. Although *The Emerald City of Oz*, published in 1910, ended with Oz apparently closed off from the outside world for ever – Frank's futile way of attempting to quell the constant requests from children for more stories – he returned to the land with *The Patchwork Girl of Oz*, which he wrote in 1911–1912 and was published the following year. From there on, he produced a new Oz book each year, with many of them taking around eighteen months from Reilly & Britton approving the plot to final publication.

Frank was also working on further stage shows, despite the financial mauling he had experienced from the

Radio-Plays. He worked with Paul Tietjens on *The Pipes of Pan* and with Arthur Pryor on the comic opera *Peter and Paul*, although neither of these was ever produced. An adaptation of *Ozma of Oz*, otherwise known as *The Rainbow's Daughter*, was meant to arrive at the Studebaker Theatre in Chicago in October 1909, but it finally materialized, considerably reworked, as *The Tik-Tok Man of Oz* in 1913. Reilly & Britton helped with the marketing of another musical comedy, *The Girl from Oz*, about Ellie, a beautiful young girl with whom everyone at an American army base falls in love.

The return to Oz in book form was prompted by the lower sales of Frank's other fantasy novels for children, following the adventures of Cap'n Bill and his young friend Trot – *The Sea Fairies* and *Sky Island*. When the first new Oz novel, *The Patchwork Girl of Oz*, sold considerably more than these, Frank and the publishers abandoned the idea of alternating books from the two series, and in the end, Cap'n Bill and Trot were incorporated into the Oz saga. Frank also penned six little books, published as *The Little Wizard Stories of Oz*, focusing on pairs of characters; these were then collected into one volume. *The Patchwork Girl* was more problematical than some of Frank's earlier Oz books: the publishers suggested that he rework one passage, which included 'meat plants', and he was not happy with Neill's illustrations, despite the publishers arranging for the two men to meet.

The stage show of *The Tik-Tok Man of Oz* opened in Los Angeles on 31 March 1913, before embarking on a tour of San Francisco and Chicago, but it did not find favour with the critics. It wasn't as panned as *The Woggle-Bug*, partly because of Louis Gottschalk's music, but it did seem as if nothing was going to compare favourably with the original *Wizard of Oz* show.

After Frank lost the rights to *The Wizard of Oz*, three short films had been made based on the story, but he had nothing to do with these. However, the Oz Film Manufacturing Company (Oz Films) was very much Frank's concern, even if he had no financial stake in it. His colleagues in the Uplifters and the Los Angeles Athletic Club raised the $100,000 stock and Frank gave the company exclusive movie rights to his stories for a block of shares; he also agreed to write the scripts for further stock. A seven-acre site on Santa Monica Boulevard, between Gower Street and Lodi Street, was purchased and Frank designed a studio which included a large concrete tank and eight smaller ones, as well as a large stage with a tunnel running beneath it, into which various trapdoors opened.

Work began on a five-reel (roughly one hour) version of *The Patchwork Girl of Oz* in June 1914, and took a month to complete. Paramount Pictures agreed to run the film at the Strand Theater in New York, but when it didn't perform as well as expected the larger studio refused to accept Oz Films' second film, *The Magic Cloak of Oz*, or their final Oz movie, *His Majesty the Scarecrow*. Believing that it might be the Oz subject matter that was causing distributors to shy away from them, they then made a version of Frank's thriller *The Last Egyptian*, and a series of short children's films entitled *Violet's Dreams*. However, when none of these was picked up either, it became abundantly clear that it was Oz Films themselves who were the problem, and after a short attempt to let the studio space out to the Alliance Company, Oz Films shut down in the summer of 1915.

The stress caused by the problems at Oz Films can't have helped Frank's health issues; the heart condition which he had had since childhood worsened, and he suffered from an irregular heartbeat, breathing difficulties, and attacks of angina. He also began to suffer from tic douloureux, agonizing episodes of severe facial pain, which could be set off by anything as mild as a breeze passing over his face. He became increasingly concerned about his workload, noting in the preface to *Tik-Tok of Oz* that he wasn't sure he would be 'permitted to write another Oz book'.

Tik-Tok, published in 1914, was based on the play of the same name, although Frank toned down some of the elements needed for a successful stage entertainment, particularly the puns and the love interest. The following year's story *The Scarecrow of Oz* amalgamated Cap'n Bill and Trot into Oz as well as enveloping some of his earlier work and continued the use of romance in the stories, this time borrowing some plotlines from the film *His Majesty the Scarecrow*, which clearly wasn't going to get the sort of audience Frank hoped for. The year 1916 saw publication of *Rinkitink in Oz*, which was a rewrite of an original novel Frank had penned in 1905; the Oz elements are imposed on the storyline, with Dorothy finally deciding to take a hand after watching the events unfold on Ozma's Magic Picture.

Frank was also still writing other tales: the Aunt Jane's Nieces series came to a close with *Aunt Jane's Nieces in the Red Cross*, published originally in 1915. The title characters head to the battlefields of Europe and tend the wounded of both sides. In 1918, Frank added some final chapters to the story, which made it clear that his sympathies were with the Allied cause – America didn't enter the Great War until 1917, so the characters' original neutrality was less surprising to that audience than it would have been to British readers. 'Edith Van Dyne' then came up with a new series featuring amateur detective Mary Louise; Frank's ill-health meant that the third of the quartet of tales, with the uninspiring title *Mary Louise Solves a Mystery*, was apparently ghostwritten by Frank's son Harry.

While writing *The Lost Princess of Oz* during 1916, Frank suffered severe gall-bladder attacks, but throughout 1917 tried to put off an operation to deal with them until he absolutely had to, all the while continuing to write. He completed *The Tin Woodman of Oz* before heading for surgery, and had finished first drafts of *The Magic of Oz* and *Glinda of Oz*, both of which were published posthumously – although he maintained to his publishers that they were actually fully complete.

Frank underwent four hours' surgery in February 1918, which weakened his heart even further. He spent five weeks in hospital, during which time he suffered from kidney complaints, and the doctors wondered if he would recover. He was confined to bed rest on his return to Ozcot, although by April he was allowed to sit up for a few hours a day to continue writing, revising *The Magic of Oz*. He was aware that his time was short, and as soon as *The Magic of Oz* was edited to his satisfaction, he began work on the revisions to *Glinda of Oz*, although most of these were completed by in-house staff at his publishers.

Although he wrote optimistically to his son Frank in September 1918 that he trusted 'before many weeks the doctors will allow me to leave my bed and at least move about the house', this was not to be. Right to the end he tried to answer some of the fan mail he received from children and those 'readers of mature years, who being children at heart still enjoy my tales'. In early May 1919, his heart and breathing problems increased, and on 5 May he started to lapse in and out of consciousness. He managed to tell Maud how much he loved her and begged her to stay living at Ozcot. The next morning, according to Frank junior's biography of his father, he surfaced sufficiently to murmur something, then said distinctly, 'Now we can cross the Shifting Sands'. Shortly afterwards, he stopped breathing.

Frank's passing was noted by the *New York Times* in a short death notice the day after, but in a fuller obituary on 11 May they noted that 'The children have suffered a loss they do not know . . . Years from now, though the children cannot clamour for the newest Oz book, the crowding generations will plead for the old ones.'

L. Frank Baum was buried at the Forest Lawn Memorial

Park; *The Magic of Oz* was published in July 1919, with *Glinda of Oz* arriving a year later. The *New York Times* was wrong about one aspect: the Oz saga did not end with Frank's death. The following year, the mantle of Royal Historian of Oz was passed to a fan of the books, Ruth Plumly Thompson.

4

THE SECOND ROYAL HISTORIAN: RUTH PLUMLY THOMPSON

Ruth Plumly Thompson was born in Philadelphia on 27 July 1891, the daughter of journalist George Thompson. The family moved to New York when her father became the night editor of the *New York Times* but his stress-related premature death, aged thirty-one, when Ruth was only four years old, led to their return to Pennsylvania. Ruth was always acutely aware of the financial pressures brought about by her father's demise, and turned down the chance of a scholarship at Swarthmore College, near her home in Philadelphia, in order to stay at home to work, supporting her mother and invalid sister, with her first material appearing in the children's magazine *St. Nicholas* – a story advertisement idea for Fairy Soap. She sold verse to various outlets, including some typical teenage angst, which she cheerfully admitted she grew out of.

Encouraged by the advertising manager at *St. Nicholas*, Thompson joined the *Philadelphia Ledger* in 1912, writing editorials for the paper that were quoted in the United States Senate. She was offered the staff position of editor of the Sunday Children's Page two years later. Unlike her predecessors, she chose to write new material, rather than simply adapt previously published work that was in the public domain. Like L. Frank Baum, she loved wordplay, with Daniel P. Mannix noting in the Oz fan magazine, the *Baum Bugle*, that she 'considered any page that did not have at least three jokes in it – usually puns – a page wasted'. She retained the copyright of the material she wrote for the *Ledger*, and much of this was reprinted in three books between 1918 and 1929.

Thompson worked as Children's Page editor from 30 August 1914 to 25 April 1921, by which time she was starting to become embroiled in the world of Oz. By chance, William F. Lee, the vice president of Oz publishers Reilly & Lee, lived in Philadelphia, and enjoyed reading Thompson's work in the *Ledger*. According to Thompson, Lee had 'one of those lightning flashes of insight and conviction' that told him she would make a worthy successor to Baum, following his death in 1919. 'Having read and been utterly devoted to the Oz stories not so long ago,' she recalled, 'I felt sure I could turn up a rousing and rollicking Oz adventure . . . Six months later, Mr Lee, with the manuscript tucked away in his briefcase, set off for Chicago.'

The transition wasn't smooth: initially the publishers wanted to rewrite Thompson's work but after she threatened to remove the Oz references and sell the tale elsewhere, they relented, and offered a flat fee of $500. Thompson was used to receiving royalties, and eventually she received two-thirds of the 10 per cent author royalty, with the remaining third going to Baum's widow.

Her work was highly regarded by illustrator John R. Neill, who had worked on all of the Oz books apart from the very first one. After finishing work on Thompson's second manuscript, *Kabumpo of Oz*, he wrote to the publishers congratulating them on 'secur[ing] an author of such superior qualifications to continue the work of supplying the "Oz books". Every feature of the child appeal is handled with the greatest skill. The whimsical, the humour, the interest and the zip of the book make me think it one of the very best Oz books so far.'

Reilly & Lee published a book a year from Thompson between 1921 and 1939, although William F. Lee's death in 1924 removed one of her key allies. Thompson wanted to create a proper franchise from the Oz books, with ambitious plans for children's records, movies, radio plays and comic strips, but whenever she put these ideas forward, either Reilly & Lee or the Baum family rejected them – the latter's attitude not helped by legal action taken by the publishers against L. Frank Baum's son Frank J. Baum after he published an unofficial Oz story, *The Laughing Dragon of Oz*, in 1935.

The only project that did get support from the publishers, probably because they could see the benefit for them in terms of immediate sales, was Thompson's short touring play, *A Day in Oz*, or *Scraps from Oz*. This ran for between thirty and forty minutes and included the key characters from the series.

It didn't help that Reilly & Lee were not interested in Thompson writing any books for them other than Oz, although they did publish *The Curious Cruise of Captain Santa* in 1926. She was a ghostwriter for Walt Disney books published by David McKay, as well as advertising booklets to help maintain the family income during the Depression years.

When Baum's widow turned down an offer for the rights to the Oz stories (other than *The Wizard of Oz*, whose rights had been negotiated separately) from the Walt Disney company, it was the last straw for Thompson, who, as she later explained, 'was reluctantly forced to resign my post of Royal Historian of Oz'. John R. Neill asked her to look over the manuscript for his first Oz novel, as did the series editor at Reilly & Lee, but she was not willing to do so unless the publishers met her terms, which they refused to do.

Although the Oz series continued without her, releases were few and far between in the 1940s and 1950s. Thompson continued to write, contributing stories to the children's magazine *Jack and Jill*. She submitted a further Oz novel, *Yankee in Oz*, in 1959, but Reilly & Lee claimed that they were working on developing a story with another author and rejected the book. Thompson created the 'Peter Puppet Page' for *Jack and Jill* and wrote it for five years until it was taken in-house and given to a staff writer. She then found it difficult to sell her material, explaining that the new editor at *Jack and Jill* was 'hard to get on with – a psychiatrist and full of notions about children, most of them wrong. Ho well! Nothing much can be done about it at present. But will not waste my dragons and princesses on him!'

Yankee in Oz was eventually published by the International Wizard of Oz Club in 1972, with Reilly & Lee's consent, and Thompson reworked a further manuscript, *The Enchanted Isle of Oz*, for publication four years later, shortly before her death on 6 April 1976.

5

THE CANONICAL OZ: BOOKS BY L. FRANK BAUM (1900–1920)

While there have been many books set within the magical land of Oz, there are forty that most fans of the series accept are the 'true' stories, from which all the others derive. That's not to say that the multiple different authors of these don't disagree in some respects with each other – indeed L. Frank Baum himself seems not to have gone back and checked his earlier work when he was writing later sequels – but the core precepts of the series are contained within these tales, published between 1900 and 1963. (The continuation novels by Sherwood Smith, which have been authorized by the Baum Family Trust beginning with *The Emerald Wand of Oz*, are discussed in part four.)

The Wonderful Wizard of Oz, published in 1900, is, of course, where it all began; everyone thinks they know the story of Baum's book because they've seen the 1939 movie version, but in fact, the original tale is markedly different.

For a start, it's clear that Oz is a real place to which Dorothy travels – and she gets there remarkably quickly. Only a couple of pages are spent in Kansas before the arrival of the cyclone. Given the silver (not ruby) shoes belonging to the Wicked Witch of the East by the Good Witch of the North, Dorothy follows a road of yellow bricks and meets up with the Lion (who wears glasses), the Tin Woodman, and the Scarecrow, on a perilous journey, in which the Wicked Witch of the West hardly features, to the Emerald City. Each eventually receives their heart's desire from the Wizard – although each visits the Great and Powerful Oz separately, seeing a different illusion. They defeat the Wicked Witch of the West, and the Scarecrow is left in charge of the Emerald City when the Wizard flies off in his balloon, inadvertently leaving Dorothy behind.

However, they have plenty more adventures before Dorothy returns to Kansas: advised that Glinda, the Good Witch of the South, can help Dorothy get home, the friends travel to her kingdom, encountering Fighting Trees, Mr Joker and the Hammer-Heads, as well as a giant spider. Glinda explains Dorothy can use the Silver Shoes as transport, and returns the others to their new kingdoms: the Tin Woodman now rules Winkie Country, and the Cowardly Lion becomes the King of the Forest.

The Marvelous Land of Oz followed four years later, when L. Frank Baum could not resist the calls for a sequel, particularly following the success of the stage show based on the original book. The attention is firmly on the Scarecrow and the Tin Woodman, whose name is revealed as (Emperor) Nick Chopper, and it includes some broad satire on the women's liberation movement.

Dorothy and the Lion are conspicuous by their absence, but instead one of the literary series' key characters is introduced: Ozma of Oz, who was kidnapped by the Wizard and given into the care of Mombi the Witch. As the story starts, Mombi is living with a boy called Tip, who can't stand her. Tip creates a wooden man with a pumpkin head who he names Jack Pumpkinhead to scare Mombi, but the witch uses the Powder of Life to bring Jack to life. When Jack and Tip escape to the Emerald City, they get caught up in a revolt against the Scarecrow by General Jinjur's all-female Army of Revolt. Tip, Jack and the Scarecrow go for help from the Tin Woodman, and are joined by the Highly Magnified and Thoroughly Educated Woggle-Bug. Mombi, who has been helping Jinjur, reveals she transformed Ozma into Tip and undoes the spell. The restored Ozma and her friends retake the Emerald City.

Ozma of Oz was first published in 1907, and widens the canvas of the Oz series considerably. The majority of the story isn't set in Oz itself although Dorothy Gale (given a surname for the first time) and the Lion do reappear. Dorothy and her Uncle Henry are travelling to Australia by ship, but Dorothy is swept overboard during a storm along with a yellow hen, Billina, who develops the power of speech when they arrive in a fairytale land. They meet Tik-Tok, a round, copper mechanical man who has three separate motors for thinking, motion, and speech, and learn they are in the Land of Ev, members of whose royal family have been taken by the Nome King. They are imprisoned by the Ev Princess Langwidere but rescued by Ozma and friends who have come to the Ev royal family's rescue. The party travels to the underground Nome kingdom, where they have to discover which ornaments are transformed Ev royalty – but if they guess wrong, they too will be changed. Billina learns the secret and forces the Nome King to allow her to guess, freeing her friends. Since her eggs are poisonous to Nomes, they're used to help the Evs and the Ozites to escape. Dorothy becomes a Princess of Oz, and uses the Nome King's magic belt they have stolen to travel to Australia to meet her Uncle Henry.

* * *

Dorothy and the Wizard in Oz followed in 1908, and has been described as the 'darkest and most troubling of Baum's Oz books', with Dorothy now on her way back home from Australia. A California earthquake sends her and her cousin Zeb – as well as cat Eureka and cab-horse Jim – plummeting down to the land of the vegetable people, the Mangaboos, where she is delighted to find the Wizard descending from the sky in his balloon just in time to prevent their execution. After a succession of terrifying adventures, in which they meet the invisible inhabitants of the Valley of Voe, as well as dragonettes and Gargoyles, Dorothy finally signals Ozma for help. They are brought to Oz, where Eureka is then accused of eating Ozma's pet piglet, and Jim is beaten in a race by Jack Pumpkinhead's animated wooden Saw-Horse. Ozma uses the magic belt to return Zeb and Jim to California, as they don't want to stay in Oz any longer; Dorothy and Eureka are sent to Kansas. The Wizard is welcomed back to Oz.

Since Baum received complaints from children about the Wizard's involvement in Ozma's kidnapping, when her backstory is explained this element has been removed. However, the Wizard still comes over quite badly: he slices a Mangaboo in half, and then dismisses burning down the wooden kingdom of the Gargoyles with 'The loss will be very small, and the Gargoyles will never be missed'.

The Road to Oz lightens the tone considerably. The 1909 book sees Dorothy and Toto meet a wandering hobo only known as the Shaggy Man, who is carrying the Love Magnet, which makes everyone love him. Travelling on the seventh path – at an intersection that normally doesn't have as many roads – they enter fairyland, where they meet Button Bright, a little boy who regularly gets lost, and Polychrome, a fairy who's the Rainbow's daughter. Dorothy realizes that she must get to the Emerald City in time for Ozma's birthday (21 August, apparently). Along the way, the king of Foxville gives Button Bright a fox's head, while King Kik-a-Bray of Dunkiton endows the Shaggy Man with a donkey's head, and they fend off the Scoodlers, who want to make them into soup. They cross the Deadly Desert on a sand-boat and meet with old friends Tik-Tok and Billina in Oz. Together with the Tin Woodman, the Scarecrow and Jack Pumpkinhead, they all go to the Emerald City where they – and a number of guest characters from Baum's non-Oz books – have a feast for Ozma. Button Bright and the Shaggy Man are returned to normal in the Truth Pond, and the Wizard reveals he can now use bubbles to send people home. Everyone disperses, except the Shaggy Man who is allowed to stay in the Emerald City.

The Road to Oz contradicts earlier stories by claiming there's no money in Oz, with many Oz scholars speculating that Baum is suggesting a very communist ethos at work.

The Emerald City of Oz was intended as the final story in the saga when it first appeared in 1910. By the end Dorothy, as well as her uncle and aunt, have moved to Oz permanently, and Glinda has ensured that its utopian walls are unlikely to come under attack again.

At Dorothy's behest, Ozma brings Uncle Henry and Aunt Em to Oz. While Dorothy introduces them to her friends, and gives them a guided tour of the country – in which a number of new and previously seen areas are described – the Nome King is eager for revenge after his defeat by Ozma of Oz. He sends his general, Guph, to recruit allies, including the large Whimsies, the Growleywogs – who are happy to help attack the Emerald City, but want to conquer the Nomes as well – and the terrifying Phanfasms, who also intend to turn on their allies once the Ozites are defeated. When Dorothy and her friends learn about this, they encourage Ozma to prepare – although Ozma doesn't take the threat very seriously. Eventually, Ozma creates a load of dust that makes the Nome armies and their allies drink the Water of Oblivion from the Forbidden Fountain – resulting in them forgetting their plan – before Ozma uses the magic belt to send them home. Ozma, Dorothy and their friends ask for Glinda's help to protect Oz, and the Witch makes it invisible. The book ends with a letter from Dorothy, explaining that Oz will never be heard from again . . .

The Patchwork Girl of Oz marked the start of L. Frank Baum's second regular stint of writing Oz stories, after his financial problems meant that he had to turn to his only sure-fire source of income once more. Baum has to jump through hoops to explain how this further tale, published in 1913, can be told (it involves wireless telegraphy, and the lucky coincidence that the Shaggy Man can use it). It introduces Ojo the Unlucky (whose sobriquet is turned around for his later appearances), who is on a quest along with the Glass Cat and the Patchwork Girl to find the Powder of Life, a solution to the consequences of the Liquid of Petrifaction: his uncle Nunkie and Margolette Pipt, the wife of Dr Pipt, the inventor of the Liquid, have been turned into solid marble statues. The problem is that the various components of the Powder include a six-leaf clover – which can only be found in the Emerald City, and have been used for evil spells so Ozma has banned them from being picked – and the left wing of a butterfly, which causes consternation, since the Tin Woodman will not allow a living creature to be harmed. In the end, the Wizard uses a spell he has learned from Glinda to reverse the effects and free Nunkie and Margolette.

Racially offensive elements of this story, featuring the Tottenhots, were removed from some reprints of *The Patchwork Girl of Oz*; Baum himself took out a chapter

showing vegetable people growing 'meat people' for food
when it was pointed out that this was not 'in harmony with
your other fairy stories'.

Little Wizard Stories of Oz, which also appeared in 1913, is
a collection of six short stories named after the lead characters in each of them: 'The Cowardly Lion and the Hungry
Tiger', in which the pair decide to follow their animal
instincts but instead end up reuniting a mother and child;
'Little Dorothy and Toto', which sees the Wizard teach
Dorothy a lesson about travelling alone; 'Tiktok and the
Nome King' sees the mechanical man trying to get some
metal for new springs; 'Ozma and the Little Wizard' deals
with three Imps: Olite, Udent and Ertinent; 'Jack Pump-
inhead and the Sawhorse' try to rescue some children but
need rescuing themselves; and 'The Scarecrow and the Tin
Woodman' take a hazardous journey on the water.

Tik-Tok of Oz, which first arrived on shelves in 1914,
betrays its unusual origins in a number of places. Based on
L. Frank Baum's musical version of *Ozma of Oz*, which
had been retitled *The Tik-Tok Man of Oz*, *Tik-Tok* sees
Polychrome meet the Shaggy Man for the 'first' time, and
also reworks the Love Magnet (the Shaggy Man has to take
it out of his pocket for it to work, rather than simply pos-
sess it). Various plots intertwine: Queen Ann Soforth of
Oogaboo wants to invade Oz; human girl Betsy Bobbin
and her mule Hank are washed ashore in the Rose Kingdom and end up helping the Shaggy Man find his brother,
who disappeared underground in Oklahoma and who has
been captured by the Nome King (who has recovered from
drinking the Water of Oblivion in *The Emerald City*). To
stop the party – which eventually includes Polychrome
and Tik-Tok – the Nome King sends them through the
Hollow Tube to the other side of the world, but the Great
Jinjin sends them back with an Instrument of Vengeance, a

dragon named Quox. After further adventures, the Shaggy Man's brother is rescued, the Nome King is deposed, and Betsy decides to stay in Oz.

Baum answered one of the persistent queries about Oz in the final scenes of this story: why is Toto the only animal that doesn't speak? It's because he chooses not to.

The Scarecrow of Oz, 1915's addition to the saga, was one of Baum's own favourite tales, and 'guest starred' Cap'n Bill and Trot, who appeared in his earlier books, *The Sea Fairies* and *Sky Island*, as well as featuring the land of Mo (the retitled Phunnyland from one of Baum's earliest works). It reworked the plot of the silent movie *His Majesty, the Scarecrow of Oz*.

Cap'n Bill and Trot find themselves in fairyland and meet Button Bright. Carried across the Deadly Desert by a giant bird, an Ork, they arrive in Jinxland, whose king Kynd was killed by Prime Minister Phearse who was then killed by his prime minister, Krewl. Now king, Krewl wants to marry Kynd's daughter Gloria, who is in love with Phearse's son Pon. Bill tries to prevent a witch named Blinkie from freezing Gloria's heart, but is turned into a grasshopper. When the Scarecrow learns of this, he is given some magic by Glinda, and goes to the rescue, enlisting the assistance of the Orks. Although he is captured and threatened with burning, the Scarecrow is triumphant, and Gloria is placed on the throne with Pon as her consort (although the Jinxlanders originally want the Scarecrow to become ruler). The others go to the Emerald City.

In a nice touch, Trot has read Baum's Oz stories, and therefore recognizes the people she meets during her journey!

Rinkitink in Oz is another story whose roots lie in earlier work by L. Frank Baum, this time in a story that he had penned as an original fantasy novel eleven years before this version finally appeared in June 1916. Reading it, you can easily see the sections that were added to make it part of the Oz saga.

Pinagree, an island in the Nonestic Ocean that surrounds the countries which themselves surround the Deadly Desert around Oz, is ruled by a king who has use of three magical pearls: a blue one for superhuman strength; a pink one to make him invulnerable; and a white one to provide pearls of wisdom. When the island is attacked, young prince Inga has to try to save the day, with only visiting King Rinkitink and a bad-tempered goat named Bilbil as aid. After many adventures during which the pearls are found, lost, recovered and used to save most of the people they realize that Inga's parents are in the hands of the Nome King. It's at this point Ozma and Dorothy, who have been watching events unfold on the Magic Picture, decide to intervene, and force the Nome King to release everyone. Bilbil turns out to have been enchanted so Glinda returns him to human form as Prince Bobo; Bobo and Rinkitink return to the latter's home, while Inga and his parents head for Pinagree.

Another brief racial insult – a tottenhot is a lesser form of man – has been excised from some later editions.

The Lost Princess of Oz, L. Frank Baum's 1917 novel, was inspired by a young girl who had written to the author saying, 'I suppose if Ozma ever got hurt or losted, everybody would be sorry'.

The story starts with the disappearance of Ozma, which would be bad enough in itself, but loads of other magical items disappear at the same time, including both Glinda and the Wizard's sets of magical tools. After the various heroes are divided into search parties, Dorothy, Button Bright, Trot, Betsy Bobbin and the Wizard head into Winkie Country to search for the missing ruler and the magic. The trail leads them to Ugu the Shoemaker who wanted more magic for himself, and kidnapped Ozma when she interrupted his thefts. Dorothy is able to use the magic belt (which, rather handily for the Ozites, hasn't been stolen along with virtually every other magic item) to turn Ugu into a dove. Ugu escapes, but a few days later returns to the Emerald City to beg forgiveness; Dorothy grants it, and offers to change Ugu back into human form, but he decides to stay as a dove.

The Tin Woodman of Oz was one of L. Frank Baum's rare examinations of the backstory of Oz. Published in 1918, it explains not only how the Tin Woodman came to be in his metallic form, but also some of Oz's history prior to the events of *The Wonderful Wizard of Oz*: some years earlier, Oz was enchanted by the Fairy Queen Lurline, who left a fairy behind to rule it.

When a young boy, Woot, questions why he never went back to find his lost love, Nimmie Amee, the Tin Woodman decides that he must rectify this error. Accompanied by Woot and the Scarecrow, he heads into Gillikin Country, but along the way they end up transformed into animals, as does Polychrome. After Ozma restores their forms, they continue their quest, and find another Tin Man rusting where Dorothy found the original. This is Captain Fyter, who was also in love with Nimmie Amee; he joins the party. The Tin Woodman also finds his original head, which is not particularly pleasant; Ku-Klip, the tinsmith responsible for both the Tin Men's predicaments, explains that he used the removed body parts to create an assistant, Chopfyt. After further adventures, they reach Nimmie Amee's house to find she's married to Chopfyt and has no intention of leaving. Although not getting the happy ending he'd hoped for, the Tin Woodman returns to the Emerald City and then back to Winkie Country.

The Magic of Oz was the first book in the Oz series published following the death of its creator, hitting stores in

June 1919, a month after Baum's death. Baum knew he was seriously ill when he wrote it, and included an apology in his foreword for not maintaining his usual diligence in replying to letters from his fans.

Once again, there's an attempt to conquer Oz by Ruggedo, the former Nome King, who this time teams up with a Munchkin boy, Kiki Aru, who has learned how to use magic to transform people simply using the word Pyrqxgl. Kiki changes the pair into birds so they can fly over the Deadly Desert, and they then try to turn the wild animal population against the Ozites by claiming that they know of a plan to enslave them. Only the arrival of Dorothy and friends – who visit the Forest of Gugu looking for monkeys to train for Ozma's birthday party – prevents the attack, and the Wizard, who overhears the correct pronunciation of Pyrqxgl, turns the villains into nuts. Before they can be properly dealt with, Cap'n Bill and Trot get in trouble on a magic island which has made them take root there; the Wizard uses Pyrqxgl to change them into bees. After Ozma's birthday, Kiki and Ruggedo are transformed back to normal and given the Water of Oblivion, so they can start fresh lives in the Emerald City.

Glinda of Oz was the final book written by L. Frank Baum. Its appearance in May 1920 marked the end of an era, and, inadvertently but appropriately, it features nearly every main character from the series – with the exception of Billina the chicken.

Dorothy and Ozma find themselves caught up in the conflict between the Skeezers and the Flatheads when they see details of the coming war in Glinda's Great Record Book. After attempting to intervene, the pair find themselves caught inside the domed island city of the Skeezers, at the bottom of the lake. Although she's wearing the Magic Belt, Dorothy simply alerts Glinda to their predicament, and the Good Witch forms the various Ozites into a rescue party, while the Skeezers try to make Ozma take over the city's combination of science and magic, which she fails to do. Eventually the Patchwork Girl, Dorothy, Trot and Betsy devise a solution and get the island back to the surface. The story ends with everyone acknowledging Ozma as the ruler of Oz, and the party then returns home.

6

THE CANONICAL OZ: BOOKS BY RUTH PLUMLY THOMPSON (1921–1939)

The Royal Book of Oz may nowadays be credited to Ruth Plumly Thompson, but when it first appeared in 1921 the cover indicated clearly that it was by L. Frank Baum on the cover. The publishers were so keen not to lose their lucrative franchise that they even claimed Thompson had written the story based on extensive notes left by Baum, which seems to be a fabrication.

The Wogglebug decides to compile a Royal Genealogy of Oz, which leads the Scarecrow to wonder about his own ancestry. Unlike many of the other inhabitants of Oz, who were created magically, he wants to know where he came from, and he heads off, followed by Dorothy and the Lion. The Scarecrow follows the pole on which he was found down into the earth, and ends up in the Silver Islands, where he is hailed as Emperor, and discovers he is the reincarnation of Chang Whang Woe. Meanwhile Dorothy and the Lion meet three new characters: Sir Hokus of Pokes; and two camels, the Comfortable Camel and the Doubtful Dromedary. They are transported to the Silver Islands when Dorothy wishes to be with the Scarecrow as they are standing on Wish Way. The Scarecrow has been trying to get away from his 'family' and the entire party manage to escape using a magic parasol and fan. On their return to the Emerald City, the Wogglebug adjusts his records regarding the Scarecrow and deems Dorothy the 'Royal Discoverer of Oz'.

Kabumpo in Oz made its debut in 1922, credited properly to Ruth Plumly Thompson, although the first-edition cover noted that it was 'Founded on and Continuing The Famous Oz Stories by L. Frank Baum' (in considerably larger text size than the author credit). This would continue to appear for many years.

Prince Pompadore of the kingdom of Pumpernick is celebrating his latest eighteenth birthday (like all dwellers in the fairylands, he's immortal so he can have as many eighteenth birthdays as he wishes) when his cake explodes, revealing a scroll threatening the disappearance of the kingdom unless Pompadore weds 'ye Proper Fairy Princess'. His elephant, Kabumpo, decides that Pompadore must marry Ozma and he sets off with the prince in tow. Meanwhile, Ruggedo, the former Gnome King (Thomson changed the spelling to the more normal version) is no longer feeling the effects of the Water of Oblivion and starts experimenting with magic, bringing a wooden doll, Peg Amy, to life, and turning Wag the rabbit into human size. He then makes himself huge, and runs off in a panic towards Ev with Ozma's palace on his head. With help from the Runaway Country (a country that's so determined to be discovered that it develops feet and sets off to find its own settlers), Pompa and Kabumpo head to the rescue – only for Ozma, quite rightly, to turn

Pompa down. However, luckily, Peg Amy is a princess, so Pumpernick is saved.

The Cowardly Lion of Oz, first published in 1923, continues Thompson's use of many hundreds of different kingdoms that readers had not heard of before – in this case, the Munchkin region of Mudge, ruled over by Mustafa, who's annoyed that he only has 9,999.5 lions. Mustafa sends two new arrivals from America – a clown called Notta Bit More, and a young orphan named Bobby Downs, who had inadvertently found themselves in Oz after accidentally casting a transportation spell – to capture the Cowardly Lion. The Lion is a bit upset anyway, as he believes he's losing the courage that the Wizard gave him, and thinks the Patchwork Girl's advice to eat a courageous man might work. However, hunters and hunted end up as friends, but Mustafa sends Crunch, a stone giant, to retrieve the Lion. Once back in Mudge, the Lion and all the other lions in Mustafa's collection (even the half) are turned to stone, but Glinda and the Wizard are able to reverse the process. Unfortunately, their spells don't work on the Lion and it looks as if he can't be turned back. However, back in the Emerald City, the tears of Dorothy and the Lion's friends, when they see his plight, do the trick.

Grampa in Oz followed in 1924. Where Baum had shown an almost utopian Oz, where everyone worked for the common good, Thompson added a small degree of realism, and set this story in the kingdom of Ragbad, which is on the point of economic collapse – for the first time since Baum's initial book, money is a key factor in an Oz tale. The king only has three servants left: Pudge, a seer who can prophesy events that have already happened; a footman; and Grampa, a veteran soldier with a game leg – it opens up into a board game. When King Fumbo's head is taken, Grampa and Prince Tatters go to look for it (and hopefully a fortune for the prince). On the way, they meet Bill, a weathervane blown from Chicago who's given life on arrival in Oz, and Urtha, a flower maiden who's really made of flowers. Dorothy, meanwhile, is helping not-very-good poet Percy Vere look for the missing Princess Pretty Good from Perhaps City in the Maybe Mountains. Fumbo's head is found, Urtha is turned back into a human – and of course, she's Princess Pretty Good. Ozma has been watching on the Magic Picture and sends everyone back to Ragbad, where a gold brick-laying hen will solve their problems.

The Lost King of Oz picks up on a brief mention of Pastoria in the second ever Oz book, *The Marvelous Land of Oz*. In this 1925 adventure, Thompson features Mombi, the former Wicked Witch of the North, who is now working as cook in the land of Kimbaloo. When she meets Pajuka, a goose that used to be the prime minister of Oz, she decides to find out what happened to Pastoria, Ozma's father whom she enchanted. (Thompson chooses to ignore some of the other variants of Ozma's past.) With the help of Pajuka, and a boy named Snip, she sets out to find him. Meanwhile, Ozma is told to 'go to Morrow today' and finds a cloak that can restore her father; and Dorothy ends up in Hollywood – where she temporarily becomes the age she would have been had she remained in our world – and brings Humpy, a live stunt dummy, back with her. They encounter the Back Talkers in Eht Kcab Sdoow, the Scooters and Kabumpo, before meeting the other group and guessing that Humpy is Pastoria. He isn't – Pastoria is really Tora, an old tailor who has been held prisoner by the invisible Blanks of Blankenburg. He doesn't want to return to the throne, and becomes a tailor in the Emerald City, helped by Snip and Humpy. Mombi however is put to death – an act that caused considerable controversy with Oz fans.

* * *

The Hungry Tiger of Oz from 1926 can be seen as a companion book to *The Cowardly Lion*, printed three years earlier. Another Arab-like ruler, Irasha the Rough, Pasha of Rash in the land of Ev, decides to solve his prison overpopulation problems by offering the incarcerated hordes to the Hungry Tiger. The Tiger eagerly comes, but then suffers pangs of conscience, particularly when he realizes that the prisoners are simply people Irasha doesn't like. Meanwhile, Betsy Bobbin (from *Tik-Tok of Oz*) meets Carter Green the Vegetable Man who has to keep moving around or he'll take root. They end up in Rash, from where they flee with the Tiger and the real Pasha of Rash, the Scarlet Prince Evered (known as Reddy) in search of three rubies that will help Reddy regain his throne. Carter has one of them; they find the second in the Gnome Kingdom. The third is held by Atmos Fere, who belongs to a race of inflated people; he tries to kidnap Ozma to prove to his subjects there are people living on the ground, but she uses a pin to bring him down to earth. When they meet Betsy and her group, Atmos passes over the ruby, and Reddy is able to get rid of Irasha, who is taken along with his henchman by Atmos to prove his point, and then dumped on an island in the Nonestic Ocean.

The Gnome King of Oz once again features Ruggedo, who is – to no one's surprise – trying to conquer Oz for what seems like the thousandth time in this 1927 novel. The former Gnome King teams up with another new American visitor to Oz: Peter, from Philadelphia, who, like Trot, has already read an Oz story (although not one featuring Ruggedo!). Peter is searching for treasure – which he finds in an old pirate ship – but realizes that Ruggedo's plans to conquer Oz need stopping. Ruggedo has found a cloak in the ship that makes the wearer invisible and transports him anywhere. It's damaged so needs repairing by the best seamstresses, who happen to be in Patch. Which is where, by pure chance (and by mistake), the Patchwork Girl has just been installed as ruler. She isn't best pleased with her new role, despite the presence of cheerful bear Grumpy, and is happy to help Peter thwart Ruggedo's plans. The trio get distracted on the way to the Emerald City, meeting an oztrich who transports them the rest of the way. Ruggedo has been causing trouble between the Ozites, but the oztrich's egg repels him for a time. However, Ruggedo manages to steal the Magic Belt back from Ozma while she is still wearing it but he is finally defeated when Peter pitches a Silence Stone at him. Peter returns home with some of the pirates' gold.

The Giant Horse of Oz is an unusual addition to the canon, in that it's named after a character who only really makes a small appearance in the book. A more logical title would have been 'The Good Witch of Oz' or similar, since this 1928 story focuses far more on Tattypoo, the Good Witch of the North (the old witch whom Dorothy meets on her initial arrival in Oz in the original book). Her assistance is sought when the kingdom of the Ozure Isles is in trouble. The wicked witch Mombi kidnapped their queen Orin and left a monster, Quiberon, to keep the inhabitants in check. Quiberon wants a mortal maiden to devour – which in Oz means it's either Dorothy, Betsy Bobbin or Trot. While the islands' soothsayer Akbad tries to kidnap one of them (and ends up with Trot, as well as the Scarecrow and an animated statue named Benny, who has arrived in Oz from Boston, Massachusetts), Prince Philador searches for Tattypoo, meeting the eponymous giant horse, High Boy, and Herby the Medicine Man. When he can't find Tattypoo, he's advised to seek help from Ozma. Trot and her party escape and meet up with Philador's group. Once in the Emerald City, they learn that Tattypoo and Queen Orin are the same person, and the elderly witch is transformed back into her younger self.

Jack Pumpkinhead of Oz continues Ruth Plumly Thompson's preference for writing about boys' adventures in Oz, rather than girls as had been the case with L. Frank Baum. Her 1929 story saw the return of Peter from Philadelphia, who wondered what had been happening in Oz since his visit there two years previously. Thanks to a magic coin, he finds out – but ends up outside Jack Pumpkinhead's house. The two decide to travel to the Emerald City, acquiring the magic dinner bell of a Red Jinn, and a new companion, Snif the Iffin (a griffin who's lost his 'gr'). They become embroiled in the villainous plots of Mogodore, the Baron of Baffleburg, who has kidnapped Princess Shirley Sunshine on her wedding day to Blefaygor, and decides to impress her by invading the Emerald City. Mogodore succeeds in imprisoning most of the Ozites (they're playing a game of Blind Man's Bluff when he attacks), but is defeated by Jack and the Red Jinn. He and his warriors are miniaturized (which was in fact their natural state before Mogodore's great-grandfather was granted human stature for carrying out good deeds), and Shirley and Blefaygor are married. Peter is then returned back to his home.

The Yellow Knight of Oz marked the start of the 1930s with an adventurous quest for Sir Hokus of Pokes (and formed the core of the only stage play based on one of Ruth Plumly Thompson's additions to the Oz saga). He heads off with the Comfortable Camel, and is joined by yet another visitor from our world – Speedy, a lad from Long Island, who accidentally arrives in Oz while travelling in a rocket apparently to Mars. Speedy's touch awakens a golden statue, Marygolden, when he crashes in Subterranea; she helps him and Sir Hokus with a quest to defeat the evil Sultan of Samandra, a place where animals – even ones who have previously been able to speak – are dumb. They manage to free both Samandra and Corabia from the spells of the Sultan, before Ozma and Dorothy arrive. It is revealed that Sir Hokus is in reality young Prince Corum and he ends up marrying Marygolden. Speedy is sent back to Long Island.

This story rewrites the origin of Sir Hokus: in Thompson's introductory tale for him, he is an Arthurian knight (and indeed most of this story plays into that background), but we learn at the end that he is a native-born Ozite.

Pirates in Oz brings Peter back from Philadelphia for a third and final time, as Thompson sets up a further threat of conquest by Ruggedo, the former Gnome King – although at least an explanation is given for his ability to menace the Emerald City once more: the people of Menankypoo wanted a 'dumb king' which meant that the silence forced on him at the end of *The Gnome King* isn't forgotten. Their speech appears as messages on their foreheads – effectively predicting texting sixty years early in this 1931 novel. His speech is returned when he's hit on the head and he ends up as pirate leader, with the help of Clocker, the former Wise Man of Menankypoo who has a clock for a face. The pirates' former leader, Captain Samuel Salt, sails around the Nonestic Ocean having various adventures, accompanied by Peter, and they are joined by a flying pig called Pigasus. When they learn of Ruggedo's escape and plans to conquer Oz, they head for the Emerald City, where they are just in time to prevent Ruggedo from using the Magic Belt, which he has managed to get off Ozma. Ruggedo is turned into a water jug; Peter once again chooses to go home – although he asks to be summoned back. Captain Salt goes sailing.

The Purple Prince of Oz's publication in 1932 marks the first time that Thompson mined her own back catalogue of creations in the Oz universe for all the lead characters (bar the obligatory appearance at the end of the story of a few old favourites). Kabumpo the Elegant Elephant is at the heart of the tale, forced to try to save the royal family of Pumpernick after their throne is usurped, with the help of his new valet Randy. Deciding not to get help from Ozma, Kabumpo instead seeks out the Red Jinn, Jinnicky. After assorted adventures, involving Queen Torpedora of Torpedo Town, the leader of a race of sentient weapons, as well as King Kumup and Queen Godown of the kingdom of Stair Way, they are helped by Polychrome across the Deadly Desert back to Pumpernick where the trio are able to defeat the evil fairy, Faleero, who had helped the usurper conquer Pumpernick. As the other Ozites come to assist, and then celebrate the restoration of the throne, a party from Regalia come crashing in to reveal that Randy is really none other than Ranywell Handywell Brandenburg Bompadoo, the King of Regalia, and that all his deeds alongside Kabumpo have been necessary for him to gain his own crown.

Ojo in Oz (1933) has attracted some negative attention from recent scholars for the highly stereotypical way in which Thompson describes the Gypsies who feature heavily within the story, and for their eventual fate – others who commit the same crimes are simply transformed into other creatures, but the Gypsies are banished to Southern Europe.

Ojo (the Unlucky as was) is kidnapped by the Gypsies and meets a captive bear, The Snuffurious Buxorious Blundurious Boroso (Snufferbux for short). The Gypsies are attacked by bandits, led by Realdbad, and Ojo, Snufferbux and Realdbad team up. Meanwhile the alarm has been raised over Ojo's disappearance, and a gang of Ozites, led by Dorothy, set out to rescue him, visiting Dicksy Land, while others check with Glinda to see if the Great Book of Records shows what's happening (it doesn't). The groups are eventually united, and it transpires that Ojo is really Realdbad's son – and Realdbad is the deposed king of See-bania, Reel Alla Bad. Ojo had been deliberately hidden to keep him from harm's way. The Gypsies are removed from Oz, while Realdbad's fellow bandits are turned into Winkie farmers.

Speedy in Oz features dinosaurs, a flying island, and the return of Long Island native Speedy in a novel that was apparently Ruth Plumly Thompson's personal favourite. The 1934 story is set on Umbrella Island (a flying island powered by umbrellas) onto which Speedy and a suddenly reanimated dinosaur skeleton (named Terrybubble) are sent by an exploding geyser in the Yellowstone National Park. The island is governed by King Sizzeroo, but unfortu-nately it's not easily steerable, and has upset a giant named Loxo by banging into his head. Loxo demands that a 'boy' he sees at the palace is to be his personal boot-lacer; in fact it's Sizzeroo's daughter Princess Guereeda. When Speedy arrives, some courtiers think they can substitute him for Guereeda, but bad luck means that both of them end up in Loxo's charge. The king requests help from Ozma and Dorothy – as they are conveniently near the Emerald City – but when Loxo refuses to release the children, he is tricked into eating and drinking items which return him to human size. He's delighted by this, and allows the children to leave. Speedy is returned to Long Island, since he knows he needs to help the United States prepare new weapons, while his friends on Umbrella Island hope for his return.

The Wishing Horse of Oz (1935) marked the point at which Ruth Plumly Thompson had written more Oz novels than its creator – unlike Baum, she didn't have periods away from fairyland – but she relied once more on the well-used plotline of someone trying to conquer Oz, although for once it's not Ruggedo behind it. This time it's King

Skamperoo, the ruler of Skampavia, who wants to get hold of the emeralds that give the Emerald City its name. With the help of a horse he conjures up, he manages to kidnap the various rulers of Oz, including Ozma, who have come to the Emerald City for Ozma's birthday party, and produce amnesia in everyone else – except Dorothy and Pigasus. The pair have to undergo various trials as they try to find a way to help their friends, but, with the help of seer Bitty Bit, they save the day, and Skamperoo is sent back to his own country.

Around this time, L. Frank Baum's son Frank Joslyn Baum published his own continuation of the Oz saga, *The Laughing Dragon of Oz*; this effectively unauthorized book became the subject of a lawsuit between Baum junior and his mother, who owned the rights to the novel.

Captain Salt in Oz (1936) sees the Pirate Captain travelling around the Nonestic Ocean, claiming the various islands that he visits in the name of Ozma. It was another move by Thompson that has subsequently proved controversial – the colonialism doesn't necessarily fit well with the ineffectual ruler Ozma usually seems to be. Apparently, Ozma is concerned about overpopulation in Oz (since children continue to be born, but nobody dies, she does have a point). Captain Salt, aided by King Ato of the Octagon Islands and Roger the Royal Read Bird, sails around the Nonestic Ocean, rescuing Tandy, the ruler of Ozamaland (who decides to stay with Salt rather than stay at home once they finally get him there), and getting captured by jellyfish-like sea people who want to put him on show. The book ends on a speculative note with Captain Salt heading back out to sea to find new lands and new civilizations.

This is the only book among the 'Famous Forty' which does not include one scene set in Oz itself, and one of only two in which neither Dorothy nor the Scarecrow says a word.

*   *   *

Handy Mandy in Oz (1937) is one of Thompson's more unusual stories, featuring at its heart a goat-girl who, like all the people from Mount Mern, has seven hands, and is rather surprised when she gets to Oz to discover that everyone there only has two. She arrives there thanks to a geyser erupting, finding herself in the principality of Keretaria in Munchkin Country, and helps Nox the Royal Ox locate the missing King Kerry. The trail leads them to the Silver Mountain, the domain of the Wizard of Wutz, who imprisons them. He plans to steal all the magical items from around Oz and use them to conquer the land. He has even got the jug containing Ruggedo and when Mandy accidentally breaks the jug, Ruggedo is freed and allies himself with the Wizard. They head for the Emerald City, but Mandy and Nox escape and get there in time to prevent the two villains from succeeding. Ruggedo is transformed into a cactus in his last appearance in the Famous Forty.

The character of Handy Mandy also appeared in the poem *Handy Mandy: Solomon T. Wise's New Cook*, although this was more like a domestic robot than a living person – and only had four hands.

The Silver Princess in Oz was Ruth Plumly Thompson's penultimate official Oz story, appearing in 1938. It centres on her own original creations once more – King Randy of Regalia, Kabumpo the Elegant Elephant, and Jinnicky the Red Jinn – as well as the eponymous metallic Princess from Anuther Planet, Planetty, and a fire-breathing Thundercolt named Thun.

Randy and Kabumpo encounter the aliens when a storm throws them out of Oz, and Randy falls in love with Planetty, who has to get back to her home planet within a week or she will die without access to Vanadium springs. They decide to ask Jinnicky for help but discover that he is no longer in control. They therefore assist him back to power, and during the various problems they encounter Planetty and Thun are turned into statues. When Jinnicky revives them, they are now suited to life in Oz, and therefore Randy asks Planetty to be his bride.

The book has attracted considerable criticism for the casually cruel way in which Planetty treats a group of black slaves, and the way in which she compares them to unthinking beasts.

Ozoplaning with the Wizard of Oz came out in 1939 to coincide with the MGM film of the very first book in the series, and Ruth Plumly Thompson brings her official run on the books to a close with a story that incorporates many of the characters from that debut story. It even begins with most of the survivors meeting for a meal in the Wizard's quarters recapping the events of their first encounter (i.e. *The Wonderful Wizard of Oz*), before the Wizard shows off his new inventions, the Ozpril and the Oztober. An accident sends the Soldier with the Green Whiskers, the Tin Man and Jellia Jamb (the maid whom Dorothy meets on her first visit to the Emerald City) flying off in the Oztober; the Wizard, the Lion, the Scarecrow and Dorothy pursue them in the Ozpril. The Tin Man gains control of the plane, and lands in the sky country Stratovania, which he proceeds to annex in the name of Ozma – much to the annoyance of King Strutoovious the Seventh, aka Strut of the Strat. Strut decides to try his hand at conquest and heads for the Emerald City; the Ozpril is blown up when it arrives at Stratovania. The Wizard and his group end up trying to help Princess Azarine of Red Top Mountain regain her throne, as well as stopping the Stratovanian invasion. With assistance from Glinda and Ozma, they finally achieve this.

7

THE CANONICAL OZ: BOOKS BY OTHER AUTHORS (1940–1963)

The Wonder City of Oz was written by John R. Neill, who had illustrated all the previous Oz stories (with the exception of *The Wonderful Wizard of Oz*). Unsurprisingly, therefore, he was expected to have a good grasp of the Emerald City and its inhabitants, although like Ruth Plumly Thompson, he didn't adhere strictly to everything that L. Frank Baum had created. However, his first book was heavily reworked by a now-anonymous copy editor at publishers Reilly & Lee, with a whole plotline added to the text – a fact Neill apparently only discovered when the final printed copies arrived in the mail.

This thirty-fourth Oz story, which appeared in 1940, is extremely confusing but follows a new character, Jenny Jump, who tries to use a leprechaun to turn herself into a fairy. However, he manages to escape from her when she's still only half transformed but has sufficient power to jump into Oz, arriving in Ozma's carriage, where she explains she wants to be queen. She sets up a Style Shop for fashion makeovers, and adopts a Munchkin boy named Number Nine whom she treats as a slave. She saves the Emerald City from attack by chocolate soldiers, but undermines it considerably when she runs for election against Ozma (the plotline added to Neill's original). When Jenny loses, she causes chaos, leading to the Wizard removing all her bad attributes. The now-calm Jenny becomes a Duchess of Oz, and the leprechaun makes her a proper fairy.

The Scalawagons of Oz (1941) continued the confusing plotlines, with the return of Jenny Jump and Number Nine, although this time it was completely written by Neill. The various problems faced by the inhabitants of the Emerald City are all connected to the Bell-snickle, a monster who enjoys making mischief, as well as the titular Scalawagons, cars that can fly, which have a rudimentary form of intelligence (and can make nice lunches). When the Bell-snickle fills the vehicles with flabber-gas they fly away; Jenny, the Scarecrow, the Woodman and the Sawhorse are sent by Glinda to retrieve them, which they finally manage to do after a number of adventures. The Bell-snickle then tries some other mischief, bringing some walking trees towards the Emerald City, but they are terrified by the Woodman's axe. The Bell-snickle is captured and put through Jenny's Style Shop, becoming a stopper that Ozma can use to put an end to any trends of which she doesn't approve.

Even less well regarded than Neill's effort from the previous year, perhaps unsurprisingly, copies of *The Scalawagons* are very hard to find!

Lucky Bucky in Oz was John R. Neill's third and final book, appearing in 1942. (He completed the text but not the illustrations for a fourth, but Reilly & Lee opted not to publish it; *The Runaway in Oz* finally appeared in 1995.)

'Lucky' Bucky is a resident of New York who finds himself in Oz after an explosion during a cruise near the Statue of Liberty. He meets a huge wooden whale, named Davy Jones, who has been the base for a group of pirates; Davy abandons the pirates but allows Bucky to live on board and they proceed to have various adventures, meeting the Dollfins (unusual wooden merfolk), and the Zenons (small snowmen) on their way to Oz. There, Ozma has been encouraging the CWO (Castle Walls of Oz) Painters' Project, in which everyone, great and small, can paint their adventures on the walls. Some of them are almost too life-like, as a picture of old Mombi flies off and stows away inside Davy Jones. She's hiding as Davy and Bucky meet the Gnomes, and go over the rainbow with Polychrome. Before they end up in the Emerald City, she flies off to hide in a volcano but she is captured and returned to her picture by the Wizard. Bucky meets all the Ozites he's previously read about, but isn't too worried about going home.

The Magical Mimics in Oz picked up the series in 1946 after a four-year break caused both by the death of John R. Neill and the various shortages caused by the Second World War. The thirty-seventh official Oz story was written by Jack Snow, and illustrated by Frank G. Kramer; Snow wasn't the first choice as author. Reilly & Lee had approached Mary Dickerson Donahey, but she had turned down the job because she felt Oz had become too complicated, and she wouldn't be able to keep track of all the characters and plots. Snow had offered his services when aged only twelve after L. Frank Baum's death and in 1954 would write the guidebook *Who's Who in Oz*, cataloguing the creations of the various Royal Historians. However, for his two novels, he only used either his own characters or those created by Baum (and in a far more coherent way than Neill had ever done). He also quite consciously modelled his story on Baum's tale *The Emerald City of Oz*.

Ozma hands control of Oz to Dorothy when she and Glinda head off for a conference with other fairies, but Dorothy and the Wizard are quickly replaced by exact copies created by the Mimics, evil beings living in Mount Illuso. However, the copies don't fool Toto, and they are exposed, but not before they find a way to free the other Mimics from Mount Illuso. The real Dorothy and Wizard escape from Mount Illuso and find the fairy Ozana who was meant to be watching over the Mimics. Together they head back to the Emerald City, where the Mimics have paralyzed the people, sedated the creatures, and tied up the non-humans like the Scarecrow and the Patchwork Girl. Ozana deals with the Mimics, who are returned to Mount Illuso. Ozana is invited to remain in the Eternal City, and brings the Pineville people (wooden puppets) and her Story Blossom Garden with her.

The Shaggy Man of Oz dragged the series kicking and screaming into the post-Second World War era. Where Jack Snow's first book had maintained the innocent, almost old-fashioned atmosphere of Oz – in line with Snow's professed intention to return it to the supposedly timeless Baum era, which reflected a pre-First World War America – *The Shaggy Man* features two children whose father is a physics teacher and own a television. In other respects, though, it owes more debt to Baum than his successors: the story is a reworking of Baum's 1906 novel *John Dough and the Cherub*.

Tom and Twink are twin brother and sister (real names Zebbidiah and Abbadiah) who live in Buffalo, New York. They find themselves in fairyland when their toy clown's third cousin Twiffle pulls them through their television screen to the island of the wizard Conjo – which happens to be where the Love Magnet that the Shaggy Man brought to Oz many years earlier was created. It's broken in half and Ozma sends the Shaggy Man to get it fixed. Conjo does repair it but steals a Magic Compass that Ozma had given the Shaggy Man to help get back to Oz. As Conjo heads for the Emerald City to try to supplant the Wizard as the chief magician of the realm, Tom, Twink, Twiffle and the Shaggy Man take a more circuitous route, eventually using the Nome King's tunnel to get beneath the Deadly Desert into Oz. They are helped by the King of the Fairy Beavers who joins them in the Emerald City and uses his water magic to squirt some of the Water of Oblivion from the Forbidden Fountain into Conjo's mouth. Twiffle takes the mind-wiped wizard back to his island, while Twink and Tom spend some time in Oz before Ozma sends them home.

There was a three-year gap between Snow's books, partly caused by his publishers refusing to accept the first half of the book, and demanding a top-to-bottom rewrite of the section – his editor was sympathetic, writing, 'How I pity your present state of mind, trying to think up an entirely new story'.

The Hidden Valley of Oz was not just the debut Oz novel by Rachel R. Cosgrove, it was the author's very first book. She would later achieve fame as a historical romance novelist, and as a science-fiction writer under the penname E.L. Arch. With Jack Snow no longer willing to write Oz novels after a spell of ill health, the publishers rushed this story out for Christmas 1951, with illustrations by Dirk Gringhuis.

The visitor to Oz in this story is Jonathan Andrew Manley (known to all as Jam), the son of a biologist from Ohio. Taking his father's experimental animals with him, he goes on a test flight of a giant kite he's built and ends up in Gillikin Country, where he's astonished to find that his animals can now talk. Percy the white rat and the two guinea pigs Pinny and Gig join him on a quest across Oz where they meet giant Terp the Terrible and the Equinots.

When they reach the Tin Woodman's castle, a group of the Ozites including Dorothy, the Scarecrow, the Lion and the Hungry Tiger agree to help defeat Terp. On the return journey, they encounter the Leopard with the Changeable Spots, as well as the King of Bookville and the inhabitants of Icetown. They manage to shrink the giant down to normal size and Jam is returned to Ohio after a feast in the Emerald City. Percy decides to remain in Oz.

Jam was meant to arrive in Oz by rocket, but the author was asked to change it because Ruth Plumly Thompson had already used this idea in *The Yellow Knight of Oz* (a rare occurrence of similar plotlines in an Oz story being stopped by the publishers). Although Cosgrove wrote a second novel, *The Wicked Witch of Oz*, this was not accepted by Reilly & Lee, following poor sales for the Oz books post-War. The next 'official' book published was Jack Snow's non-fiction guide, *Who's Who in Oz*, in 1954.

Merry Go Round in Oz was the final official book published, and arrived in bookstores in 1963, twelve years after *The Hidden Valley of Oz*'s debut. It was credited to mother and daughter Eloise Jarvis McGraw and Lauren McGraw Wagner; McGraw had won the Newbery Medal on two occasions, for *Moccasin Trail* in 1952 and *The Golden Goblet* a decade later. In fact, McGraw wrote the actual text of *Merry Go Round in Oz*, but she felt that her daughter's contributions merited a co-author credit.

Three separate story strands feature in *Merry Go Round*. Robin Satchiverus Brown, an orphan from Cherryburg, Oregon, finds himself in Oz with a talking roundabout horse named Merry (who has serious problems travelling in straight lines), and has assorted adventures in View Halloo and Roundabout. Dorothy and the Lion go to order Easter eggs from the Easter Bunny, while in the kingdoms of Halidom and Troth, three Golden Circlets have gone missing, and pageboy Fess is sent with Prince Gules to try to retrieve them. Dorothy and the Lion exit Bunnyland from the wrong tunnel and meet Fess and Gules and their assorted menagerie of friends. Following clues given to them by an oracle, they travel to Roundabout where they meet Robin and Merry, and find the circlets. After everything is sorted out, Robin and Merry ask if they can stay in Oz, and Ozma grants their request. The final words in the official Oz canon are addressed to Merry by the Cowardly Lion: 'Welcome home'.

Seven further books are considered by some Oz historians as part of the canon since they were written by Royal Historians or illustrators of the Famous Forty.

Ruth Plumly Thompson's *Yankee in Oz* was written in 1959, and published in 1972 by the International Wizard of Oz Fan Club; *The Enchanted Island of Oz*, also by Thompson, was released in 1976. *The Forbidden Fountain of Oz* was written by the final official Royal Historians, Eloise Jarvis McGraw and Lauren Lynn McGraw (the latter reverted to her maiden name after divorce) and published in 1980. Illustrator Dick Martin, whose drawings graced *Merry Go Round*, penned his own tale, *The Ozmapolitan of Oz* in 1986, while (now going by her married name) Rachel Cosgrove Payes' *The Wicked Witch of Oz*, a sequel to *The Hidden Valley of Oz*, finally saw print in 1993, forty years after it was written.

Books of Wonder produced a version of John R. Neill's *The Runaway in Oz* in 1995; Neill had written this in 1943, but didn't complete the illustrations. It was edited and illustrated by Eric Shanower. Hungry Tiger Press provided an edition of Eloise Jarvis McGraw's *The Rundelstone of Oz* in 2001, a year after the author's death; this had originally formed part of *The Forbidden Fountain of Oz*.

With the renewed interest in Oz following the success of the book and stage show of *Wicked* (see part 3), the Baum

Family commissioned Sherwood Smith to pen four new authorized books set in Oz. *The Emerald Wand of Oz* and *Trouble Under Oz* appeared in 2005 and 2006, with the author announcing that the third volume, *Sky Pirates of Oz*, had been delivered in May 2013.

2. OZ ON SCREEN

I

SILENCE IN OZ

Ask the average person what the most famous movie remake is, and you're likely to get a wealth of different answers. What's not very likely is that they will suggest *The Wizard of Oz* as a possibility, yet the 1939 version of L. Frank Baum's story was at least the fourth different adaptation of the original story for the silver screen. Long before Judy Garland went over the rainbow, there were plenty of other Dorothy Gales.

The earliest surviving Oz movie dates from 1910, and was produced by Selig Polyscope, who had provided the film segments for Baum's travelling version of the tale, *The Fairylogue and Radio-Plays*, two years earlier (for more details, see pp 164–6). The show had been a financial failure, and Baum had been forced to sell all the rights to *The Wizard of Oz* and some of his other books. The four films that Selig made based on Baum's material were an attempt to recoup some of that money.

The Wonderful Wizard of Oz is a 1,000-feet, one-reel film, which runs for a mere thirteen minutes. It can be seen on YouTube, and at times prefigures the rather surrealist version of Oz that John R. Neill presented in his books by thirty years.

The plot is necessarily simplified, although a lot is packed in. On a Kansas farm, Hank the mule is kicking out at farmhands shortly before Dorothy discovers that the Scarecrow out in the field is really alive. He warns her to take refuge in a haystack during a cyclone, which blows them, as well as Hank, Imogene the Cow and Toto, into Oz. Meanwhile, Momba, the Wicked Witch, asserts her authority over the Wizard and he prepares a proclamation stating that he will pass over the crown of Oz to anyone who helps him to beat her since he wants to return to Omaha. (He also notes that as a wizard he's a Humbug, and he's 'tired of this King business'.)

Glinda the Good Witch transforms Toto into a 'real protector' (i.e. replaces the real dog with a much larger pantomime animal), who promptly saves Dorothy from the Cowardly Lion. The Scarecrow spots the Wizard's proclamation and the motley troupe goes to investigate. After finding the Tin Woodman, they are joined by Eureka the Kitten before being captured by Momba. When Dorothy throws water over her, she's killed. They then all go to the Emerald City to claim the crown, and after Dorothy refuses it, the Wizard appoints the Scarecrow as his successor. He prepares to fly off in his balloon, although he faces strike action from his assistants since they don't have to work after 12 noon. He eventually leaves; Dorothy is lifted up to his balloon but he flies off without her.

There is a menagerie of pantomime animals involved and a great deal of vaudevillian slapstick – all the actors playing animals seem to have to show how acrobatic they are. There is no surviving contemporary documentation to confirm the actors or director, although it has been suggested that Bebe Daniels played Dorothy, with Hobart Bosworth as the Wizard, Robert Z. Leonard as the Scarecrow, Olive Cox as Glinda, Winifred Greenwood as Aunt Em, and Eugenie Besserer as Momba.

Selig Polyscope produced two further one-reel Oz films in 1910, but no copies of either exist. According to descriptions in their catalogue based on press releases, though, *Dorothy and the Scarecrow in Oz* dealt with the attempts by the Scarecrow, the Tin Woodman and the Cowardly Lion to get brains, heart and courage respectively from the great Oz, as well as situations involving the carthorse Jim as recounted in Baum's 1908 book, *Dorothy and the Wizard in Oz*. Some sources suggest that this film also included a battle with a giant spider, and Glinda sending Dorothy home, but the documentation is confusing and contradictory.

The Land of Oz, described as 'the crowning effort of the Oz series', added 'new characters, new situations and scintillating comedy' as Dorothy deals with the rebellion army of General Jinger [*sic*] – a plotline derived from Baum's second book, *The Marvelous Land of Oz*.

Selig also produced a version of Baum's 1906 novel *John Dough and the Cherub*, which tied the plotline into the Oz universe, with Princess Ozma of Oz making an appearance. Again, this is lost, and little is known beyond its basic retelling of the original story.

None of the films was successful enough to wipe out Baum's debt to the company; when he declared bankruptcy in 1911, he still owed Selig Polyscope $1,000.

The next set of Oz silent films were produced four years later, and were the creations of the Oz Film Manufacturing Company, set up by Baum to 'produce quality, family-oriented entertainment suitable for children'. Baum reworked material from his seventh Oz novel *The Patchwork Girl of Oz*, published in 1913, for the first film, removing the character of the Shaggy Man, but adding the donkey Mewel, and 'the Lonesome Zoop' (a new creation somewhere between a Flying Monkey and Dr Seuss' Grinch in looks). Instead of the Love Magnet that the Shaggy Man was carrying in the book, there's a small statue created of one of the characters that women find irresistible. The film is based around the same central quest as the novel, as various characters team up to look for the items needed to create the antidote to the Liquid of Petrifaction, but, as with the 1910 films, the plot is often held up to allow for various vaudeville and slapstick routines – as well as a couple of stop-motion effects sequences which are surprisingly sophisticated for 1914.

Scraps, the titular Patchwork Girl, was played by French acrobat Pierre Couderc, since Baum couldn't find an actress who could perform the necessary stunts, with Violet MacMillan as Ojo, Todd Wright as the Wizard, Lon Musgrave as the Tin Woodman and Herbert Glennon as the Scarecrow. Playing the Cowardly Lion – as well as one of the blacked-up Tottenhots – was 'Al' Roach. Better known as Hal, he got along so well with one of the uncredited players on the film, Harold Lloyd, that they went on to work together on some of the best-known silent films of the 1920s.

It was probably the only success story to derive from *The Patchwork Girl*. Paramount Pictures distributed the film on behalf of the Oz Film Manufacturing Company, but after it failed at the box office, partly because it was perceived very much as a movie for children, they refused to accept the other two films in the Oz cycle, which Baum had already made!

The Magic Cloak of Oz, based on Baum's 1905 novel *Queen Zixi of Ix*, was supposed to be released on 28 September 1914, but Paramount declined to do so. The five-reel film was acquired by the British company Alliance Film Productions, and shown in Great Britain in its full form, before being reworked into two separate two-reelers, entitled *The Magic Cloak* and *The Witch Queen*, for distribution both in the UK and in America in 1917. The version of the film that appears on DVD releases of *The Wizard of Oz* is derived from splicing elements of these together, with the 2009 edition containing further footage previously believed lost. Like *The Patchwork Girl*, the film was scripted by Baum himself and directed by J. Farrell Mac-Donald; however, despite its title, its only real connection to Oz is one of the first intertitle cards that notes that some of the characters are 'fairies of Oz' (and these cards have so many other inaccuracies in them that this might well be a mistake). By this point, though, Baum was well aware that his Oz stories were more popular than his other books, so any connection to them – no matter how tenuous – would hopefully draw audiences into theatres.

Whereas *The Patchwork Girl* had been a full-length movie – running for 84 minutes, if projected at the current standard of 24 frames per second – the other two films were only designed to last for 59 minutes. The version of *The Magic Cloak* that we now have runs for 38 minutes, since a complete reel of the film was effectively lost during the conversion into two separate movies. However, the third film, *His Majesty, the Scarecrow of Oz* exists complete, and is by far the best of the three. Alliance Film Productions released it in October 1914, and although critics seemed to like it, the public weren't so impressed. When it was re-released in 1915, under the title *The New Wizard of Oz*, it fared a bit better, but still nowhere near well enough to recoup the money that the Oz Film Manufacturing Company had expended on the trio of films.

In a way, it's a retelling of the original *Wizard of Oz* story, with Dorothy meeting the characters for the first time, and the Scarecrow gaining a new origin – according to this movie, he's animated thanks to the Spirit of the Corn. This was partly because Baum no longer controlled the rights to his original book, so had to steer carefully around elements from that story.

Pon, a gardener's boy, has met his true love, Princess Gloria, the daughter of King Krewl, ruler of the Emerald City. However, Krewl uses Mombi, a wicked witch, to freeze Gloria's heart so she won't love Pon. With the help of Dorothy, the Scarecrow, the Lion, the Tin Woodman, Button Bright, and the Wizard (who is travelling around in a red wagon pulled by the Sawhorse), the lovers are reunited and King Krewl deposed.

If elements of this sound familiar, it's because, never one to miss a chance to cannibalize material, Baum used the storyline of the film as the basis of his next Oz book, *The Scarecrow of Oz*. Violet MacMillan played Dorothy, with Frank Moore as the Scarecrow, Pierre Couderc as the Tin Man, and probably Hal Roach as the Lion. All the animals are credited to Fred Woodward on the titles prepared decades later, but since there are scenes featuring multiple creatures, he couldn't have played them all, and the three films were shot within days of each other.

The failure of *The Patchwork Girl of Oz* spelled the end for L. Frank Baum's dreams of making his own versions of his Oz stories, and a decade passed before another film was completed (Ray C. Smallwood, the director of Rudolph Valentino's *Camille*, worked on a version in 1921 that was never finished or released). This one also claimed to be *The Wizard of Oz*, but treated its source material in a quite cavalier manner – in its own way, it was as drastic a reworking of Baum's Oz stories as *Wicked* would later prove to be. As American Home Entertainment president James Russo warned in 1996, when it was reissued for American audiences alongside Baum's three films from 1914, 'It's not the greatest of the four, because it doesn't hold up to the image we have of the MGM movie.'

Available to watch online, or in a restored version as an

extra on the various anniversary DVDs of the 1939 film, the 1925 film, simply titled *Wizard of Oz*, is probably best known for an early role for Oliver Hardy shortly before he teamed up with Stan Laurel. Director and writer (and former silent comedian) Larry Semon obtained the rights to the story from L. Frank Baum's son Frank Joslyn, and persuaded the younger Baum to write the screenplay, which Semon and another writer, Leon Lee, reworked prior to filming.

Wizard of Oz is often cited as the film that shows how not to handle Baum's gentle and innocent land. It's framed as a story told by an old toymaker to his granddaughter, who wants to hear the familiar tale of Dorothy, the Scarecrow and the Tin Man. That's not what she gets.

In this tale, the Emerald City and Oz aren't governed by Ozma or the Wizard: eighteen years before the start of the film, the townsfolk of Oz woke up to learn that their baby princess had vanished. Since then Oz has been ruled by Prime Minister Kruel, with help from Lady Vishuss, Ambassador Wikked, and the Wizard, who carries out magic tricks (rather than use real magic) to distract the hordes from following Prince Kynd's attempts to foment revolution. Meanwhile, in Kansas, young Dorothy is about to turn eighteen, and is told that she's not actually related to her Aunt Em and Uncle Henry – she was abandoned on their doorstep with a letter that was to be opened when she turned eighteen. When Ambassador Wikked turns up at the farm, he demands to be given the letter: Dorothy is the missing princess, but under Ozian law, if she doesn't actually read the letter explaining this, she will not legally become queen. Although he's treated Dorothy badly, Uncle Henry refuses to hand the letter over to Wikked. Two of the farmhands, played by Semon and Hardy, are in love with Dorothy, a fact that Wikked exploits to try to get hold of the letter. Hardy steals it but Semon retrieves it before they're all swept into Oz by a tornado.

Once there, Dorothy reads the letter, which means that Kruel and Wikked, with Hardy's help, have to come up with various other schemes to maintain their position. At various points Hardy masquerades as the Tin Man, Semon as the Scarecrow, and a third farmhand (Snowball, played by Spencer Bell credited as 'G. Howe Black') as the Cowardly Lion, but eventually Prince Kynd and Dorothy fall in love and live happily ever after – by which point the Toymaker's granddaughter has fallen asleep!

The cast, including Semon's wife Dorothy Dwan as Dorothy, Charles Murray as the Wizard, Josef Swickard as Kruel and Otto Lederer as Ambasador Wikked, try valiantly with the material but there's no disguising the fact that the 93-minute movie is a mess.

According to the full-page ad that Chadwick Pictures took out in *Variety* on 14 January 1925, the film was 'The Greatest Sensation Among Screen Classics Since The Birth of a Nation. The World's Most Famous Fantastic Spectacle The Wizard of Oz [*sic*] starring Larry Semon, The Screen's Greatest Eccentric Comedian.' Assuring the readers that these were 'REAL FACTS!' the ad maintained that 'six months of conscientious effort was required and over $300,000 was spent in the production of this stupendous masterpiece'. Urging potential 'broadcasters' to 'wire now!' it pointed out that *The Wizard of Oz* 'has the unique distinction of being the most famous play ever produced since the beginning of the American Theatre! [It] has the largest ready-made aggregate public in the world, consisting of the millions who saw the original play and the million who have read the famous Oz books! Every year edition upon edition is reprinted of the Oz books series to supply the inexhaustible demand of the lovers of Oz stories. Up to date 1,256,792 copies have been sold!'

It didn't help matters when the National Film Corporation tried to prevent *Wizard of Oz* from opening in February claiming that they had rights to Baum's book, based on their distribution of *The Magic Cloak of Oz* a decade earlier. Chadwick threatened to counter-sue, and National backed down.

Variety seemed to love the film – in their review in April, they noted that despite the fact that 'Larry Semon must have tried every conceivable manner possible to ruin this picture, he has failed to do so and has probably turned out one of the best pictures of all times to take the kids to see.' (It's worth noting that *Variety*'s reviewer 'Fred' took Semon to task for giving Bell the screen credit of G. Howe Black – 'he deserved [a] better fate'.)

Despite the lavish exhortations in the advertisements, and Chadwick Pictures' attempts to drum up business by taking the film out as the centrepiece of a 'roadshow' (unconsciously reflecting L. Frank Baum's failed *Radio-Plays* from two decades earlier, and described by *Variety* as being in a 'pretentious manner'), *Wizard of Oz* failed to do well at the cinemas, and came close to bankrupting the studio.

There was another version of *The Wizard of Oz* which can very much be seen as a halfway house between Semon's black and white silent film and the 1939 all-singing all-dancing colour movie. This colour cartoon, running for roughly eight minutes, was made by Canadian animator Ted Eshbaugh in 1933. The only dialogue is a sung 'Hail to the Wizard of Oz! To the Wizard of Oz we lead the way!', otherwise the film is scored by Carl Stalling with arrangements of folk songs and classical themes.

The screenplay is credited to Colonel Frank Baum (i.e. Frank Joslyn Baum), who was in the United States Army at the time. Although the film was made in Technicolor, various sources have suggested that Eshbaugh apparently didn't apply for the proper licence from the Technicolor Corporation, so it was originally released in monochrome – many home-video releases are also in black and white,

although an unrestored colour version can be seen on You-
Tube. It has also been mooted that Frank Baum's sale of
the rights to *The Wonderful Wizard of Oz* to Samuel Goldwyn, which led eventually to the 1939 movie, may have
been behind the film's rapid disappearance from availability, if indeed it was ever released at all. What seems most
likely is that it became the subject of so much litigation that
it vanished from sight.

Surviving documentation from the period shows that
John Booth, the financier of the film, brought an action
in March 1934 against Technicolor, who were refusing to
let him have the negative and the soundtrack for the film,
although the reason they were holding on to it is not clear;
soon afterwards Technicolor cross-claimed. In June 1934,
L. Frank Baum's estate (i.e. Frank Baum junior, as the
assignee of the rights to the book) accused Technicolor of
infringing the copyright on the original book; according
to them, 'distribution of the Technicolor cartoon would
greatly diminish the value of Oz as literary property with
picture sales prospects. He demands that the negative be
destroyed.' This action presumably failed, since Frank
Baum brought a different case against Eshbaugh in May
1935, when he believed that Technicolor and the producer
were apparently ready to release the film, claiming that
Eshbaugh had 'failed to finish' the film 'within agreed time.
Contract is therefore regarded as void by Baum,' according
to a report in *Variety*. Unfortunately, there are no further
references to the various court cases in *Variety*'s records.

Eshbaugh's cartoon begins by loosely following the initial beats of the original Baum story: Dorothy and Toto
are swept by a tornado into Oz, although they land directly on the Scarecrow. They then meet the Tin Woodman,
oiling him so he can join them. They pass some mating
animals, and arrive at the Emerald City, where a great
parade greets them before they are led to the Wizard. He's
portrayed as a mad Merlin figure who performs various

conjuring tricks and then produces a hen who lays assorted eggs, which crack to reveal different animals. The last egg refuses to stop growing; the Woodman's axe and other weapons are useless against it. Eventually it hatches to reveal a baby chick, and the cartoon finishes with them all singing 'Rock–a-bye Baby' to the chick.

Perhaps the most interesting aspect of this cartoon is its use of colour: the Kansas sequences are monochromatic (but blue and white, rather than the more common black and white). Once Dorothy arrives in Oz, everything switches to colour. This was a trick that was emulated by the 1939 film (and later by Sam Raimi for *Oz the Great and Powerful*).

Eshbaugh announced that his *Wizard of Oz* was the start of a series of cartoons, but, perhaps not surprisingly given the legal minefield that resulted from the first one, no further tales materialized. He wasn't the only animator to tackle the Oz series during the 1930s. Kenneth L. McLellan produced a short puppet film in 1938 featuring the Scarecrow in his Corncob House, but this failed to attract investors – something that may have secretly pleased Ruth Plumly Thompson. Baum's successor as Royal Historian of Oz had tried to persuade Maud Baum and the publishers of the Oz books to sell the rights to Walt Disney's son Roy for a series of animated short films. They had elected to go with McLellan instead, and thus were not in a position to capitalize on the success of the MGM movie, when it stormed into cinemas in the summer of 1939.

2

THE MGM OZ

'We scenarists did have problems,' admitted Florence Ryerson and Edgar Allen Woolf, two of the primary writers on the 1939 version of *The Wizard of Oz*. 'But they were those that involved satisfying Oz readers. We left in the most memorable incidents, never altered the characters; and we inserted most of the magic. After that, it was the problem of those technical geniuses to figure out how to do those strange things. And they did.'

Ryerson and Woolf may have been playing a little fast and loose with the truth in their statement – the differences between L. Frank Baum's original 1900 novel and the 1939 Metro-Goldwyn-Mayer (MGM) version were larger than they were making out – but what cannot be denied is their intention to translate the first of the Oz books onto the silver screen in as close a way as possible. Just as sixty years later, fans of J.K. Rowling's Harry Potter series wrote to the producers worried that the films wouldn't translate the books word for word, so fans of Baum's book wrote to the studio 'warning us to follow the book and to leave out no characters'.

The road to Oz was a complicated one, and many rumours and tales have grown up over the years about what exactly happened when, where, and to whom. Some have entered into the realm of urban legend (the claim, for example, that you can see a Munchkin who committed suicide hanging from one of the branches of a tree; clearer sight of the scene in question would suggest it was one of the birds borrowed from the Los Angeles zoo – and in any case, the Munchkins hadn't begun filming at the point the scene in question was shot); others were simply the result of the passage of time and fading memories.

After Larry Semon's interesting take on *The Wizard of Oz* failed to ignite the box office – and the earlier silent films hadn't exactly played to packed audiences – it did seem as if Baum's fantasy world was destined to remain firmly on the printed page. But on 26 January 1934, on the advice of story scout George Oppenheimer, Samuel Goldwyn (the 'G' of MGM) purchased the film rights to the novel from Frank Joselyn Baum for $40,000, with a view to making it a starring vehicle for musical comedian Eddie Cantor, who was under contract to the studio. Cantor would probably have played the Scarecrow, with other parts given to W.C. Fields, child star Marcia Mae Jones, Mary Pickford and Helen Hayes.

Nothing came of this though, but when the success of Disney's *Snow White and the Seven Dwarfs* proved the popularity of fantasy films, the studios all started looking for properties that they might be able to woo audiences with. Twentieth Century Fox were seeking an appropriate idea for their child star Shirley Temple; some at MGM were also trying to find something that would suit their ingénue, Judy Garland. Both studios therefore went to Goldwyn to obtain the rights to the Oz stories, and the producer accepted the MGM offer. The studio purchased the rights from Goldwyn in February 1938. Some sources suggest they paid $20,000, others $75,000 – either way, it justifies Oz historian David McClelland's description of the deal as 'one of the best buys since the sale of Manhattan'.

The force behind the purchase was new producer Arthur Freed, who was determined to make his mark at MGM. However, the songwriter, best known for composing 'Singin' in the Rain', did not have a solid track record behind him, and therefore the head of the studio, Louis B. Mayer, turned to Mervyn LeRoy, who had recently signed with the studio, to produce what everyone expected would be a hugely demanding project. Freed remained involved as associate producer. (LeRoy maintained that the project was always destined for him, although his contract with MGM only began on 3 February 1938, a mere fortnight before Sam Goldwyn sold the rights.)

On 24 February *Variety* announced that 'Metro has acquired the screen rights for "The Wizard of Oz" from Samuel Goldwyn and has assigned Judy Garland to the role of Dorothy. Mervyn LeRoy will produce the Frank Baum childhood fantasy.' Gossip columnist Louella Parsons also reported that Garland was set to play Dorothy.

Various directors were considered for the movie – and indeed although Victor Fleming is given sole credit on the final version, many others handled portions of the film. Norman Taurog was originally put in place, but by the time shooting began on 13 October 1938, thriller director Richard Thorpe was at the helm. He lasted a mere nine filming days – Mervyn LeRoy later commented that Thorpe 'didn't have the feeling for it. I think you have to have the heart of a kid to make *The Wizard of* Oz.' George Cukor was therefore brought on board (although in the end he simply helped deal with some of the practical problems that had arisen during the first few days of shooting), before Victor Fleming arrived at the start of November.

Margaret Hamilton, who played the Wicked Witch of the West, later recalled that 'Lewis Milestone, who had directed *All Quiet on the Western Front* was on the film for a while too.' This constant change unsurprisingly unsettled the cast: 'As each director left, we went in for an interview,' Hamilton remembered. 'Each time we thought we'd get the axe, but LeRoy wanted us. Mr LeRoy had wanted to direct the picture himself, you see, and had very firm ideas about how the thing should be done.'

The creation of the screenplay was no less fraught, with some of the top writers in Hollywood tapped to work on the film. Even as negotiations with Samuel Goldwyn for the rights were being finalized in January 1938, a four-page outline was prepared by LeRoy's assistant William H. Cannon, but this deviated too far from the magical elements of Baum's creation – indeed, its ideas of the Scarecrow being a man who's so stupid that he could only get work as a scarecrow, and the Tin Man as a hardened criminal who had been placed in a tin suit as a punishment, were considerably closer in tone to Larry Semon's movie from a decade earlier than the whimsy to be found in Baum's writings.

Irving Brecher was the first screenwriter to work on a script, but before he could get very far, he was reassigned to work on *At the Circus*. Herman J. Mankiewicz was the next to take a shot, producing seventeen pages for the Kansas scenes, and a further fifty-six before he too was removed from the movie at the end of March. Poet Ogden Nash came on board for a short time, working with both Mankiewicz and Noel Langley, who had separately been hired to work on the film in early March – the idea of parallel scripts being prepared for a film of this size wasn't uncommon, and it's unlikely that Mankiewicz or Langley were aware of the other's involvement. Langley completed the first draft on 5 April and continued revising it until early June. Both Herbert Fields and Samuel Hoffenstein took a look at the screenplay during this time, but apparently made no major contributions.

On 4 June, Langley left the project, to be replaced by Florence Ryerson and Edgar Allan Woolf who penned drafts through June and July. They were transferred to work on *Babes in Arms* at the end of July, and Noel Langley returned, working with Jack Mintz through August on revisions, and then completing the work on his own ready for the start of filming. The final screenplay was credited to Langley, Ryerson and Woolf, with the adaptation by Langley – his key changes to Baum's original included switching from silver to ruby slippers, and mirroring the three farmhands from Kansas in the trio of Tin Man, Scarecrow and Lion. Minor revisions were made to the screenplay during shooting by Langley – the final ones are dated 28 February 1939; Langley left the film on 3 March, two weeks before the production wrapped on 16 March.

The composition of the all-important songs was slightly less chaotic. MGM originally sent out a press release on 17 March 1938 stating that Mack Gordon and Harry Revel were going to write the songs for the film, which was superseded by a report in *Variety* on 18 April that Nacio Herb Brown and Al Dubin were the chosen pair. According to the eventual composer Harold Arlen, 'There were plenty of other major songwriters who were damned unhappy when they heard we'd gotten [*The Wizard of Oz*] because they'd all been sitting around waiting for that job.' Arlen and his lyricist partner E.Y. 'Yip' Harburg were selected over other key musical figures of the period, including Jerome Kern, Ira Gershwin, and Dorothy Fields, by Arthur Freed, whose own musical background made him the ideal person to choose the composers whose songs were felt vital to the production.

Harburg and Arlen were announced as composers in July, although they had begun work on the film at the start of May. Freed had been impressed with their Broadway musical *Hooray for What?*, in particular its lead musical number. ' "New Apple Tree" got us *Wizard of Oz*,' Arlen admitted later; Freed felt that Harburg 'had a wonderful feeling for fantasy', according to a biography of Arlen, 'that, coupled with Arlen's musical fancy, might produce the right songs'.

According to Harburg's son, Ernie, it was Yip Harburg who came up with the idea of incorporating the songs into the ongoing storyline, rather than simply stopping the story to allow for a song – an idea that would cause problems later on, when the decision was made to axe 'Over the Rainbow' from the film prior to opening. Ernie Harburg also claimed that 'Yip also wrote all the dialogue in that time and the set-up to the songs, and he also wrote the part where they give out the heart, the brains and the nerve, because he was the final script editor . . . He pulled the whole thing together, wrote his own lines and gave the thing a coherence and a unity, which made it a work of art.'

'I loved the idea of having the freedom to do lyrics that were not just songs, but scenes,' Harburg himself told biographer Max Wilk. It meant they weren't tied to short songs that fit a normal musical pattern but were writing 'what would amount to the acting out of entire scenes, dialogue in verse and set to Harold's modern music'.

One of the most persistent stories told about *The Wizard of Oz* is that Shirley Temple was originally intended as the lead, and Judy Garland was simply a replacement when that didn't pan out. It's certainly true that had the film been made by Fox, Temple would have played Dorothy, and before Arthur Freed became involved with the production, and persuaded Louis B. Mayer to back the project, it seems that early discussions at MGM centred around arranging a swap between Fox and MGM to bring Temple across for Oz, in return for Clark Gable and Jean Harlow working on a Fox film. Even Temple's own autobiography states this to be the case, but Harlow's premature death in 1937 brought this idea to a halt. Talking about how much she enjoyed returning from a holiday in Bermuda, Temple joked that 'There's no place like home' in newsreel footage from 1937, which has often been cited as proof that she was to be involved. It has been suggested that she had an 'unofficial' audition for the role with Freed's assistant Roger Edens, but although he was charmed by the young star, he didn't think she would be able to do what was required.

Even with Temple out of the picture, Garland wasn't a shoo-in for the role. Deanna Durbin, who had co-starred with her in the 1936 movie *Every Sunday*, was also under consideration, but was physically more mature than Garland, and also had a more operatic singing style. Arthur Freed had been pushing for Garland from the start – and would continue to work with her for many years after *The Wizard of Oz* was complete. He believed the then sixteen-year-old Garland would perform the songs better than the ten-year-old Temple.

The fresh-faced Kansas look that Garland adopted in the picture wasn't there from the start. Under first director Richard Thorpe, Garland wore a blonde wig, with her teeth capped and the shape of her nose subtly altered with putty. When Mervyn LeRoy reviewed the footage that had been shot in the first two weeks, he realized that this look simply wasn't working, and ordered it changed, and pigtails altered. Interim director George Cukor agreed and suggested that much less make-up was applied to Garland, reminding the young girl to remember her character's background at all times. These key changes helped to ensure that Garland's Dorothy retains the freshness and innocence of the character that generations of children had already grown up reading.

The roles of her three companions on the Yellow Brick Road also went through various metamorphoses before reaching the familiar line-up. Ray Bolger was the first to be cast – with an announcement hitting the press as early as 5 March 1938 – but he was initially set to play the Tin Man (as the character was known in the script, rather than the Tin Woodman of the books). Bolger wasn't happy about this, since he wanted to play the Scarecrow. The original stage Scarecrow, Fred Stone, had been Bolger's inspiration for going into vaudeville in the first place, and Bolger wanted to pay homage, particularly because, as he pointed out to Mervyn LeRoy, he felt that 'I'm not a tin performer; I'm fluid'. LeRoy consented to the swap.

But it wasn't the man now indelibly linked with the part of the Tin Man, Jack Haley, with whom Bolger was changing places; the original casting was Buddy Ebsen, later to become best known for his role as hick Jed Clampett in *The Beverly Hillbillies*. Ebsen had worked with Garland previously, and the producers had felt that he would be able to replicate the odd shuffling gait that Stone had adopted as the Scarecrow. He didn't have a problem with the swap either. What Ebsen had a major problem with was the make-up that had been created for the Tin Man.

To produce a sheen that would reflect properly in Technicolor, Ebsen was covered in an aluminium facial dust spray over a clown-white base. He was inhaling this powder for hours each day, and after ten days of shooting, he had serious problems breathing. Ebsen was rushed to hospital, and put into an iron lung. Although his condition was kept quiet for many years, it was eventually revealed that MGM studio bosses refused to believe that he was genuinely ill, and only realized how serious the situation was when they visited the hospital, and were told in no uncertain terms by the nurse looking after Ebsen that there was no possibility of him returning to the set for some time. (A press release simply noted that he was suffering from 'pneumonia'.)

A lot changed during the production shutdown that

followed: LeRoy reviewed the footage so far and changed Garland's costume, replaced Thorpe as director, and hired a new actor as the Tin Man, who would be wearing a different form of make-up. Jack Haley was unaware of what had happened to his predecessor: like everyone else, he assumed, wrongly, that Ebsen had been fired from the film. Incoming director Victor Fleming asked Haley how he would approach the role, and was pleased when the actor explained that he would talk in the same way that he told stories to his young son.

The final member of the trio, Bert Lahr, had worked with lyricist Yip Harburg on a couple of Broadway shows; although Harburg and Arlen had been working on the songs for a few weeks before Lahr was cast as the Cowardly Lion, their familiarity is clear.

It looked for some time as if the Wizard himself would be played by W.C. Fields; reports differ as to whether he was holding out for more money for his fee and his demands were refused, or was unable to extricate himself from his commitments to Universal on the movie *You Can't Cheat an Honest Man*, which he was both writing and starring in. Ed Wynn and Wallace Beery were also considered but the former supposedly claimed the part was not big enough (which seems a little odd given that whoever played the Wizard was also turning up in five other guises across the film). The latter did a screen test, but it was felt that he might unbalance the movie. The part went to Oscar nominee Frank Morgan.

Finding his counterpart, the Wicked Witch of the West, took some time. Edna May Oliver was the first choice, but since she was known for playing the sort of character whose gruff horse-faced (her own description) exterior hid a heart of gold, she was eliminated. Gale Sondergaard was Mervyn LeRoy's next choice, since he seemed to be going for a slinky and seductive portrayal of evil, as seen in Disney's *Snow White*; Sondergaard screen-tested for the part, but given that Glinda the Good Witch points out to Doro-thy that bad witches are ugly, changes had to be made. The actress tried out an 'ugly' make-up, but shortly before shooting began, she bowed out of the production. 'I was not about to make myself ugly,' she pointed out.

She was replaced by Margaret Hamilton, a former school-teacher turned actress. Hamilton loved to regale audiences later in life with the tale of how she was approached for the part – her agent contacted her to say that she was being considered for a role in the film. Hamilton, who had grown up reading and loving the Oz books, was excited by the prospect, but was a little disheartened when her agent told her it was for the Witch. She queried that, and was rather knocked back by his reply: 'Yes – what else?'

Glinda the Good Witch was played by Billie Burke, the widow of the famous impresario Florenz Ziegfeld; she too had worked with Garland previously. She was a last-minute replacement for starlet Helen Gilbert, who apparently had disappeared on holiday with Howard Hughes. Aunt Em and Uncle Henry were played by Clara Blandick and Charley Grapewin. And in the great tradi-tion of dogs swapping gender in the movies, Toto the dog was played by Terry the bitch.

And then, of course, there were the Munchkins, cred-ited as 'The Singer Midgets'. Over a hundred small people were brought to Hollywood to appear in the film, and the stories about their behaviour have become magnified in the retelling over the years. Liza Minnelli, Judy Garland's daughter, has been keen to point out that her mother was an entertainer, who was very good at amplifying a story, so the many tales Garland regaled interviewers with in later life did not necessarily have much of a grounding in real-ity. One particular story was repeated regularly: one of the Munchkins, aged around forty, according to Garland, was keen to ask her out. Garland didn't want to offend him by saying that she didn't want to go out with someone so small, so said she didn't think her mother would let her go. This didn't faze her would-be paramour, who suggested that she bring her mother along!

After most of the songs were recorded between 30 September and 7 October, the shoot for the film began in mid-October 1938 and lasted until mid-March 1939. As Jack Haley would later recall, 'Like hell was it fun'. A lot of the actors were barred from the studio commissary (the dining area used by cast and crew from whatever productions were filming on the lot) because even with some of their make-up removed, they scared the other diners. The Technicolor process required special lighting that meant that the temperature on set reached over 100° Fahrenheit (38° Celsius) even in the Californian winter, which caused some considerable problems for the actors encased within the heavy costumes.

The Lion costume weighed around fifty pounds, and was made from real lion skins, which the wardrobe department had taken two months to sew together. Rubber pieces were applied to Bert Lahr's upper lip, which meant that he was unable to eat normally – for the duration of the shoot while he was in costume, he had to sip through a straw. Margaret Hamilton had the same problem when she was fully made up, and, as she recalled to interviewer Jerry Vermilye, 'It was deathly hot under the lights, and I couldn't go too long without nearly perspiring it all off'. For the Scarecrow, Bolger's face was covered with transparent burlap, glued on and then painted. Jack Haley was unable to sit down in his Tin Man costume, and had to rest against a 'leaning-board'.

Unsurprisingly the atmosphere on set could easily become tense, but the veteran vaudevillians teased each other to keep their spirits up. 'If we couldn't have laughed, we would have been tearing each other apart,' Bolger recalled. They were also delighted whenever Judy Garland was called from the set for her statutory lessons: 'That meant we could take the make-up off,' Haley explained.

Garland's youthful energy also helped to keep the older professionals engaged. 'Her freshness and vitality are things I will never forget,' Margaret Hamilton noted, while Bolger initially thought she was 'a dumpy little kid', but was amazed by the difference once the cameras were rolling. 'When the Klieg lights shone on her, she was marked by a total lack of inhibition and an amazing intensity.'

Director Victor Fleming was very well aware of the problems faced by his cast, and tried to find many ways of avoiding them becoming irritated by the inevitable delays during production. If he thought they were tiring, he'd call them over and ask for their advice on the next scene.

Judy Garland embellished her tales of shooting – she claimed on television that her three co-stars tried to upstage her while they were walking up the Yellow Brick Road. They were so large, she claimed, that she was constantly pushed to the back behind them. 'And Mr Fleming, a darling man who was always on a boom,' Garland would conclude, 'would yell, "You three dirty hams, let the little girl in there!" '

All three men denied that this ever happened, although Haley did concede, 'After a while, I guess she just started to believe it.' As he pointed out, the four of them are locked arm in arm in a long shot in the sequences Garland was talking about – 'how can you push someone out of the picture with a long shot?' Ray Bolger told the US *TV Guide* that none of them had time to upstage anyone else; each was concentrating on his own part. 'I was constantly falling, Lahr had that tail to manage, and Haley just clogged along.'

Haley was also very clear that, no matter what Judy Garland might have alleged in the latter days of her life, the film's star was not given drugs by people involved with MGM to help her get through the movie. 'She used to love to laugh,' he recalled. 'She was full of laughter. And pep. She didn't need pills but the poor sucker got hooked on them. Not while she was on Oz. The pills started when she turned out pictures faster than Metro could make money on them.'

The logistics of the shoot were immense. The Munchkin sequences involved hundreds of small people, who came from all over the world. According to the casting director, Bill Grady, although they were credited as 'Singer's Midgets' they weren't actually provided by Leo Singer. The impresario was only able to provide 150, but far more were needed. Grady therefore approached a midget monologist called Major Doyle, who was happy to assist – on condition that Grady didn't get any from 'that son of a bitch' Singer following a previous disagreement. Grady agreed, and Doyle danced a jig in delight. To get the midgets from New York to Los Angeles, Grady hired buses, but routed three of them to Singer's apartment on Central Park. Stopping outside, he asked the doorman to get Singer to look out of his window. When Singer did so, he was greeted with the sight of three busloads of midgets all baring their backsides at him. This, perhaps unsurprisingly, became known as 'Major Doyle's revenge'.

Other sources suggest that Singer did provide some of the Munchkins, but although some of his performers sang his praises and looked up to him as a father figure, there were stories that he kept half of the fees due to the actors.

Once they had arrived in Hollywood, each Munchkin was sketched and then had their own individual costume and make-up designed, which was photographed so it could be meticulously recreated each day that they were on set. Twenty make-up artists worked on the troupe, trying to get through nine per hour to ensure that everyone could be ready on set when required. Victor Fleming and his cameraman Harold Rosson created a special 'rubber lens' camera which floated on a crane above the action, and allowed them to incorporate details of the action that would otherwise have become lost in the melee of multi-coloured Munchkins.

Some took the job more seriously than others. Bert Lahr recalled one of the midgets, known as the Count, was 'never sober' but because he was at the head of the Witch's Monkeys, they had to wait for him to arrive before shooting on those scenes could begin. When a whine was heard coming from the men's restroom, one of the crew investigated and discovered that the Count had got so drunk during the lunch break that he had fallen into the latrine and had been unable to get himself out. (It should be noted, though, that some of the small actors complained vociferously at their portrayal – particularly by Bert Lahr's son John in his biography of his father – as 'midgets who, in fact, made their living by panhandling, pimping and whoring', pointing out that the hours on set meant that such behaviour simply couldn't have gone on.)

At least some of the stories must have been true. 'Disney can thank Christ his Seven Dwarfs weren't real,' one of the MGM publicity team commented wryly towards the end of the Munchkins' time on set, and even Mervyn LeRoy was glad to see the back of them.

Although there were many visual and post-production effects in the film, including some spectacular matte painting backgrounds that were seamlessly incorporated into the live action, a lot of effects needed to be carried out on set during filming. When the group reach the Emerald City, they meet the 'horse of a different colour'; to keep changing the colour of one horse would simply not have been practical, so the scene was filmed with a number of different white horses, all of whom had been prepared earlier. However, they couldn't be painted the requisite colours – the American Society for the Prevention of Cruelty to Animals made that very clear – so they had to be covered in various flavours of the gelatine dessert, Jello, which unfortunately the horses were very tempted to lick off prior to filming!

One practical effect went badly wrong on 28 December, and saw Margaret Hamilton retire injured from filming for six weeks with second- and third-degree burns. The sequence in which the Wicked Witch departs from Munchkinland in a sheet of flame used a classic piece of stagecraft. As she explained, 'There was a little elevator that was supposed to take me down, with a bit of fire and smoke erupting to dramatize and conceal my exit. The first take ran like clockwork, I went down out of my clothes, the fire and smoke erupted and that's the one you see.' But on the retake, the timing was slightly off, and the hat and broom both caught fire. Hamilton was in 'excruciating pain' but couldn't understand why those helping her insisted on removing her green paint before taking her for treatment. But, as she was later informed, 'the green paint had copper in it. If they hadn't gotten the paint off, my face would have been a mass of holes.' On her return to the set, she made one thing very clear: 'No more fire work!' She was quite happy to be released from the picture if necessary: 'I let go of the idea that the show must go on!' This meant that when it came to film the 'Surrender Dorothy' scene in which the witch is seen with her broomstick billowing smoke, Hamilton refused to take part. Betty Danko, Hamilton's stand-in, therefore was called upon – and was badly injured during filming on 11 February 1939. A smoking pipe had been dressed to look like the broomstick, and on the third take, it exploded. Danko was hospitalized for eleven days and received permanent scarring.

At some point during the filming of *The Wizard of Oz*, every single one of the twenty-nine sound stages on the MGM lot was used; if all sixty-five sets had been erected simultaneously, they would have covered twenty-five acres. The poppy field alone covered an acre and a half, with 40,000 separate red poppies on two-foot wire stems – it took twenty men a full week to stick them into the set. Cedric Gibbons and the art department sometimes had to create items from scratch to provide the effect that was needed, but on other occasions, more prosaic items came in useful. The yellow brick road itself caused a number of problems, since the team couldn't find a dye or paint that would show up in the correct bright yellow that the director wanted. In the end, Mervyn LeRoy asked Gibbons if he had tried simple yellow fence paint, and once that was applied to the set, it did the job perfectly.

It wasn't just that particular shade of yellow that presented difficulties for cinematographer Harold Rosson. When a number of characters were in a scene together, the particular lighting requirements of their costumes could conflict: the Witch, with her black costume and green skin, was usually kept in front of a dark-grey background, with the outfit lit brilliantly. But the Tin Man's shining metallic costume could reflect the light on set, and if Rosson wasn't careful, could look blue, so straw-yellow lighting was required. The ruby slippers may have been enchanted, but they also reflected the light, so again care had to be taken to ensure that nothing reflected into the camera. The scenes in Munchkinland were the worst in this respect: the two-acre set of tiny villages contained more than a hundred tiny homes, and dozens of shades of primary colours. Rosson later reckoned that the lighting on that set was sufficient to light 550 five-room homes!

The Winged Monkeys were achieved by a combination of practical effects and stunts involving some of the small actors hired to play the Munchkins. Ray Bolger recalled that they were to be paid $25 each time they swooped down on wires to attack Dorothy, but when Victor Fleming called for a fourth take, they started to become uneasy. 'We could hear them saying to each other, "They'll never pay us all this money. Never!" To make sure Metro did fork out the cash, the midgets struck the picture. Stopped it cold for a while.'

Initially, special-effects designer Buddy Gillespie considered creating the full Winged Monkey Army in animation, but after a number of tests he realized that it would look too much like a cartoon on the screen. 'We did it with miniature monkeys we cast and supported with 2,200 piano wires,' he later recalled. 'The wires supported them on an overhead trolley and moved their wings up and down. It was an awful job to hide the wires. They had to be painted and lighted properly so they blended into whatever the background might be.'

For the famous shot of Dorothy's farmhouse flying through the twister towards the camera, Gillespie filmed a model of the building being dropped from the roof of the studio down onto the floor, which had been painted with a cloud background. This was then shown backwards and in slow motion, so it appeared to be coming at the audience.

The cyclone itself was actually a woman's silk stocking filled with fuller's earth, pulled across a sound stage while wind machines blew it into different shapes. This was then intercut with the live-action scenes of Dorothy running towards the house.

The transition from black and white (or sepia-coloured) footage for the Kansas sequences into the full Technicolor Oz scenes required some sleight of hand on set to replace the original plan of painstakingly repainting each frame of the film by hand. The inside of the farmhouse was repainted in the sepia tone, and Judy Garland's stand-in, Bobbie Koshay, went to the door, wearing a sepia version of the gingham dress. She then backed out of the frame, and Judy Garland, wearing the full-colour bright-blue dress, walked forward into the Technicolor Oz.

A month before principal photography on *The Wizard of Oz* was completed, the director left the picture. Victor Fleming was needed elsewhere, to rescue the filming of

Gone with the Wind, whose star, Clark Gable, had fallen out with the director George Cukor. *Gone with the Wind* producer David O. Selznick had originally wanted King Vidor to take over from Cukor; Vidor wasn't happy with the idea of working on the huge Civil War movie at such short notice, but he was prepared to complete *Oz* if Fleming – a great friend of Clark Gable, who the star wanted working on the film – would take on *Gone with the Wind*. Fleming agreed, and gave Vidor a hasty tour of the *Oz* sets before vanishing.

Vidor was responsible for the sepia sequences set in Kansas, including the filming of 'Over the Rainbow'. Vidor received no credit on the final movie, and never revealed that he had been behind the camera for the shooting of the film's most famous song until after Victor Fleming's death in 1949. Vidor had always wanted to work on a musical, and used the same guidelines that he had when helming silent pictures – keep the movement going. Fleming returned to oversee the editing of the movie, working simultaneously on this and *Gone with the Wind*. As a result, he missed two weeks of filming on the latter from exhaustion.

Many of the musical sequences that are synonymous with *The Wizard of Oz* underwent changes during the production, editing and previews of the movie. Even 'Over the Rainbow', which has become the film's hallmark, was removed after one of the previews until wiser heads prevailed.

'Over the Rainbow' was one of the last songs to be written for the film across the summer of 1938. When reviewing the various pieces already composed, Arthur Freed decided that the movie needed a ballad to balance what writers Yip Harburg and Harold Arlen described as the 'lemon drop songs'. Arlen admitted that he struggled with the piece for some time, but one evening his wife was driving them down into Hollywood, and as they went past Schwab's

Pharmacy on Sunset Boulevard, inspiration hit. Telling her to pull over to the side of the road, Arlen scribbled the tune down rapidly. The middle eight bridging part of the song was suggested by Harburg, who drew his partner's attention to a dog whistle he had at home.

Garland recorded the original on 7 October, and it was set to appear twice in the film – once in a more fearful version when Dorothy is captured in the witch's castle. This was removed quite early on. The main rendition, as Dorothy stands in the Kansas barnyard, fell out of favour following the first preview of the movie in San Bernadino. The executives present thought it slowed the movie down. 'All the other songs were in a faster, catchier tempo,' LeRoy explained later. 'They were the sort of melodies the public could latch on to quickly. "Over the Rainbow", on the other hand, was a ballad, and it always takes a private ear several hearings before it appreciates a ballad . . . I tried to persuade them that the song was a good one, but I seemed to be arguing in vain.'

The argument raged throughout June 1939, with Sam Katz, the executive producer of MGM's musical division, claiming that the whole score was 'above the heads of children' and music publisher Jack Robbins disparaging the composition by comparing it unfavourably with children's piano exercises. Eventually Arthur Freed made it clear that either the song was reinstated into the film, or he would resign. Louis B. Mayer agreed to its return before Garland premiered it for the public on a radio programme at the end of June.

Other musical numbers also had chequered histories. Ray Bolger's song 'If I Only Had a Brain' was re-recorded prior to the number being filmed: the first version was quite sedate so a more upbeat rendition was laid down. The song also originally included a huge musical interlude during which Bolger threw himself around the set, and chased after a crow that had stolen some of the Scarecrow's stuffing. This was rethought during shooting, and a revised choreography was prepared by Busby Berkeley to replace Bob Connolly's original.

That took a day or so to film, beginning on 28 February 1939. Five weeks' worth of filming was consigned to the cutting-room floor after the first preview of the film when 'The Jitterbug' was unceremoniously cut out – this time, at Arthur Freed's suggestion.

The sequence comes when Dorothy and her friends enter the Haunted Forest, and see an insect in the trees. It's a huge dance routine – 'everything danced!' Harburg recalled – and its excision did lead to a continuity error in the film, since the Witch tells the Winged Monkeys that she will send an insect ahead of them that will take the fight out of them, but we never get to see it.

The jitterbug dance was popularized in the years leading up to the filming of *The Wizard of Oz*, in particular by Cab Calloway whose 1934 song 'Call of the Jitter Bug' emphasized the link between the dance and alcohol – the movements were meant to be like alcoholics suffering from the 'jitters' (delirium tremens).

Various reasons have been suggested for its deletion. Freed told Victor Fleming that he felt that it slowed the movie down 'and is irrelevant to the story'; it also meant that the movie became a more acceptable length. Arlen and Harburg later claimed that once everyone saw the film, they felt that they had produced a classic movie, and that including the jitterbug would date the movie too quickly. It's also been claimed that it was removed to lessen the impact that Bert Lahr was making in the film.

Its removal, however prompted, did mean that the latter part of the film lacks a big musical production number. Oddly, Judy Garland recorded a studio version of the song as late as July 1939, only two weeks before the first press previews of the film in New York and Los Angeles.

* * *

The Wizard of Oz begins with young Kansas farm girl Dorothy Gale getting in the way of her Aunt Em, Uncle Henry, and their three farmhands Hunk, Zeke and Hickory. She's worried that the nasty Elvira Gulch is going to do something terrible to her dog, Toto, since the terrier has been chasing Miss Gulch's cat. Dorothy is told to find somewhere where she won't cause trouble (leading into 'Over the Rainbow'). Miss Gulch arrives with an order to take Toto, but the little dog escapes and runs back to Dorothy, who decides to run away from home. On her way, she meets Professor Marvel, a charlatan who claims that he's seen a vision of a farm woman crying; this worries Dorothy, who heads home – as a storm approaches.

A twister is heading for the farm and the others take refuge in the storm cellar. But when Dorothy gets back, the storm is at its height. The front door blows away, and the window in her bedroom is blown out, hitting her on the head and rendering her unconscious. When she wakes, she finds the house has been pulled up into the twister, and she sees various odd sights, including an old lady knitting, two men in a rowboat, and Miss Gulch on her bicycle, who suddenly transforms into a witch on a broomstick.

The house lands and Dorothy is amazed when she opens the door to find herself in the brightly coloured Munchkinland. She's told by Glinda, the Good Witch of the North, that she is in Oz, and her house has landed on, and killed, the Wicked Witch of the East. Festivities break out until the Wicked Witch of the West comes looking for her sister – and she's not at all happy that Glinda has given Dorothy her sister's ruby slippers. Vowing revenge, she vanishes in a flaming explosion. Dorothy decides she wants to go home, and Glinda tells her to 'Follow the Yellow Brick Road' to the Emerald City to ask the Wizard of Oz for his help.

On the way Dorothy and Toto meet a Scarecrow, who joins her hoping to get a brain; a Tin Woodman, who is in need of a heart; and a Cowardly Lion, who desperately wants to get some courage. When they get within sight of the Emerald City, the Wicked Witch sends them to sleep in a giant poppy field, but Glinda makes it snow, waking them. The gateman lets them in to the Emerald City when he sees Dorothy's slippers, and as they prepare to see the Wizard, the Witch skywrites 'Surrender Dorothy' with her broom, scaring the Lion even further. They are taken to the Wizard but only see the huge head of the Great Oz, who booms that he will grant their requests – as long as they bring him the Wicked Witch's broomstick.

The quartet (plus Toto) head into the Haunted Forest where they are attacked by the Witch's Winged Monkeys (this is where the 'Jitterbug' song originally came). The Monkeys carry Dorothy and Toto off to the Witch's castle. Before the Witch can kill Dorothy to get the slippers back, Dorothy's friends sneak into the castle, past the Winkie guards – but just as they are about to leave they are confronted by the Witch, who sets the Scarecrow on fire. Dorothy douses him with a bucket of water, but some hits the Witch, who melts and dies.

They take the broom to the Wizard, but as he's playing for time before granting their requests, Toto pulls a curtain aside, to reveal the real Wizard, a harmless fraud. He explains that he was a balloonist who was blown to Oz from a Kansas fair; when the inhabitants called him a Wizard, he accepted the job. He gives the Scarecrow a diploma that shows he has a brain; the Cowardly Lion gets a medal for bravery; and the Tin Man gets a clock shaped like a heart. Since he still has his balloon, he agrees to take Dorothy back to Kansas.

Unfortunately, the balloon, with the Wizard on board, flies off without Dorothy, and Glinda explains that now Dorothy realizes she has everything she wants at home, the ruby slippers will transport her there. Saying goodbye to her friends, she taps her heels together three times, saying, 'There's no place like home'. Back home in Kansas, she wakes from her dream and is greeted by her family and friends (all of whom appeared in Oz in various guises); the movie finishes with Dorothy telling her aunt there is no place like home.

Although the screenplay veers very close to Baum's original story, many different approaches were considered during the pre-production preparation. The overall look of the film was initially going to be more contemporary: two days after the official announcement of the movie was made, Mervyn LeRoy's assistant, William Cannon, sent a memorandum noting, 'The whole background should be more modernized than it is in the book to appeal to the modern person's idea of a Fairyland. When L. Frank Baum wrote this story which was before 1900, there were no autos, no radios, no airplanes and I do believe if he had written it today he would have in some manner made it a little more acceptable to the audience on a basis of using some of the modern contrivances that we use today. I think our Wizard of Oz background should be a Fairyland of 1938 and not of 1900.' This is in accord with the philosophy in the continuation books that Reilly & Lee were publishing, in which more up-to-date methods of getting to Oz were used.

A plotline that was removed quite early on would have seen Dorothy ('an orphan in Kansas who sings jazz') involved in a singing contest with a 'Princess of Oz, who sings opera'. The Witch was going to use a crystal and mirror to monitor Dorothy's progress, rather than the crystal ball, while ideas for a 'book opening routine' were requested from the Visual Effects department in June. Noel Langley's final draft from late June included the Wicked Witch trying to conquer the Emerald City, while *Mrs* Gulch had a son, Walter, who would become Bulbo in Oz. The central quartet at one point try to see the Wizard by making a human pyramid to look into a window at the back of the Wizard's palace, while the Wizard's balloon was going to be attacked by a woodpecker preventing the Wizard and Dorothy from using it.

A draft completed in early July included the idea that the Witch has clipped Nikko, her personal Flying Monkey's wings, and that Nikko later gives Dorothy the pail of water that she uses on the Witch. A late July version made the Winkies into 'huge figures with grotesque and hideous headdresses like the deather's head helmets [*sic*] in Japanese armour'.

The Wizard of Oz officially premiered in Oconomowoc, Wisconsin, in the heartland of the United States, on 12 August 1939. A big gala premiere was held at Grauman's Chinese Theatre in Los Angeles on 15 August, and again at Loew's Capitol Theatre New York two days later, which was followed by a live performance by Judy Garland and Mickey Rooney – which they continued to do to promote the movie for the next fortnight, with Bert Lahr and Ray Bolger replacing Rooney for a third and final week. The movie opened across the country on 25 August 1939.

In his review published in the *New York Times* on 18 August, Frank S. Nugent noted that *The Wizard of Oz* was a 'delightful piece of wonder-working which had the youngsters' eyes shining and brought a quietly amused gleam to the wiser ones of the oldsters . . . The Baum fantasy is at its best when the Scarecrow, the Woodman and the Lion are on the move.' *Time* magazine noted that 'it floats in the same rare atmosphere of enchantment that distinguished *Snow White and the Seven Dwarfs*', and *Variety* called it 'a pushover for the children and family biz'.

Not everyone was so positive. William Boehnel felt that the film 'cries out for the light, deft, humorous touch of a Walt Disney. This may sound like carping criticism of a film which has more than a generous share of fun in it, but the fact remains that much of the charm which is inherent in this engaging fairy tale is lost because of heavy-handed treatment.'

The film cost $2.6 million, and only took around $3 million on its initial release. A re-release in 1949 added a further $1.5 million to the coffers, but only when it became an annual ritual on American television did it really show the profit that MGM hoped for. After an initial broadcast on 3 November 1956, CBS began their yearly showings at Christmas 1959 on the second Sunday of December until 1964 (it wasn't shown in 1963, perhaps because America was still reeling from the Kennedy assassination). The first nine telecasts included introductions and commentaries with the first hosted by Liza Minnelli, Bert Lahr and Oz historian Justin Schiller. Not a year has gone by since without it being repeated.

3

RETURN TO OZ

While the 1939 film was a moderate success, it didn't translate into an increased awareness of Oz. Ruth Plumly Thompson resigned as Royal Historian of Oz and was replaced by illustrator John R. Neill, whose two Oz books were not as well received. Wartime paper shortages meant that the saga wasn't added to between 1943 and 1946, and the series never really recovered: only half a dozen new books were published in the post-war years.

Nor were there immediate sequels for the big screen, despite the fact that there were over thirty ready-made stories available for adaptation. MGM did consider a sequel, referred to as 'Wizard of Oz II', in the early 1940s, but decided against it. There were various television versions (described in chapter four), and Walt Disney hoped to bring some of the books to the screen, but the first big-screen follow-on that actually got made was *The Wonderful Land of Oz*, which arrived in American cinemas at Halloween 1969.

The film was prepared for what was known as the 'kiddie matinee' audience: rather than cinema owners showing the same film in the afternoon and the evening, they screened movies that were especially made for a children's audience. Many of these derived from Mexico's Churubusco Studios, with the films suitably dubbed, but there was some American home-produced fare, including movies shot around the Pirate World amusement park by producer Barry Mahon, otherwise known for films such as *Fanny Hill meets Dr Erotico* and *White Slavery*.

Mahon's contribution to the screen Oz was a moderately faithful version of L. Frank Baum's second novel, *The Marvelous Land of Oz*. This introduced a number of new characters to the saga, including Ozma, the true ruler of Oz, Jack Pumpkinhead and the Wogglebug, while not using either Dorothy or the Cowardly Lion. Mahon's version retains the gender-swap plot of Baum's original (the hero Tip is actually a transformed Ozma) although it muddies the water somewhat at the end when Glinda (a good fairy in this version, rather than a witch) states that 'When I transform you, Ozma will be the girl, and Tip will be your spirit, a wonderful, adventurous spirit, that will float out into the land beyond, and become a part of every little boy.' The lead role of Tip was played by Mahon's son Chan; Mike Thomas, who played the Scarecrow, became better known for his work behind the scenes providing make-up for films such as *Ghostbusters*.

The film was scripted, produced and directed by Mahon, with songs by George Linsenmann and Ralph Falco. When the project was announced in *Variety*, on New Year's Day 1969 (in an article headlined 'Fanny Hill Producer's Sideline'), Mahon was described as 'the king of sexploiters' and told the trade paper that he 'expects to utilise some of the "better actors" from his previous efforts.' He also hoped to 'pull a "coup" via having narration spoken by Judy Garland', although this never materialized. The film had a

$50,000 budget but needed to recoup around $300,000 to cover distribution costs.

Although *The Wonderful Land of Oz* has been described as being 'like a high-school pageant laid to film', it gains some credibility for its willingness to stay faithful to Baum's story. For a long time it was one of the many 'lost' Oz projects until its release first on DVD in 2001, and then, rather surprisingly, on VHS the following year.

A Turkish adaptation of the original story was produced in 1971, written by Hamdi Değirmencioğlu and directed by Tunç Başaran. *Aysecik Ve Shihirl Cuceler Ruyular Ulkesinde* (literally *Little Ayse and the Magic Gnomes in the Land of Dreams*) is a pretty faithful version of L. Frank Baum's tale.

A young girl, Aysecik, lives on her uncle's farm with her dog Banju and is transported by a tornado into the dreamland of Ulkesinde, where the house lands on and kills a Wicked Witch. The Good Witch, and her seven dwarf friends, send Aysecik on the path through Dreamland to find the Wizard who can send her home. She meets a Scarecrow, a Tin Man, and a Lion, and they encounter trees that try to attack them. After being rescued by the dwarfs when they are stranded in the middle of a stream, they arrive in the Emerald City, where Keşkin Zeka, the Wizard, tells them to kill Kötü Cadi, the Wicked Witch of the South [*sic*]. The Witch captures them and wants to take the silver ballet shoes that the Good Witch gave Aysecik, but ends up melted by water from a pail. Returning to the City, Banju unveils the real Wizard, who gives the three friends an inspiring speech that seems to sort them out. He then leaves by balloon, leaving Aysecik behind; the dwarves take her to Doll Country, where they dance with the china dolls, then rescue Aysecik and her friends from cavemen before reuniting her with the Good Witch by a lake. There the Good Witch explains how the girl can get

home, and she and Banju are reunited with her uncle and
aunt.

Aysecik Ve Shihirl Cuceler Ruyular Ulkesinde was one
of around forty films starring Zeynep Değirmencioğlu as
Aysecik. The dwarfs were added to the story after they
had been popular in an adaptation of Snow White: most
of the movies were other stories into which the character
of Aysecik was interjected, such as Pollyanna. The movie
is obviously low-budget – the make-up for the various
characters doesn't bear close examination – but it has an
infectious energy. It can be viewed in its original form on
YouTube, but there are also versions that marry it up with
the Pink Floyd album *Dark Side of the Moon* to sometimes
quite surprising effect.

The next Oz film to appear in American cinemas had a very
long gestation. Work began on the animated feature *Journey
Back to Oz* as early as 1962. It was eventually released in
1974, with an amended version, including live-action segments featuring Bill Cosby as the Wizard, debuting in 1976
on ABC television. With numerous links to the 1939 original, it too took some of its story cues from L. Frank Baum's
second Oz book, although it replaced Tip/Ozma with
Dorothy and returned the Cowardly Lion to the line-up.

The project was produced by Filmation Studios' Lou
Scheimer, who was approached by Norm Prescott in 1962.
Prescott had acquired the rights to produce an animated
sequel to *The Wizard of Oz*, and had put together a vocal
cast including Paul Lynde, Ethel Merman, Milton Berle,
Mickey Rooney, Danny Thomas, and Paul Ford. Making
the project especially interesting, Liza Minnelli was set to
play Dorothy, while the original film's Wicked Witch of
the West, Margaret Hamilton, was signed up to play Aunt
Em. Although the soundtrack was recorded around 1960,
the original Yugoslav animation house had been unable to
cope with the workload.

Work began on the film in Hollywood, and survived Filmation's split with Paramount Pictures; when the company later hit financial difficulties, Prescott bought half of Scheimer's 80 per cent share to ensure it could continue. By late 1965 though, the cash flow caused problems again: according to Scheimer, it was being financed from the profit made by a private airline in the Congo, and when the crisis there was resolved, the airline ceased to make a profit. Prescott and Scheimer showed the finished footage to Universal, but neither they nor any of the other studios were interested in becoming involved. Although Filmation managed to survive when DC brought *The Adventures of Superman* to them, they were not able to continue work on *Oz*.

Nearly five years passed before new drawings were added to the animation, with 12 October 1970 marking the official date that production resumed; confidently, Scheimer announced that the film would be released for Easter 1972. By the following summer, they were sure they could bring the release date forward to autumn of that year, and were hoping to start a series of live *Oz* roadshows, which, like L. Frank Baum's ill-fated *Radio-Play* from 1908, would integrate actors, music and filmed segments. At this point, Liza Minnelli offered to re-record her vocals, although Filmation was keen to retain the rougher edge of her younger voice.

The vast amount of other work that Filmation was undertaking meant production on *Oz* slowed down, and the film was in fact finally premiered for Warner Bros. International representatives in Hong Kong in May 1973, and was shown to other reps over the next few months. Filmation handled the US and Canadian distribution, while Warner Bros. covered the rest of the world. Test screenings began in Sacramento, Fresno, Portland and Seattle from June 1974, and the film opened around the US across the rest of the year. Although it got good reviews, it didn't perform as well financially as had been expected, although it gained a second life in its television version.

For this, Filmation shot extra scenes with Bill Cosby – with whom they worked regularly – as the Wizard, flying around in a balloon with a talking parrot and two Munchkins named Sprig and Twig. Cosby only contracted for two uses of the film, so Filmation later reshot these sequences with Milton Berle, which allowed the project to enter syndication. The company contemplated working on two further Oz-connected projects: *The Assistant Wizard of Oz*, as a vehicle for Buddy Hackett; and *The Yellow Brixx Road*, in 1980, which would have been a live-action series. Neither progressed beyond the concept stage.

The animated feature makes Mombi rather than General Jinjur the clear villain of the piece: she has created an army of green elephants to attack the Emerald City and allow her to take control of Oz. Dorothy and Toto are returned to Oz after getting caught in a tornado, and learn Mombi's plans. Dorothy therefore needs to gather as many allies as possible to overcome her, including Pumpkinhead, Woodenhead Stallion III (who is remarkably similar to the character of Merry Go Round from the final Oz book, although that did not appear until some years after the soundtrack for *Journey* had been recorded), the Tin Man, the Cowardly Lion, the Scarecrow and Glinda the Good Witch of the North. A dozen original songs were written by Sammy Cahn and Jimmy Van Heusen, which were separately released as a soundtrack album.

The next version of Baum's story to reach cinemas was the 1978 adaptation of the stage play *The Wiz*, which is discussed, along with the play, in part three. Four years after that came an even more unlikely adaptation: the Japanese anime *Ozu no mahôtsukai*. Originally shown at the Cannes Film Festival under the title *The Wizard of Oz*, this is notable for its close adherence to Baum's original text: when the quartet are brought before the Wizard, he appears to each of them as something completely different; Dorothy is nearer to Denslow's illustrations than a replica of Judy Garland's brunette from the feature film – although many of the Oz buildings resemble the illustrations from John R. Neill's later Oz books. The 1939 film amalgamated the Witches of the North and the South into the character of Glinda; there are still four Witches in the anime.

The film was directed by *Gundam 0080* & *Patlabor III*'s Fumihiko Takayama, but was produced by American distributor Fred Ladd, and didn't arrive in Japan until four years after its US debut. Dorothy was voiced by Aileen Quinn with John Stocker as the Tin Woodman, Billy Van as the Scarecrow and Thick Wilson as the Lion. *Bonanza* and *Battlestar Galactica* paterfamilias Lorne Greene provided the voice of the Wizard. Lyrics for the English version came from Sammy Cahn and Allen Byrns to tunes by Jō Hisaishi and Yuichiro Oda. Contrary to some accounts, though, this was not connected to the later Japanese TV series about the Wizard (which shared the same title in Japanese, although it was known as *The Wonderful Wizard of Oz* for its American broadcast).

Before that came the culmination of Disney's long quest to bring an Oz story to the screen. Walt Disney had acquired the rights to eleven of L. Frank Baum's original books in 1954, and set Dorothy Cooper to work on an adaptation of *The Patchwork Girl of Oz*, to be used as an episode of their new ABC television series *Disneyland*. Cooper supplied an outline for a two-part episode (i.e. a feature-length running time), under the title *Dorothy Returns to Oz* in April 1957, but by the time she completed the draft teleplay, it was entitled *The Rainbow Road to Oz*.

Never one to miss an opportunity, Walt Disney decided that the screenplay was too good to use on television; it deserved a cinematic audience. Interest in *The Wizard of*

Oz was heightened by the positive reception given to the first CBS telecast of the 1939 movie the previous Christmas, and the time must have seemed ripe to capitalize on that. According to contemporary Disney studio publicity, *The Rainbow Road to Oz* would start filming in November 1957, produced by Bill Walsh and directed by Sidney Miller.

Walt Disney shrewdly intended to bring some of the television audience along by using the Mouseketeers from their popular children's series *The Mickey Mouse Club* for the majority of the lead roles, with Annette Funicello starring as Ozma. Designs were quickly commissioned, and costumes prepared: they are reminiscent both of the original drawings by John R. Neill and those prepared for the 1939 film (the sketch of the Cowardly Lion as a king can also be seen almost as a prototype for King John in the 1973 Disney version of *Robin Hood*). The rights to a twelfth book were added to the Disney roster, in case elements from *Dorothy and the Wizard in Oz* were required.

The season opener of the *Disneyland* TV show featured the Mouseketeers trying to persuade 'Mr Disney' to make a live-action version of the Oz tales, since it would take him 'seven or eight years' to produce an animated film. Mr Disney seems suitably enthusiastic, but somewhere between the recording of that episode and the projected start date Walt Disney lost faith in the production. In the absence of paperwork giving a clear reason, it has been suggested that he didn't think that the Mouseketeers were capable of sustaining a whole feature film; or that the score by Tom Adair and Buddy Baker for the musical numbers lacked the polish and style of the Arlen/Harburg compositions in the earlier film; or even that the cost was simply spiralling out of control.

The Rainbow Road to Oz didn't begin filming in November as planned, and by February 1958, it was clear that the project was not proceeding. Instead, Disney opted to go ahead with a version of Victor Herbert's 1903 oper-etta *Babes in Toyland*, which was eventually released in 1961 – featuring Funicello in one of the lead roles, and guest starring the original Scarecrow, Ray Bolger. Disney didn't lose all interest in Oz: when he was contemplating extending the Storybook Land Canal Ride at Disneyland, it was going to feature various tableaux of Oz situations and characters, although this project also stalled. A few years later, Ray Bolger reprised his role of the Scarecrow in a series of 'storyteller albums', based on the Baum stories, and, in the case of *The Cowardly Lion*, supposedly includ-ing some of the songs that Adair and Baker had written for the proposed movie.

But no movie was greenlit or put into production. By 1980, Tom Wilhite, the new head of production at Walt Disney Studios, knew that they had to do something with the rights in the next five years, before the books entered the public domain. He was also keen to work with an up-and-coming film-maker who had made his mark as the sound designer on Francis Ford Coppola's *Apocalypse Now*: Walter Murch.

Although Murch at the time wryly commented, 'Tom had to work his way down to the Ms before he finally found me', when he looked back twenty years later, the director recalled that Disney had 'pulled my name from a shortlist of people who were doing interesting things in film and might someday direct'. Wilhite and Murch met for what the latter described as 'a fishing expedition on both of our parts. But one of the questions he asked was, "What are you interested in that you think we might also be interested in?", and I said, "Another Oz story". I had grown up with the specific books on which *Return* is based – *The Land of Oz* and *Ozma of Oz* – in fact, they were the first "real" books I ever read on my own. And Tom sort of straightened up in his chair, because it turned out, unbe-knownst to me, that Disney owned the rights to all of the

Oz stories. And they were particularly interested in doing something with them because the copyright was going to run out in the next five years.'

As a result, Murch was signed to write and direct Disney's new take on Baum's material, known for a time simply as *Oz*. An official announcement was made in August 1981: Walter Murch and Gill Dennis had been signed to write a screenplay for *Return to Oz*, 'based on L. Frank Baum's books which inspired the original Judy Garland hit.' According to Disney's chief operating officer Ron Miller, 'This will not be a sequel or continuation of MGM's 1939 film but it will draw on characters and situations from other books in the formation of a totally new story with an entirely different look.' (In the end, one element of the MGM production did cross over – the ruby slippers that Dorothy wore in the film, rather than the silver shoes of the book, were used, after a suitable fee was paid to MGM.)

By the time that *Star Wars* producer Gary Kurtz was brought aboard to oversee the project in the summer of 1982, the storyline was clearer. Tom Wilhite told *Variety* that the new film would pick up nine months after the tornado occurred in *The Wizard of Oz*. The live-action film would not be a musical, would 'feature Dorothy and relatives' and would incorporate characters from the other Oz books. Wilhite did not expect the movie to be confined to a soundstage, and would 'include flying characters, and underground world and special effects'. Filming was planned for summer 1983.

Pre-production on the film took considerably longer than Wilhite had anticipated. Indeed by the time that Wilhite left the studio in the autumn of 1983, $6 million had been spent, and it looked as if the costs were getting out of control. New boss Richard Berger shut down production in November 1983, a mere six weeks before filming was due to start at Elstree Studios in London the following January, telling *Variety* the projected spend 'had climbed beyond

$20,000,000, or past what Disney wanted . . . The project
got out of hand. We want to make the picture; we're talking
to Kurtz but it's hard to tell what will happen.' Berger had
a problem on his hands, because other recent Disney films,
such as *Something Wicked This Way Comes*, had gone over
budget. In July 1985, he told the *New York Times* he had
had little option but to close down the movie and write off
the money spent: the budget was in fact 'up to $27 mil-
lion', partly because the producers were aiming to shoot in
Algiers, Sardinia, Spain, Canada, Kansas and England, and
partly because of the high costs connected to the new characters, which would be created with special effects rather
than by performers as in the 1939 movie.

By December, a compromise was reached. Two of the
seven soundstages that were booked were cancelled, and
Variety noted that they believed a cap of $20 million
was set for the film. This impacted on the special-effects
budget, as well as removing all location work (apart from
a few scenes on Salisbury Plain, near Stonehenge) – some
scenes intended for Italy were the last to be dropped,
shortly before filming got underway. '[T]he decision was
based upon confidence in director Walter Murch's creative
approach to the material and a firm commitment from the
production team to adhere to the studio's budgetary guidelines,' the official press statement noted.

And Walter Murch's creative approach was dark. Much
darker than the Technicolor world created for the 1939 film,
much darker than L. Frank Baum's literary Oz, although
Murch did believe that he came closer to presenting something that looked and felt more like the books than had
been seen on screen previously. The humour and wordplay
that was so essential to the books was missing – as Oz historian John Fricke explained in a 2007 documentary about
the making of the film, the official Oz fan club had supported the creation of the film, but when Fricke saw it, he
headlined his review, 'The Joy That Got Away'.

'I thought enough time had passed for a different sensibility to have a chance, to present a somewhat more realistic view about Dorothy and her life on the farm,' Murch maintained later, adding, 'I definitely felt that if we had tried to really do a sequel, which is to say, do something in the style of an MGM musical, we would have been in even greater trouble, because there's just no way you can reinvent that particular combination of people, technology and attitude.'

Return to Oz opens a few months after the twister has hit Kansas, and Dorothy is being given electric-shock treatment by Doctor Worley and Nurse Wilson to help her deal with her obsession with Oz. After finding a key with an Oz symbol on it, which she believes her friends have sent, Dorothy is rescued during a huge thunderstorm by a mysterious girl, and only survives drowning after being chased by Nurse Wilson by pulling herself onto a chicken coop. When she wakes, she's back in Oz, and her pet chicken, Billina, can talk – but it's an Oz in ruins. Following the damaged Yellow Brick Road takes her to the Emerald City where she finds her friends the Tin Woodman and the Lion turned to stone. The key opens a room inside which is Tik-Tok, a clockwork mechanical man. Tik-Tok explains that King Scarecrow has been captured by the Nome King.

Dorothy, Billina and Tik-Tok try to get information from the witch Mombi, but she is the Nome King's ally and imprisons them. They're freed by Jack Pumpkinhead, and use the Powder of Life to create a flying Gump to get across the Deadly Desert to the Nome King's lands. There they are able to free the Scarecrow, who has been turned into an ornament, and Billina's egg poisons the Nome King. The King has the ruby slippers, which Dorothy repossesses, and uses to escape to the Emerald City. There she revives her friends and sees the mysterious girl again, who turns out to be Princess Ozma. Ozma sends Dorothy

home – where she is found on the riverbank. The hospital
has been struck by lightning during the storm and burned
down, killing Doctor Worley – and Nurse Wilson has been
arrested. Arriving home, Dorothy sees Billina and Ozma
looking out through her mirror but this time, keeps their
existence a secret.

Shooting *Return to Oz* was no less fraught than its pre-
production. Fairuza Balk, who had been selected to play
Dorothy, was only nine years old, which meant that there
were strict rules governing how many hours a day she
could work. Given that Dorothy was in nearly every scene
of the film, there wasn't even the normal backstop of such
productions, where the adults could continue working on
something else during the mandated breaks for the child
star. Murch was full of praise for her hard work – 'she was
absolutely great, a fantastic ally in the making of the film'
– but the conditions were very difficult for the first-time
director. Far from obeying the old adage about not working with children or animals, 'We had not only a child
and animals, talking chickens and dogs and all of that,' he
recalled, 'but also puppets, each operated by three or four
people, radio-controlled devices, front projection and clay-
mation that wasn't there at the time of shooting . . . When
Fairuza had to act with the Nomes, she was just looking at
a piece of tape on a wall, having to imagine it as something
else.'

  Disney was concerned about the production before
filming began, and when the shoot started to fall behind
schedule, and the dailies (the compilation of everything
filmed on a particular day, before editing) weren't living
up to expectation, Murch was fired from the film. He was
only reinstated after his friend George Lucas, the producer
of the *Star Wars* and *Indiana Jones* films, insisted to Disney
management that they should back him after viewing the
footage that Murch had already shot. According to Murch,

Lucas 'met with the Disney executives and said, "No this is going to be great, you guys just have to be more patient with this process, let's see what can be done to facilitate it." ' Lucas offered to guarantee the production, and he and Murch's other high-profile friends, including Coppola and Steven Spielberg, gave the novice director the benefit of their experience.

By the time that the 114-day shoot was complete, and the film entered the lengthy period of post-production to complete the many special-effects sequences, there was yet another change at the top of Disney. The new bosses, Michael Eisner and Jeffrey Katzenberg, seemed to have little interest in a film that had been set up two regimes earlier, which meant that Murch had a freer hand to complete the film the way he wanted it – but also that they didn't really promote the film as well as they could have done. True, it was the centrepiece of a presentation at New York's Radio City Music Hall, but it didn't get the attention it deserved.

The critics weren't overly kind to *Return to Oz* when it opened in June 1985. 'Children are sure to be startled by the film's bleakness,' Janet Maslin maintained in the *New York Times*. Roger Ebert, who believed that 'elements in *The Wizard of Oz* powerfully fill a void that exists inside many children', said, 'Somebody should have thought at the very first when they were starting out with *Return To Oz*, somebody should have had this thought: "It oughta be fun, it oughta be upbeat, it oughta be sweet, it oughta be wondrous. It shouldn't be scary." ' His colleague Gene Siskel agreed: 'Kids under six are gonna get nightmares from this picture. Kids over six, they'll just have a bad time at the movies.'

Return to Oz did not make its budget back at the box office, nor was it garlanded with awards (an Oscar nomination for Best Visual Effects was as good as it got). Controversial American writer Harlan Ellison even suggested that the new team at Disney wanted *Return to Oz* to fail so that any projects they did looked better by comparison (he claimed that he 'began to smell the odour of filmic crib-death' even before the film opened.) Any hope of a revival of Oz films – at least under the Disney banner – was dashed, for a few decades anyway.

Although various reimaginings of *The Wizard of Oz* were prepared for television or as direct-to-video films (including versions reworked to incorporate the Muppets, and combative cartoon duo Tom & Jerry, discussed further in chapter four), there was nearly a twenty-five-year gap before serious work began on any form of proper theatrical return to the franchise.

The life story of Oscar Zoroaster Phadrig Isaac Norman Henkel Emmannuel Ambroise Diggs, aka the Wizard of Oz, is touched upon in various parts of L. Frank Baum's novels – some of which contradict each other, as Baum realized that the Wizard was a character whom his young audience liked, despite his humbuggery. But he was one about whom movie audiences really knew comparatively little, as the producer of the most recent Oz film, former Walt Disney chief executive Joe Roth, pointed out, 'This character is only in the last few minutes of [*The Wizard of Oz*] and we have no idea who he is'. Nor does he make an appearance in *Return to Oz*. But he's the star of the most recent Oz film, *Oz the Great and Powerful*.

The success of the stage show *Wicked* led to a degree of interest in the Oz saga, but, as screenwriter Mitchell Kapner wryly noted, he had been keen on scripting an Oz film previously but felt that now *Wicked*, with its reworking of the whole Oz mythos in which the Wizard is very much the villain of the piece, was part of the zeitgeist, he had missed the boat for a straight tale. In 2009, he was pitching various ideas to Joe Roth, but none was getting the producer interested. Roth asked Kapner what he was reading, and the writer explained he was reading the Baum books to his children. Roth had believed that there was just the one Oz book and was intrigued to learn more.

When Kapner reached the story about the Wizard's arrival in Oz, Roth stopped him, recognizing 'this was an idea for a movie that was genuinely worth pursuing'. As well as the connection to one of the top movies of all time, Roth knew from his time at Disney 'how hard it was to find a fairy tale with a good strong male protagonist. You've got your Sleeping Beauties, your Cinderellas and your Alices ... But with the origin story of the Wizard of Oz, here was a fairy-tale story with a natural male protagonist.'

Once Kapner had prepared a story treatment, incorporating elements of Baum's tales as well as some twists of his own, Roth and his production partner Palak Patel took the idea to Sony, who turned it down. But Dick Cook, then-chairman of Walt Disney Studios, liked it and commissioned a screenplay. Concerned in case other studios fast tracked their projects when they knew of Disney's interest, it became codenamed 'Brick' and everyone involved was sworn to secrecy.

News of the project broke in March 2010 in the *Los Angeles Times*: 'As conceived in Kapner's script, the wizard is a charlatan who's part of a traveling circus but goes on a similar odyssey as Dorothy when he mysteriously lands in Oz,' the paper reported. A month later, the same paper suggested that Robert Downey Jr, a hot property following the success of the *Iron Man* comic book adaptation, was being eyed to play Diggs in what was now known as 'The Great Powerful', and either Sam Mendes (who was suddenly available when his Bond movie *Skyfall* was postponed), or *Hairspray*'s Adam Shankman were potential directors.

The eventual director refused initially to read the script. Sam Raimi's office on the Sony lot was adjacent to Joe Roth's and the producer asked Raimi to read the script.

He refused because he was such a big fan of the 1939 MGM musical, and had no intention of touching *The Wizard of Oz*. When Roth explained it was a prequel, Raimi read it, and realized, 'Oh, it's not just treading on the good name. It's its own story, and one that I really liked.'

That didn't mean that he accepted Kapner's script as it stood; Raimi refined it and brought in Pulitzer Prize winner David Lindsay-Abaire to help. Out went some of Kapner's Baumian touches – such as a tribe of humanoid knives and forks – and in came more multi-ethnic touches and a larger emotional arc for Oz (as he was now known throughout the film). Out also had to go any overt references to the MGM movie (although astute audiences will notice some sly nods): Warner Bros. owned the rights to the various elements created for this, such as the ruby slippers, and the make-up used for the Wicked Witch of the West, so Raimi had to work around the legal minefield. In the end the Witch was green, but the shade is technically a different enough colour to satisfy the lawyers. 'We had to go 180 degrees in the other direction,' Raimi commented. 'I thought, "We're just going to have to make our own Oz." '

Even so, Raimi still wanted the film to have a similar look and feel to its predecessor by emulating its production values. 'Sam insisted we use as little green screen as possible on this picture,' Roth recalled. 'He wanted his actors to be standing on real sets with their feet on the ground, so that this fantasy world could then be tactile.' As a result, seven different soundstages were used at the Raleigh Michigan Studios in Detroit to bring Oz to life.

To play Oz, Raimi first met with Robert Downey Jr, but this didn't pan out; Roth then spoke with Johnny Depp, but the actor was committed to working on *The Lone Ranger*, and wasn't able to sign up. Eventually, five months before the scheduled July 2011 start of filming, James Franco was approached. Franco had played Harry Osborn in Raimi's *Spider-Man* trilogy of movies, and was delighted to work with the director again. He was also a fan of the original books.

In *Oz the Great and Powerful*, the Great Oz (Oscar) is a philandering fake magician who is trying to escape yet another debacle when he is carried away by balloon through a tornado into the land of Oz. He meets the witch Theodora who believes he's the Wizard who is meant to come to rid the land of the Wicked Witch who killed the king of Oz. As they travel to the Emerald City, Theodora falls in love with him. They also meet flying monkey Finley, who Oscar saves from a lion, which runs away. In the Emerald City, Theodora's sister Evanora is dubious about Oscar being the foretold wizard, and sends him to destroy the Wicked Witch's wand. On their way to the Dark Forest, Oscar and Finley meet a China Girl, the only survivor of an attack by the Wicked Witch.

Oscar realizes he's been duped when the 'Wicked Witch' turns out to be Glinda the Good Witch, who explains that Evanora is the true Wicked Witch. When she sees what has happened, Evanora turns Theodora against Oscar, and persuades her to eat a magic apple to remove her heartache. This it does – by transforming her into a heartless green-skinned Wicked Witch.

Glinda takes Oscar and his friends to her domain and although she knows that he's not a real wizard, she wants him to help them. The tricks that formed part of Oscar's magic act then come in handy, as Oscar pulls off a major illusion to capture the Emerald City. Theodora flees, while Evanora is banished and carried away. Oscar then uses the projector he has created to maintain the illusion of his power and he and Glinda embrace.

The schedule for *Oz the Great and Powerful* was only a week shorter than that of *Return to Oz*, at 109 days, and it was equally gruelling. Mila Kunis's skin took two months to recover from the regular applications of the green make-up for her role as Theodora. Actors such as Zach Braff, who voiced the Wizard's simian pal, and Joey King, who played the China Doll, would rehearse the scenes in situ with the actors, and then for the takes they would go to a soundproof booth to the side of the soundstage. Their places would be replaced by a pole at the correct eyeline. At the end of the pole was a monitor showing the performance from the booth to the actors on set, as well as a camera to record their characters' point-of-view shots. On other occasions, a marionette would be used to give the animators the correct positioning for the China Girl.

James Franco learned how to perform real magic tricks with Las Vegas stage magician Lance Burton – and the set had to be cleared of all but non-essential personnel when they were filmed, to maintain the magicians' code. (Sadly none of them made the final cut of the film.)

The producers had to work around various other commitments: Franco's father died during the filming, which meant he was off set for three days, while Rachel Weisz (Evanora) was filming *The Bourne Legacy*, and Michelle Williams (Glinda) was promoting her lead role in *My Week with Marilyn*.

Through it all, Raimi gave a strong lead. 'One can become a bit edgy,' Williams remembered. 'But Sam was able to fight it off. When you see that your brave leader, with the world on his shoulders, is able to have a new enthusiasm every day and be patient and kind, you wake up to your own possibilities.'

With its black-and-white opening sequences that develop not just into full colour, but change aspect ratio as well, *Oz the Great and Powerful* is definitely the 'love poem to *The Wizard of Oz*' that Sam Raimi set out to make. Although it grossed sufficiently well at the box office to warrant Disney green-lighting a sequel, it received mixed reviews. Kim Newman wrote in *Empire* magazine that

'long-term Oz watchers will be enchanted and enthralled
. . . Sam Raimi can settle securely behind the curtain as a
mature master of illusion'. *Variety* was less fulsome: 'In a
real sense, *Oz the Great and Powerful* has a certain kin-
ship with George Lucas' *Star Wars* prequels, in the way it
presents a beautiful but borderline-sterile digital update of
a world that was richer, purer and a lot more fun in lower-
tech form,' Justin Chang wrote. 'Here, too, the actors often
look artificially superimposed against their CG backdrops,
though the intensity of the fakery generates its own visual
fascination.'

Sam Raimi is unlikely to be at the helm of a sequel. 'I did
leave some loose ends for another director if they want to
make the picture,' he told website Bleeding Cool in March
2013. 'I tried to make it a complete ending, so that the
audience would be fulfilled, but I also let Evenora and
Theodora get away . . . I was attracted to this story but I
don't think the second one would have the thing I would
need to get me interested.'

According to Mila Kunis, all the cast were signed up for
sequels and the indications are that any new film will continue to be set prior to the events of *The Wizard of Oz* – Joe
Roth told Slashfilm that there are no plans to involve the
character of Dorothy Gale, while Mitchell Kapner pointed out that 'It's twenty years before Dorothy. A lot can
happen in that time.'

4

OZ ON THE SMALL SCREEN

The very first appearance of Oz on the small screen came on a fondly remembered American children's puppet show called *Kukla, Fran and Ollie*, which featured radio comedienne and singer Fran Allison interacting with various puppets operated by Burr Tillstrom. These included Oliver J. Dragon (Ollie for short) and Kukla (taken from the Greek word for doll). The episode, broadcast on NBC on 22 May 1950, three years into the series' decade-long run, included Fran explaining how Tip and Mombi created Jack Pumpkinhead, as related early on in *The Marvelous Land of Oz*. The Scarecrow and the Tin Woodman made brief appearances.

As discussed in the last chapter, Walt Disney's plans to produce *The Rainbow Road of Oz* as a feature film derived originally from his purchase of the rights to the majority of L. Frank Baum's Oz series – bar *The Wizard of Oz* and a couple of others. If *The Rainbow Road of Oz* had formed a two-part episode of the *Disneyland* series, as intended, then it might have opened the floodgates for a slew of adaptations of the entire Oz canon.

Instead, the first television version of Baum's stories came on *The Shirley Temple Show* in 1960. 'The Land of Oz' was the opening episode of the NBC show's second season. The one-hour programme (which can now be seen in the United States via the Hulu website or on DVD) was 'intended for the childlike eye' according to the write-up in *TV Guide*, and was hosted by the former child star, who sometimes, as she did in the case of 'The Land of Oz', starred in the stories.

Temple played dual roles in the story, which was based on *The Marvelous Land of Oz*, one of the two Baum novels to which Disney did not have the rights by this stage. 'It all starts when Lord Nikdik, wickedest denizen of Oz, hits upon a scheme to take over the kingdom,' ran the promotional material. 'His assistant – Mombi the Witch.' Unfortunately, the cast list gave away one of the key elements of the story, that Tip and Princess Ozma are one and the same!

Temple's Tip was assisted by Frances Bergen as Glinda the Good, Ben Blue as the Scarecrow, Gil Lamb as the Tin Woodman, and Sterling Holloway as Pumpkinhead. Facing them was Agnes Moorehead (soon to become famous as mother-in-law from hell, the witch Endora in *Bewitched*) as Mombi, and Jonathan Winters as Lord Nikdik. The adaptation was by Frank Gabrielson, and directed by William Corrigan.

'The Land of Oz' adhered pretty closely to Baum's original story, avoiding the temptation to include Dorothy or the Lion, but in this Ozma ruled Oz for some time before being captured by Mombi, on the instructions of Lord Nikdik, and her memory being wiped. (Nikdik was simply a magician in the original story; it was General Jinjur who was trying to conquer the Emerald City.) The story ends with Glinda sentencing Nikdik to perform one good deed a day for the rest of his life. 'What will my friends say?' he demands!

It was a smart choice for a season opener: this was the first episode made and broadcast in colour, and the costumes and scenery of Oz were a perfect fit. Older audiences may have remembered that Temple was supposed to have been the original choice for the big-screen Dorothy, so tuned in to see how she fitted into Oz. It's perhaps a shame that rights issues prevented any further such adventures – although Ruth Plumly Thompson offered the use of some of her later adventures for adaptation, the producers decided not to return to Oz.

Oz did come back to the small screen a year later, but in an animated form. *Tales of the Wizard of Oz* was made by the Canadian company Crawley Films for Videocrafts (who eventually became known as Rankin/Bass from the names of its executive producers, Arthur Rankin Jr and Jules Bass). Perhaps the best indication of how seriously the producers took their Oz lore can be judged from a synopsis of a random episode, 'The Last Straw': The Wicked Witch puts a fake advertisement in the Oz newspaper for a 'handsome-judging' contest (i.e. a male beauty pageant), which will be adjudicated by the famous movie actress Zelda Zowie. It's a plot to grab the most handsome man in Oz and make him her slave. All of the characters – including the Wizard, Rusty the Tin Man, and Dandy Lion – prepare for it, with the exception of Socrates, the ragged old Scarecrow. To give him a fair chance, Dorothy prepares a new head and body for him. The Witch disguises herself as the actress (who is wearing typical early 1960s clothing) and grabs this incredibly handsome man of straw, not guessing that it's Socrates. But when she hears him speak, she realizes that she has made rather a large mistake . . . Other episodes include 'The Witch Switch', 'Leapin Lion', 'The Munchkin Robin Hood' and 'To Bee or Not to Bee'.

Tales of the Wizard of Oz was the second series to be made by Videocrafts, and their first using cel animation – *The New Adventures of Pinocchio* was appropriately enough made with puppets. Reports differ as to how many episodes were made, but there were around 130 three- to five-minute long cartoons. As the episode titles might indicate, this was 'suggested' by *The Wizard of Oz*, rather than a faithful rendition: Dorothy Gale (voiced by Corinne Corley) is stuck in Kansas with her little dog Toto, who's a white Scottish Terrier in this account. The Wizard (Carl Banas) is a midget magician, who does a remarkably good impression of W.C. Fields, to the extent of using Fields' catchphrase 'my little chickadee' to Dorothy from time to time. The Scarecrow (Alfie Scopp) is known as Socrates, but he doesn't have the brains of the Athenian philosopher; he's a brainless fool. Rusty the Tin Man (Larry D. Mann) is not a very pleasant character who rides rough-shod over people's feelings (ignoring his creator's comment in *The Wonderful Wizard of Oz*, 'The Tin Woodman knew very well he had no heart, and therefore he took great care never to be cruel or unkind to anything'), while Dandy Lion (Paul Kligman) lives up to his name while retaining his Cowardly characteristics. The Witch, also voiced by Mann, is small, green and desperate for a boyfriend.

The success of the series, which started syndication on 1 September 1961, led to a movie using the same designs, which was called *Return to Oz* but really should have been entitled 'Rewrite of Oz'. Designed as a ninety-minute film, it was cut back to fit a one-hour slot, and acts as a sequel to *The Wizard of Oz*, while also revisiting most of its key plot points. Romeo Muller was responsible for the teleplay, which starts with Dorothy receiving a letter from the Scarecrow saying how much they are missing her. Finding her silver slippers, she is sent back in another twister to Oz (in an apple tree rather than a farmhouse), to learn that the Wicked Witch has been reconstituted, and is wreaking

Dorothy Dwan as Dorothy and Larry Semon as the farmhand who is in love with her in Semon's idiosyncratic version of *Wizard of Oz* (1925).
(©Chadwick Pictures/Kobal)

Dorothy Dwan as Dorothy, who believes she's a simple Kansas farmgirl but is really Princess Dorothea of Oz in Larry Semon's *Wizard of Oz* (1925). (©Chadwick Pictures/Kobal)

Producer Mervyn LeRoy, star Judy Garland and director Victor Fleming with some of the hundreds of Munchkins on the set of *The Wizard of Oz* (1939). (©MGM/Kobal)

One of the lobby cards for the 1939 version of *The Wizard of Oz* showing a rather surprised Frank Morgan as the Wizard. (©MGM/Kobal)

An unusual shot featuring Ray Bolger (the Scarecrow), Jack Haley (the Tin Man) and Margaret Hamilton (the Wicked Witch) in character if not fully in costume for *The Wizard of Oz* (1939). (©MGM/Kobal)

MGM studio head Louis B. Mayer with two of his biggest stars: Mickey Rooney and Judy Garland. The pair performed live for audiences during the initial run of *The Wizard of Oz* (1939). (©MGM/Kobal)

A rare picture showing preparations underway to shoot a scene during filming of *The Wizard of Oz* (1939). (©MGM/Kobal)

Margaret Hamilton as The Wicked Witch of the West plans a horrible fate for Dorothy and her little dog too in *The Wizard of Oz* (1939). (©MGM/Kobal)

A vision of Oz the Great and Powerful as played by Frank Morgan in *The Wizard of Oz* (1939). (©MGM/Kobal)

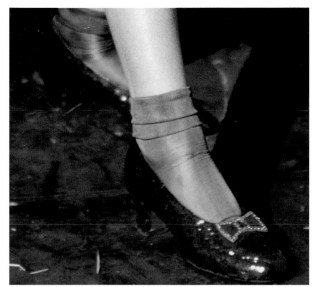

A close-up view of the infamous ruby slippers worn by Judy Garland in *The Wizard of Oz* (1939). In all other versions of the story, they are silver. (©MGM/Kobal)

Dorothy realizes that she and Toto aren't in Kansas anymore in this scene from *The Wizard of Oz* (1939). (©MGM/Kobal)

Judy Garland as Dorothy on the Munchkinland set. Note the curve of the backdrop painting at the top of the picture.

(©MGM/Kobal)

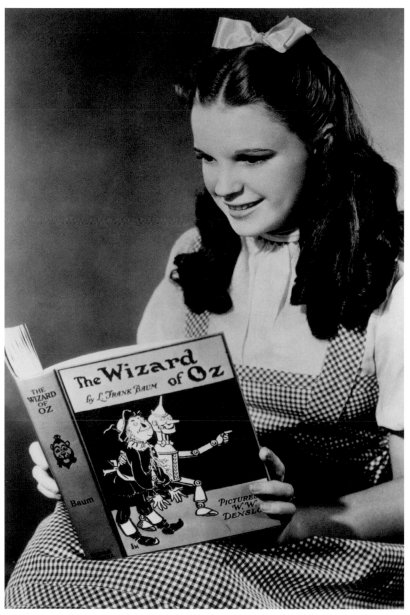

A publicity still showing Judy Garland reading a copy of L. Frank Baum's original book with the title suitably altered to fit the new movie's name. (©MGM/Kobal)

Nipsey Russell, Diana Ross, Michael Jackson and Ted Ross come face to face with one of the Monkeys in this scene from *The Wiz* (1978). (©Universal/Kobal)

(*left*) Michael Jackson strikes a pose as the Scarecrow in Sidney Lumet's version of *The Wiz* (1978). (©Universal/ Kobal)

(*below*) The land of Oz as you've never seen it before − within the World Trade Center, as imagined for the 1978 film adaptation of *The Wiz*. (©Universal/Kobal)

Dorothy (Fairuza Balk), Bilina the chicken and Tik-Tok the Mechanical Man – the heroes of Disney's *Return to Oz* (1985). (©Buena Vista/Kobal)

Dorothy tries to help the residents of Oz – Jack Pumpkinhead, King Scarecrow, the Gump and Tik-Tok – in a scene from Disney's *Return to Oz* (1985). (©Buena Vista/Kobal)

(*left*) Dorothy faces one of the dreaded Wheelers as she walks down the ruins of the Yellow Brick Road in Disney's *Return to Oz* (1985). (©Buena Vista/Kobal)

(*below*) Jean Marsh in villainous mode as the witch Mombi, who tries to trap Dorothy in her attic when she makes a *Return to Oz* (1985). (©Buena Vista/Kobal)

havoc once more. The Scarecrow, the Tin Man and the Lion all have to retrieve the items that the Wizard gave them, and the Witch wants the silver slippers. The perils they face are slightly different from the original movie – flying alligators and lightning bolts – and the Witch is turned to stone rather than destroyed with water. Dorothy's trio of friends triumph because they have heart, brains and courage; Dorothy is returned to Kansas by another twister.

Return to Oz first aired on Sunday 9 February 1964, as part of NBC's *General Electric Color Fantasy Hour.* Like the series it was directed by F.R. Crawley, Thomas Glynn, and Larry Roemer. Mann reprised his roles as the Witch and the Tin Man from the TV series, with Banas returning as the Wizard and also playing the Lion; Scopp once again played the Scarecrow. Dorothy, though, was played by two actresses: Susan Conway for the spoken parts, and Susan Morse for the songs. According to a report in the *Calgary Herald*, 140,000 individual pieces of artwork were created by forty animators for the special.

The *New York Herald Tribune* described *Return to Oz* as 'a charming sequel for the very young, its action and sentiment – cut from the original pattern – probably evoking more delight and some youthful nostalgia . . . Children were the ones this musical was aimed [at] although its commercials were directed at adults.' Talking to a website dedicated to the Rankin/Bass shows some years later, Susan Conway recalled that 'In a climactic part of the story Dorothy speaks some words that have always resonated deeply within me: "Golly, I'm no wizard, but I know you should never give up hope – there's plenty of magic. Why a little Robin poppin' out of its shell in the middle of May . . . what's that but magic? When you're with those you love and who love you, there's magic there with you." The message is simple but profound and I'm proud to have been a part of a production that reminds people of those values.'

* * *

The next production, *Off to See the Wizard*, arrived three years later, although this can be seen as MGM capitalizing on their ownership of the movie rather than a true continuation of the Oz saga. In much the same way that cast members and their families as well as Oz historians provided introductions to the annual screenings of the 1939 film, this one-hour series saw animated versions of the characters from the film present assorted movies from the MGM library, usually divided into two parts. These included *Clarence, the Cross-Eyed Lion*, the movie that inspired the hit series *Daktari*; the 1959 version of *Tarzan*; and dolphin adventure *Flipper*. The animation was directed by the legendary Chuck Jones, with Mel Blanc providing the voices for the Cowardly Lion and Toto; Daws ('Yogi Bear') Butler as the Scarecrow, the Tin Man and the Wizard of Oz; and June Foray as Dorothy and the Wicked Witch.

There wasn't a great deal of animation: the titles show Dorothy travelling over a rainbow with Toto into Oz where she meets her three friends, and they sing as they travel to the Emerald City. There they stand on a balcony overlooking the Great Oz's courtyard, and the Wizard comes out from behind the curtain, firstly to thank that episode's sponsors, and then to have some repartee with the characters before the film begins. At the end, there's a bit of introduction to the highlights coming up next week, and then the four friends reverse their path, adding a new verse to the classic lyrics: 'Each week a new adventure/A magic carpet ride/There's loads of fun for everyone/With the Wizard as your guide.' A brief snatch of 'Follow the Yellow Brick Road' leads into 'Somewhere Over the Rainbow' as the titles roll.

The 1970s were a quiet time for Oz on television, barring brief reworking of the iconography for episodes of various TV series (see part four). However, in 1980, you could spend *Thanksgiving in the Land of Oz* 'as Dorothy and Toto embark on an exciting new adventure, and meet friends old and new' in a CBS special that added Jack Pumpkinhead, Tic Toc [sic], Ozma and the Hungry Tiger to the roster of animated Ozites. This animated special isn't well regarded, even though it incorporates some elements of the original Baum saga that rarely turn up elsewhere.

Dorothy on this occasion returns to Oz in a green turkey-shaped balloon as she prepares for her final Thanksgiving with Aunt Em and Uncle Henry before they move to a retirement home. She then becomes embroiled in yet another slightly altered rerun of her original adventure, this time battling against Tyrone the Terrible Toy Tinker. She manages to persuade Tyrone that with Christmas coming up, maybe his time would be better spent using his toy-making skills to make children happy. As a thank you, Ozma allows her to bring Aunt Em and Uncle Henry to Oz.

Also released on DVD as *Dorothy in the Land of Oz* (with some of the Thanksgiving references removed), the half-hour animated musical was directed by Charles Swenson and starred Sid Caesar as the Wizard, the Narrator, and a new character, U.N. Krust, who, according to the publicity release, is 'a living, talking mince pie who speaks with a different accent every time he utters a phrase!' Other voices were provided by Mischa Bond (Dorothy), Robert Ridgeley (Tyrone and Jack Pumpkinhead) and Joan Gerber (Tic Toc and Ozma). The author was once again Romeo Muller.

A year after Disney's *Return to Oz* had failed to reignite major interest in L. Frank Baum's wonderful world, a new Japanese anime series returned to his original stories about Oz. *The Wonderful Wizard of Oz*, known in Japan as *Oz no Mahōtsukai*, comprised four separate story arcs – in the English-dubbed version these were 'The Wonderful Wizard of Oz', 'The Marvelous Land of Oz', 'Ozma of

Oz', and 'The Emerald City of Oz' – which roughly corresponded to the events of the first three and the sixth story of Baum's saga. However, the longer the series went on, the further the story strayed from the source material.

Not connected to the similarly titled anime from 1982, these fifty-two twenty-five-minute episodes were first broadcast in Japan on NHK and TV Tokyo between 1986 and 1987. HBO bought the rights to an English-language version, with former Superman actress Margot Kidder acting as narrator, and it first aired from 1987–1988, before being re-edited (severely) into four TV movies.

The English-language version starred Morgan Hallet as Dorothy Gale with Richard Dumont as the Scarecrow, George Morris as the Tin Man and Neil Shee as the Cowardly Lion. Sumi Shimamoto, Yoshito Yasuhara, Takuzo Kamiyama and Ichiro Nagai played the parts on the original Japanese soundtrack. The episodes were directed by Tonogawa Naisho and Hiroshi Saito, and scripted by Akira Miyazaki; the English adaptation was by Don Arioli and Tim Reid, who was also credited as the director.

The music score was by Joe Hisaihi, who had also composed the music for the 1982 anime feature, while the English version included a song 'Searching for a Dream' by the Parachute Club over the new opening titles, a CGI rendition of a farm in Kansas hit by a twister, which pulls up a yellow brick road (and a hen, for no readily discernible reason).

The first seventeen episodes adapt *The Wonderful Wizard of Oz*, and those wanting to see a story that translated Baum's text to the screen will have been pleased. Little touches like the field mice rescuing Dorothy and her friends from the poppy fields, and the individual audiences with the Wizard are retained – ideas that would have been very hard to create in live-action.

There were a few changes along the way. Before she's transported to Oz in the twister, Dorothy has a dream about strange events that are about to happen to her interspersed with her desperately trying to run back to the farm, which recedes from her into the distance – a two-and-a-half-minute-long trailer for everything that's coming up within the series. Uncle Henry and Aunt Em aren't present on the farm when Dorothy disappears; this leads to scenes with her uncle believing that she's dead, while Aunt Em is certain that she's alive. The Wicked Witches of the East and West are sisters, as are the Good Witches of the North and the South – for once, these characters aren't amalgamated into one. The magic shoes that the Wicked Witch of the East was wearing only become Silver Slippers once Dorothy's wearing them (of course, there was no question of these being ruby). And the plotline of the second book impinges as Mombi and Tip arrive at the Wicked Witch of the West's castle while Dorothy and her friends are resting there after the death of the Witch.

The following thirteen episodes adapt *The Marvelous Land of Oz*, but incorporate Dorothy into the action (although the Lion remains conspicuous by his absence). This means that the writers have to explain how she gets back to Oz. This is quite ingenious: the story begins with Toto and Dorothy reappearing in Kansas but the girl has lost one of her magic shoes. Dorothy meets the Wizard at a circus but when Aunt Em finds the missing slipper, Dorothy eagerly heads back to Oz, this time leaving Toto behind in Kansas. She arrives in time to find Tip creating Jack Pumpkinhead, and the story then progresses much as in Baum's second novel – including the Wizard's part in placing Ozma with Mombi, something that Baum wrote out of Oz history in later novels (a process known to comic-book fans nowadays as 'retconning', retroactively changing continuity). Other changes are comparatively minor: the Wogglebug doesn't appear; Glinda and Mombi have a fight as transformed animals; and Jinjur refuses to reform her ways, and has to be magicked into a new outlook, whereas Baum had her changing of her own accord.

The next eleven instalments are based on *Ozma of Oz*. This time Dorothy arrives in Oz thanks to the magic power of the silver slippers, although once again these, and Toto, remain in our world rather than travelling across (there's no suggestion in this version that Oz isn't a distinct and separate place – Dorothy vanishes from one land and appears in the other when magic is involved). The writers clearly looked at the original story and decided that there were elements that could be simplified from the way Baum wrote them: Ozma doesn't head off with the party into the Nome Kingdom, since she has a kingdom of her own to deal with, and she's not been back in charge for long. There aren't as many members of the Royal Family of Ev – Princess Langwidere in the book becomes Princess Lulu on screen, and is the sister of the Crown Prince, who has been kidnapped by the Nome King. The Nome King doesn't have a Magic Belt (although quite what the literary Ozma would have done if she hadn't possessed that isn't worth thinking about: it was considerably overused as a plot device in the books). The Deadly Desert isn't as deadly as it is in the books – rather than being fatal to anyone touching it, it simply has a large number of hazards including a giant beetle and a lack of oases.

One element that was changed does throw up some questions: in the original story, Dorothy arrives in Oz together with the chicken Billina, who develops the power of speech. Her eggs are important to the resolution of the plot, since the Nomes are frightened of them. In the anime, Dorothy arrives alone, and she and her friends encounter Billina on the way to the Nome Kingdom; according to the tale she tells them, she used to be the Nome King's chicken, raising the question why would a species scared of eggs (which remains a plot point) keep one?

The final eleven episodes follow directly on from the conclusion of the third arc, with Dorothy still in Oz rather than starting with her finding a new way to arrive. *The*

Emerald City of Oz was the sixth novel, with the Nome King plotting revenge for the theft of his Magic Belt; because that element was removed from the adaptation, he's simply out for revenge against the Ozites from the Emerald City. Also vanished from the original is the subplot regarding Aunt Em and Uncle Henry's arrival in Oz – probably a good move, since the scenes don't show Ozma at her finest. Although these seem minor changes, their effect is felt throughout the story, which maintains the plot beats of the original, while making the Nome King's desire for revenge on Dorothy more personal. At the end of the entire series, Dorothy says goodbye to her friends and returns to Kansas, where Aunt Em and Uncle Henry are waiting for her.

On 18 November 1987, around the same time as the Japanese series was receiving its US premiere, another take on *Ozma of Oz* was released direct to video, although this lasted a tenth of the running time, at a mere twenty-eight minutes – and two and a half minutes of that was spent on an introduction by Michael Gross, and a ghastly piece of 1980s pop about 'a place of princes, girls and dreams'! The adaptation was by Jim Carlson and Terrence McDonnell and directed by Pierre DeCelles and Georges Grammat. Voice cast included Sandra J. Butcher, Nancy Chance, Jay David, Janice Kawaye as Dorothy (credited as Hiromi Kawaye), Fredie Smootie and Matthew Stone.

The key beats are here: Dorothy and Billina are swept overboard from a voyage to Australia and find themselves in Oz. They meet the Wheelers, Tik-Tok and their other friends, and go to try to save the royal family of Ev from the Nome King. They have to guess which ornaments are transformed people, and Billina helps by scaring the Nomes. It even includes the Magic Belt and its ability to change everyone back to normal, and transport Dorothy across the dimensions. Its only real difference is that

it suggests that, as in the 1939 movie, it's all a dream –
although Dorothy finds an egg that proves to her it wasn't.

To mark the fiftieth anniversary of the MGM movie,
DiC Entertainment produced a thirteen-part animated
series, which aired on ABC in the United States between 8
September and 1 December 1990. Unlike most new Oz
adventures, which were capitalizing on the release of the
books into the public domain, DiC licensed the iconic
imagery from the MGM film, so, for once, Dorothy has
ruby slippers, although sensibly the creators didn't try
to portray her as Judy Garland, but veered closer to the
design of Ariel in the Disney cartoon *The Little Mermaid*.
(Vocally, though, it's a Judy Garland imitation, consciously
or unconsciously.) The cast included Liz Georges as Dorothy, Charlie Adler as the Cowardly Lion, Hal Rayle as the
Tin Man, David Lodge as the Scarecrow, Tress MacNeille
as the Witch, and erstwhile bionic surgeon Alan Oppenheimer as the Wizard.

Talking to Lynne Heffley in the *Los Angeles Times* the
day before *The Wizard of Oz* premiered, DiC president
Andy Heyward explained that everyone involved 'felt a
great sense of responsibility. We felt that we were dealing
with something that was almost sacred – not based on toy
products or something transitory, but one of the treasures
of American film.'

His colleague Mike Maliani, DiC producer and vice
president of development, added: 'Thirteen episodes take
them all through Oz. They're in Munchkin village, then
Fort Nutcracker with wooden soldiers, Pop Land, full
of jack-in-the-boxes; Mechanica, where everybody is
mechanical – they get caught up in all kinds of adventures
as they're trying to find the Wizard.'

Each episode was deliberately created as a variation on
the quest theme central to the movie, with Dorothy summoned back to Oz to help her friends after the Wicked

Witch has been resurrected and stolen the items the Wizard has given them (a very similar conceit to the 1964 *Return to Oz* cartoon). The Wizard is constantly being blown around in his hot air balloon thanks to a spell. As the revised lyrics explained, Dorothy and her friends were now off to 'save the Wizard'.

'I think we kept the integrity of the classic and mixed in enough new for today's audience,' Maliani said. 'Kids would be instantly turned off to see something old.'

DiC may have been hoping for the series to be renewed for a second year: certainly the last broadcast episode, 'Hot Air', finishes with the Witch escaping yet again, and the Wizard still being blown around in his balloon. However, it was aired opposite *Muppet Babies*, and ABC declined to order more episodes. The company turned its attention to other properties including G.I. Joe and *Bill & Ted's Excellent Adventure*. ABC ordered a new take on *The Wizard of Oz* six years later with *Oz Kids* (discussed in part four).

A fresh adaptation of the original story by Barbara A. Oliver followed in 1991 as part of the anime series *Funky Fables* (not to be confused with the more recent CBBC series). The production design was, to put it mildly, eclectic: the Tin Man looked rather more like Tik-Tok than the traditional idea, with a clockwork key on the top of his head. 'Once upon a time, in a place called Kansas, there lived a girl named, wait a minute . . . No, don't tell me . . . Doris, no, that's not it . . . Dorothy . . .' starts the narration, which gives a pretty good idea of the tack that Oliver took, which has to be seen to be believed. This over-the-top hilarious take can be found on YouTube and was one of a series of reworkings of well-known stories.

The first decade of the twenty-first century saw further reimaginings of the Oz story (also discussed in part four) including the Muppets' reworking of the story. A very basic computer-animated version of *The Patchwork Girl of Oz* was promised for 2005 from Thundertoad Animation, which eventually surfaced a few years later – it is faithful to L. Frank Baum's seventh Oz novel but suffers from a low budget.

The first attempt to return to either the Baum original or the 1939 movie came when MGM decided to amalgamate two of their most popular properties: *The Wizard of Oz* and cartoon enemies Tom and Jerry. The cover for the DVD simply put the two logos together with an ampersand to connect them and showed the famous cat and mouse caught up in a twister along with the characters from the Oz saga.

Tom and Jerry and the Wizard of Oz follows in the footsteps of the stage version of *Wicked* by showing some of the action that's going on simultaneously with the Judy Garland movie but had not previously been seen – a trick used most memorably by Tom Stoppard in *Rosencrantz & Guildenstern Are Dead*, his reworking of Shakespeare's *Hamlet*. This is definitely the film version of Oz: Dorothy has ruby-red slippers, and the story concludes midway through the book.

Tom and Jerry are workers on the Gale farm, and become caught up in the twister that takes Dorothy to Kansas. There Tufty, Jerry's cousin, brings them up to speed, and the trio follow Dorothy and her friends along the Yellow Brick Road to the Emerald City. Tom and Jerry disguise themselves as Winkie guards to help rescue Dorothy once she's been captured by the Witch, and find morose dog Droopy there as one of the instructors (in his usual way, Droopy keeps appearing wherever the pair try to hide while they're being chased). They realize the Witch has a severe problem with water; after some considerable difficulty getting hold of some, they manage to splash the Witch. On the return to the Emerald City, like Dorothy, they fail to take off in the Wizard's balloon, but are taken back with her thanks to Glinda's intervention.

Spike Bradt's direction of Gene Grillo's script for the hour-long special manages to combine the two franchises successfully without the Oz characters feeling shoehorned into the tale. The strong voice cast included a number of veterans of the fantasy genre: Michael Gough (Alfred in the 1980s and 1990s *Batman* films) as the Scarecrow, *American Horror Story*'s Frances Conroy as Auntie Em, *Heroes*' Todd Stashwick as the Cowardly Lion, and the latest voice for Daphne in *Scooby Doo*, Grey DeLisle, as Dorothy. It was first broadcast on the Cartoon Network in the US on 13 August 2011.

Further TV series are being contemplated in light of the success of *Oz the Great and Powerful*. *Abraham Lincoln: Vampire Hunter* director Timur Bekmambetov is working on Warriors of Oz, a 'fantasy-action' miniseries, for the US Syfy Channel, in which a warrior from contemporary Earth is transported to a post-apocalyptic future Oz where he must team up with three other warriors, Heartless, Brainless, and Coward, to defeat the evil Wizard who has enslaved the land. CBS is developing *Dorothy*, a medical soap based in New York inspired by *The Wizard of Oz*, with Carl Beverly and Sarah Timberman, the executive producers for the Sherlock Holmes contemporary update, *Elementary*. NBC has picked up the dark reimagining *Emerald City*, written and executive produced by *Siberia*'s Matthew Arnold, which will draw on all of Baum's original fourteen novels. Both *Emerald City* and Warner Bros' proposed TV series *Red Brick Road*, created by concept artist Rob Prior, have been pitched as 'the Wizard of Oz story . . . told in a *Game of Thrones* fashion, filled with politics, intrigue and violence'. It remains to be seen how many of these survive in the cutthroat world of peak-time television.

5

OZ IN OTHER MEDIA

Although L. Frank Baum named his financially disastrous 1908 Oz stage show *The Fairylogue and Radio-Plays*, the Radio referred to in the title had nothing to do with audio broadcasts through the air. Although there were various amateur radio stations by this time, regular licensed broadcasting didn't begin until 1920.

The first programme to feature Oz was *Topsy Turvy Time*, broadcast by WMAQ (which supposedly stood for 'We Must Ask Questions') in Chicago, which began transmitting in 1922. This daily children's show, which encouraged its young listeners to tell the truth and sent them certificates to remind them, regularly included readings of some of the Oz books between 1926 and 1927. As part of their drive to publicize the new books by Ruth Plumly Thompson, publishers Reilly & Lee also commissioned her to write *The Enchanted Tree of Oz*, a new short story. This followed adventures for the Scarecrow and Dorothy, but stopped as they disappeared into the Magical Tree of Whutter Wee – and the young listeners were invited to submit their own endings. Sadly, none of these survives, although Thompson's start was reprinted in Oz fan-club newsletter, the *Baum Bugle*.

In 1927, radio station WTAM ('Where the Artisans Meet', allegedly) in Cleveland, Ohio considered adapting the various 'Junior League' versions of the stage plays published by Samuel French (see p 168) for their younger listeners. However, in the end they decided to proceed with their own version, and negotiated for the rights with Baum's widow, Maud Gage Baum. This only lasted for twelve weeks before the sponsor decided not to proceed further. Two years later, the National Broadcasting Company (NBC) included readings from the Oz saga as part of their *Children's Hour*, as well as the Cream of Wheat sponsored show *Jolly Bill and Jane*. This wasn't confined to the Baum tales, but excerpted from Ruth Plumly Thompson's books as well.

The first proper dramatization for radio could also be heard on NBC. Fifteen-minute-long episodes of *Wizard of Oz* ran between 25 September 1933 and 23 March 1935, three nights a week (Monday, Wednesday and Friday), from 5.45 p.m. It covered elements from the saga from *The Wonderful Wizard of Oz* through to *The Emerald City of Oz*, with suitable interjections to the plot made to allow for sponsor messages from Jell-O – the most infamous of these was when the Nome King turned the characters into ornaments, the narrator had to explain that the worst tragedy that they faced was that they could no longer eat Jell-O!

The scriptwriters had no compunction about reordering events, or changing them completely. The Phanfasms from *The Emerald City*, Johnny Dooit from *The Road*, and the burial in popcorn snow that features in *The Scarecrow of Oz* were all incorporated into one single quarter-of-an-hour episode. Dorothy remained in Oz after the events of *The Wonderful Wizard* because she's lost one of the silver slippers, and then meets Tip and Jack before finally getting home. Once that story has been told, Dorothy then returns after the shipwreck that begins *Ozma of Oz*.

Jell-O unfortunately decided not to continue sponsorship of the programme, transferring their allegiance to Jack Benny's radio show – which would go on for many years. NBC was unable to find another sponsor, and the show came to an end, replaced by the adventures of college boy Frank Merriwell.

Twelve-year-old Nancy Kelly played Dorothy, with Bill Adams as the Scarecrow, Jack Smart as the Cowardly Lion and Jack Pumpkinhead, and Parker Fennelly as the Tin Woodman and Tik-Tok. Agnes Moorehead, who went on to threaten Shirley Temple's Tip in the 1960 TV version of *The Land of Oz*, played Mombi and Langwidere. Reilly & Lee reprinted four of L. Frank Baum's *Little Wizard Stories of Oz* in separate booklets to accompany the series.

Rival network CBS also produced a version of *The Wizard of Oz* during the 1930s, from which the first and the seventh episodes survive. They were written and directed by John Elkhorn, with music provided by Charles Paul and His Munchkin Music Men.

The MGM movie dominated the 1940s, and Lux Radio Theater, which adapted stage plays and movies for radio audiences, brought the screen story to audio on Christmas Day 1950. The entire script, as well as a recording of the hour-long play, can be found online, and it was released on LP and CD. The big draw of this production, of course, was Judy Garland returning to the role of Dorothy after a dozen years. Herb Vigran played the Tin Woodman, Hans Conried was the Scarecrow and Ed Max played the Lion. Noreen Gammill was the Wicked Witch.

The lack of visuals are made up for with the normal prerequisites of radio drama from those days – 'There's a big sign on the wagon. Wait, I think I can see what it says. "Professor Marvel, acclaimed by the crowned heads of Europe. Let him read your past, present, and future in his crystal," ' Dorothy announces to Toto, and later the tornado scene has her explain, 'Now she's on a broomstick! She *is* a witch!' At the end, listeners could hear Judy Garland explain how her four-year-old daughter Liza ('says three in the script, but she's really four') is being taught to dance by the Scarecrow – much to the annoyance of the Lion.

Another fifteen years would elapse before new audio dramatizations appeared. Ray Bolger narrated and reprised his role as the Scarecrow from the 1939 film on the 12-inch LP, *Walt Disney Presents the Scarecrow of Oz*, adapted by Jimmy Johnson. Robie Lester, Martha Wentworth and Dal McKennon joined Bolger in the tale based on L. Frank Baum's ninth Oz tale. *The Wizard of Oz* and *The Cowardly Lion of Oz* followed in 1969. Bolger wasn't involved in either of these, and the latter, despite sharing its title with Ruth Plumly Thompson's 1923 tale, was an original story by Johnson.

Disney's final story was 1970's *The Tin Woodman of Oz*, which starred future *Happy Days* actor and film director Ron Howard as Woot. Johnson loosely based this on the twelfth of Baum's novels, but rewrote the ending so that all the main characters – the Tin Woodman, Woot, Polychrome, the Scarecrow and the Cowardly Lion – get married. Disneyland Records later released an LP featuring the songs from the first three tales.

Around 1967, Golden Records provided a sequel story whose LP cover opened out to form a new Oz board game. Written by Sid Frank, with songs by Ralph Stein, it was an attempt to continue the story, but didn't really tie in with either the original book or the MGM musical. Both Dorothy and the Wizard return to Oz, and persuade the Good Witch of the North to pretend to be evil to persuade the Ozites that they need a Wizard again. Of course it all goes horribly wrong. The album was re-released as *Further Adventures of the Wizard of Oz* in 1972.

Other adaptations of the original story were released during the early 1970s. The Famous Theatre Company version was part of United Artists Records' *Tale Spinners for Children* collection, which was 'an exciting new concept on records for young people. Every album in the series combines three major ingredients: classic stories for young people; a fine theatrical company plus a famous actor or actress playing the title role; and the music of the Hollywood Studio Orchestra providing the finest background possible. Through the magic of *Tale Spinners*, young listeners are exposed to the finest literature, and a form of classical music presented in a most attractive setting.' Graced with some of the most psychedelic art to be found in an Oz tie-in, this was a standard shortening of the story.

Robert Lewis produced a longer double-album version for Jabberwocky Records in 1972, narrated by Fay DeWitt. The script was by Patti Mortensen and featured Tricia Metz as Dorothy, Steve Covington as the Scarecrow, Rick Cimino as the Tin Woodman and Terry McGovern as the Lion. With around ninety minutes to fill, further adventures could be included in the story, rather than simply using the first two-thirds of the book in common with the MGM film.

Apart from an LP or cassette version of *Return to Oz*, to tie in with the 1985 Walt Disney film, audio versions of the Oz tales during the 1970s and 1980s tended to be reissues. The next major audiobook was a release of the 1994 radio series, starring Maureen Lipman as the Wicked Witch of the West. This was adapted in three forty-five-minute episodes by Marcy Kahan, who had previously written a version of *The Railway Children*, and would go on to co-adapt *War and Peace* for the BBC. Barbara Barnes played Dorothy, with Patrick Barlow as the Tin Woodman, Philip Franks as the Scarecrow and Bradley Lavelle as the Cowardly Lion.

The US National Public Radio (NPR) network broadcast a four-hour unabridged version of *The Wonderful Wizard of Oz* on Thanksgiving Day, 23 November 2000, with an all-star cast. *Buffy the Vampire Slayer* co-star Michelle Trachtenberg was Dorothy, with Robert Guillame (*Benson*) as the Lion, Disney and *Star Trek: Deep Space Nine*'s René Auberjonois as the Scarecrow, and *Homeland*'s Nestor Serrano as the Tin Woodman. Phyllis Diller reprised her stage role of the Wicked Witch and Harry Anderson was the Wizard, with cameos from Annette Bening, Mark Hamill, John Goodman and Joanna Gleason. David Ossman's adaptation was highly praised but is now very hard to track down.

Colonial Radio Theatre also marked the centenary of publication of the original book with a ten-cassette, eleven-and-a-half-hour version of the first five books in the Oz story. They recorded the first story in May 1999 but weren't happy with the end result, so re-recorded it in November 2000 after they had completed the other four books. They finally recorded the sixth book – *The Emerald City of Oz* – in 2011 (although some sources suggest that this may be replacing an earlier recording from 2002), which was released in December 2012. Amy Strack played Dorothy in the early stories, replaced by Kerry Donovan for *The Emerald City*; Tom Berry was the Scarecrow throughout, although Mark McGillivray took over from David Krinnit as the Cowardly Lion, and Joe Caliendo Jr was the Tin Woodman in the later story, replacing Frederick Rice. (It's worth noting that the Audible releases of the original five stories have been slightly edited.)

A few minor changes were made: the Fighting Trees don't appear in *The Wonderful Wizard of Oz*; the Woggle-Bug becomes the Woogle-Bug; Queen Zixi isn't invited to the party in *The Road to Oz*; and the Braided Man and the Dragonettes aren't in *Dorothy and the Wizard in Oz*. One nice touch is the inclusion of L. Frank Baum's introductions to the stories. The entire set was released as 'The Oz Family Collection' on CD in June 2013.

With the growing popularity of audiobooks, there have been assorted readings of *The Wonderful Wizard of Oz* (and the odd version of some of the later books), but the most recent dramatization also came from the BBC. Linda Marshall Griffiths condensed the story of *The Wonderful Wizard of Oz* down to a single hour for a Saturday Drama presentation on 19 December 2009. The play was advertised as a conscious attempt to return to Baum's version of the story, with silver slippers and separate witches of the north and the south. Amelia Clarkson played Dorothy, who acts as narrator for a lot of the tale. Kevin Eldon, Burn Gorman and Zubin Varla played the Scarecrow, Tin Woodsman and Lion respectively. It was a well-received production: the *Guardian*'s Elisabeth Mahoney noted: 'all the essentials were established: a magical journey; the possibilities of friendship; the virtue of focusing on what you have instead of what you don't; the incontrovertible importance of shoes. "The magic of the shoes," we heard, "is that they grant your heart's desire." '

Producer Nadia Molinari admitted she was consciously making the play for a generation of children brought up on J.K. Rowling's *Harry Potter* books. 'Some people who love the Judy Garland film will hate this version because there are no songs and it's much, much darker in tone,' she told *Mancunian Matters* magazine. 'While others I think will appreciate it as a dramatization of the book and a piece of work that stands on its own.'

The Radio Drama Reviews website summed up the 2009 version with words that any future director of *The Wonderful Wizard of Oz* will no doubt wish to be applied to their work: 'a new and intriguing slant on a well-loved work'.

While many of the comic-book versions of Oz have allowed their authors to create new dimensions for L. Frank Baum's wonderful world, over the years there have been multiple visualizations of the stories – as well as some new ones that were told by Oz's creators purely in this form. The plural is deliberate: both Baum and the original illustrator, William Wallace Denslow, were responsible for separate, and potentially contradictory, comic-strip versions of the characters from *The Wonderful Wizard of Oz*, which appeared in the years following publication.

Queer Visitors from the Marvelous Land of Oz was the first to arrive, written by Baum and illustrated by Walt McDougall. It was part of the publicity blitz that Baum's publishers Reilly & Britton devised for the second book, *The Marvelous Land of Oz*, and began on 4 September 1904. It was foreshadowed by various articles the previous month which chronicled the discovery of a mysterious flying object approaching the United States.

The object was the Gump, which was bringing the Scarecrow, the Animated Saw-Horse, the Tin Woodman, the Woggle-Bug and Jack Pumpkinhead on a visit to the United States – incidentally, although little was made of this at the time, making it clear that as far as Baum was concerned, at least for these stories, Oz was a land on another world. Each story saw the friends travelling around America and experiencing different aspects of life; at some point in the first seventeen tales the Woggle-Bug would answer a question, but the audience weren't shown his reply. At the end of each strip they were asked 'What did the Woggle-Bug say?' and invited to send their responses in. Cash prizes of around $500 a month were available.

The travellers were there as ambassadors for Ozma of Oz, as explained in a proclamation that appeared on Sunday 28 August 1904. The characters are 'on their first vacation away from the Emerald City and the Land of Oz. They want to romp with the children of the United States.' Ozma explained she had permitted them to come 'in order that they may accumulate great stores of Wisdom

and Experience', and Baum added for the readers' benefit that 'it is possible [the visitors'] ignorance of our ways
and manners may get them into a few scrapes before their
return to Princess Ozma'.

These weren't comic strips in the way that we know
them today. Baum penned a short adventure, which was
lavishly illustrated by Walt McDougall, a highly respected
cartoonist. Some of these drawings had speech bubbles,
others were simply images. They wouldn't be out of place
in British children's comics from the 1960s and 1970s.

Denslow's illustrations for his series, on the other hand,
were considerably more detailed. Since he shared the copyright for *The Wonderful Wizard of Oz* with Baum, he was
perfectly within his rights to use the characters from that
book as he saw fit – and as Baum had chosen not to incorporate Dorothy into the narrative of either *The Marvelous
Land of Oz*, or the *Queer Visitors* strip, it seemed logical to
start his stories off with her return. 'Dorothy's Christmas
Tree' appeared on 10 December 1904.

Although the stories were headed 'Denslow's Scarecrow and the Tinman', they also featured the Cowardly
Lion. Denslow took a leaf out of Baum's book, and his
stories were also about the characters' adventures in
North and South America – the pair encounter Aztec vil-
lagers and Bermudan customs officials, travel to the New
Orleans carnival, as well as meeting up with cowboys.
The format began similarly to Baum's, with illustrations
dotted around the page, but eventually followed a more
structured pattern, with the text beneath the pictures to
which it referred.

Denslow had a neat conceit for the tales. The Scarecrow and the Tinman were the characters seen on stage
in the long-running show: they had come from Oz and
were playing themselves in the production. However, the
strip only lasted for fourteen weeks, as opposed to Baum's
twenty-six instalments. While a gifted illustrator, Denslow

was not a natural storyteller like Baum – his stories are a series of incidents – and increasingly fewer papers carried the strip until it was stopped.

The next major comic strip ran from May 1932 to October 1933, drawn by Walt Spouse. *The Wonderland of Oz* (and there was no connection intended to Lewis Carroll's *Alice in Wonderland* stories) featured adaptations of five of Baum's stories: *The Marvelous Land of Oz, Ozma of Oz, The Emerald City of Oz, The Patchwork Girl of Oz* and *Tik-Tok of Oz*. Like *Queer Visitors*, these were intended as a publicity gimmick to promote the sales of the newer books, with the heading explaining that they were 'based on the stories by L. Frank Baum and Ruth Plumly Thompson'.

Spouse's art emulated the drawings created for the original editions by John R. Neill, although there were a number of elements that he had to create from scratch, given how long the stories were and comparatively how few illustrations in the printed books. These included all of Mombi's transformations in *The Marvelous Land of Oz*, and the Saw-horse kicking the Nome King in *Ozma of Oz*.

A few changes were made to the text, particularly to *The Emerald City*. The Shaggy Man wasn't included, so his scenes were shared between Uncle Henry and the Wizard; a bank official comes to visit Uncle Henry and Aunt Em to explain their financial predicament; and Baum's attempts to bring a close to the saga, by creating an impenetrable barrier around the Emerald City, were ignored.

In their original form, these were like Denslow's later comic strips: text (adapted by a staff writer from Baum's books) ran beneath Spouse's pictures. When some of the stories were reprinted in Dell Comics' book *The Funnies* in 1938–1940, and again in Hawley Publications' Hi Spot Comics, they were turned into more traditional comics, with speech and thought balloons, often without too much consideration as to placement. A further reprint followed from Hungry Tiger Press, beginning in 1995, which included new speech balloons prepared and carefully placed by Eric Shanower to present the artwork as cleanly as possible.

A couple of adaptations of the first story appeared in the 1950s from Dell Junior Treasury Comics, written by Gaylor Dubois, and in the Classics Illustrated junior series, the latter of which has recently been made available in digital form. Dell also produced a single-issue tie-in to *The Wizard of Oz* cartoon series as part of their Four Color line (#1308) in 1962 which promised: 'Wicked Witches! Flying Broomsticks! Magic Lions! Silly Scarecrows! . . . They Are All Here'.

The next major Oz comic came in 1975 and required two of the biggest names in the comics business to join forces to create it: MGM's *Marvelous Wizard of Oz* was published by Marvel Comics and DC Comics jointly, the precursor of a number of specials between the two companies over the coming years. This Giant Size Treasury Edition – or tabloid size – was the result of both companies working on an Oz book simultaneously.

Writer Roy Thomas recalled in the mid-1980s that Marvel had intended to create a faithful rendition of the Baum story, as the start of an Oz line, but when they heard of DC's plans, they decided to collaborate on the project rather than compete. Although Thomas believed DC may have been bluffing, comics historian John Wells noted that Sheldon Mayer was working on the DC book as writer and artist; Carmine Infantino mentioned this in passing to Marvel's Stan Lee. Perhaps because so much of the iconic imagery belonged to MGM, the studio became involved, and the comic book turned into a highly accurate version of the film instead, starting in monochrome and turning to colour when Dorothy visits Oz, and including full-splash pages for key moments.

Publicized as 'the most magical, most magnificent, most merriest comics masterpiece of all time!' the book spawned a sequel, just from Marvel. *Marvel Treasury of Oz* #1: *The Marvelous Land of Oz* was an accurate retelling by Roy Thomas of the second Oz book, featuring 'the Scarecrow and the Tintinnabulatin' Tin Man!' according to the cover. The imagery by Alfredo Alcala was drawn heavily from John R. Neill's pictures, although the contract with MGM insisted that the likenesses of the Scarecrow and the Tin Man matched the movie portrayal.

The back page announced 'coming Oztractions: Next issue: Marvel's miraculous adaptation of L. Frank Baum's *Ozma of Oz* . . . on sale February 3rd, 1976 to Gillkin and Munchkin alike!' It was completed, with art by Alcala, layouts by Marie DeZuniga, front and back covers for the Treasury Edition by John Romita, but Roy Thomas's version was never seen. According to Thomas, Marvel's lawyers discovered that the book was not yet in the public domain, and he was told to stop work on the next book, *Dorothy and the Wizard in Oz*. Eric Shanower acquired a partial set of photocopies of the pages but noted in a 2010 interview promoting his version of the story that rights issues pertaining to the MGM likenesses would probably prevent the 1976 version from ever appearing.

Thirty years later, David Chauvel and Enrique Fernandez created their own version of *The Wonderful Wizard of Oz*. Published in France in 2005 as *Le Magicien D'Oz*, it won the prestigious 2005 Grand Prix de La Ville De Lyon Award for Illustration and was translated into English by Kat Amano and 'remixed' by Image Comics' Joe Keatinge. The ninety-six-page graphic novel doesn't try to copy the designs of Denslow or Neill, nor does it fit with the stereotypes of the MGM movie – it's a new take on the world.

Puffin Graphics also published a version the same year, commissioned by Byron Preiss Visual Productions, and adapted and illustrated by up-and-coming artist Michael Cavallaro. Although he updates the imagery – Dorothy wears boot-cut jeans and Wonder Girl bracelets – the story remains faithful to the original but the trip to Glinda's palace at the end is abbreviated.

Oz: The Manga was an eight-part version of the first story, written and drawn by David Hutchison between 2005 and 2006, to which an epilogue was added, to cover the conclusion of the book that was covered in brief in the original run. As the title implies, this version adopted the manga look – characters with impossibly large eyes, for example. Although one reviewer noted that 'it has the same relationship to actual Japanese comics as food in American Chinese restaurants has to actual Chinese food', the 2006 run was successful enough that Antarctic Press commissioned a reworking of *The Marvelous Land of Oz* which came out as *The Land of Oz: The Manga* from 2008–2009.

Hutchison made a few changes to the text: the backstories for the Scarecrow and the Tin Woodman are revealed later than in the book; and the Lion runs from the Wizard (which may have been a homage to the MGM movie). He portrays the witch as a younger woman (perhaps in the way it might have been in the movie had Gale Sondergaard played the part) and gives her an advisor, Nestred – which of course allowed more use of dialogue. He also made clever use of speech balloons to match the type of person or creature speaking.

Marvel Comics returned to Oz triumphantly with Eric Shanower and Skottie Young's adaptations of the Baum stories which began with *The Wonderful Wizard of Oz* in 2008. An Oz fan since the age of six, Shanower had previously created his own Oz tales (see part four), and had also overseen the reprinting of the classic Walt Spouse tales.

Shanower revealed in a 2008 interview that he was glad

he wasn't asked to draw the book as well as write the adaptation, since he wouldn't have had time in his schedule. Working on the script gave him a new slant on Baum's writing: 'I'd never been over it so closely or thoroughly before. One quirky detail that stands out to me from writing this adaptation – something I'd never paid attention to before – was that the Soldier with the Green Whiskers has Dorothy and her friends wipe their feet before they enter the Wizard's palace. It's so minor, but so characteristic of Baum's writing.' He also ensured that the new comic didn't set up any contradictions with later books, where possible, and consulted the occasions in the Royal Histories where Baum retold elements of the original tale, using them when they seemed better thought out (although that eliminated the new origin for the Scarecrow that was devised later). The eight-part series spent twenty-three weeks on the *New York Times* Graphic Books bestseller list and won the 2010 Will Eisner Comic Industry Awards for 'Best Publication for Kids' and 'Best Limited Series or Story Arc'.

This was followed by an eight-issue version of *The Marvelous Land of Oz*, for which Shanower borrowed some elements from Baum's own stage version of the story. *Ozma of Oz*, which Shanower described as his favourite of the Oz books when growing up, came next, with *Dorothy and the Wizard in Oz* (adapted in six parts), *Road to Oz* (Shanower's first ever Oz book, another six-parter), and *The Emerald City of Oz* each receiving the lavish treatment. Shanower even acted as artist for variant covers for some of the later runs.

In an interview for website iFanboy promoting the release of *The Emerald City*, Shanower explained what set his and Young's versions of the stories apart from their predecessors: 'We stick very closely to Baum's tone and intent, so that if you like the original vision of Oz, you'll find it in our Oz comics.' Young's artwork may take some getting used to – it's very different from the Denslow and Neill characterizations – but the books have proved popular. With sales encouraging the continuation of the line, fans are hoping that all fourteen of Baum's books will eventually be published by Marvel.

3. OZ ON STAGE

I

THE EARLY STAGE SHOWS

L. Frank Baum knew pretty much straightaway that, for once in his life, he had really come up with a successful idea when *The Wizard of Oz* started to sell well following its publication in September 1900. In those pre-motion picture days, a stage adaptation was the logical follow-up, but who actually came up with the idea is a matter of some debate. At the time the musical extravaganza opened, Baum claimed that he started off thinking of it as a comedy which grew in scope with the addition of composer Paul Tietjens, and even further once producer Fred Hamlin and director Julian Mitchell became involved. Equally, three years later, Baum said he'd been given the idea 'of making my story into an American fairy extravaganza' by a lady, but by 1910 the tale had changed yet again. 'The thought of turning my fairy tale into a play had never even occurred to me when, one evening, my doorbell rang and I found a spectacled young man standing on the mat,' he wrote.

The latter version of Tietjens' and Baum's first meeting seems apocryphal. The two had actually been introduced in 1899 and by 1901 were working on a musical that had nothing to do with Oz. That June, Oz illustrator William Wallace Denslow heard Tietjens playing at a dinner party and suggested that his style of music would perfectly suit Oz. Baum wasn't happy with the idea, partly perhaps because he didn't want to work with Denslow again after the two had clashed during the preparation of *The Wonderful Wizard of Oz* (Denslow never illustrated another Oz book after the first; John R. Neill took over). However by July, Baum became more receptive to the idea, and worked out a five-act structure for an Oz stage play, to which Tietjens began contributing musical ideas.

Since the copyright to *The Wonderful Wizard of Oz* was shared between Baum and Denslow, the artist became part of the trio creating the musical play, although right up to the signing of the contract there were arguments as to what a fair division of the spoils should be, with both Denslow and Tietjens arguing at different times that they were entitled to more. While Baum and Tietjens worked on the book and score, Denslow approached various producers, eventually finding Fred Hamlin who in his turn brought in Julian Mitchell. According to Tietjens' diaries, Mitchell didn't like the script, and it's not hard to see why.

Although Baum had retained much of the basic structure of his novel, there had been many changes, making his script neither a straight adaptation of the book nor a musical extravaganza in its own right. The Wicked Witch of the West was eliminated altogether: a Forest Witch makes a brief appearance, but otherwise the story becomes about Dorothy trying to get home, rather than the Witch trying to retrieve the silver slippers. The whole section in which Dorothy and her friends are sent to get the Witch's broom is therefore also excised.

The Cowardly Lion is a non-speaking role, and

disappears from the play before the end of the first act. Toto doesn't even get to appear in the first place! A brief romantic subplot is established for the Tin Woodman: he offers the heart he's given by the Wizard to the Captain of Glinda's guard, who turns out to be his lost sweetheart. Glinda also acquires four Wise Men – Socrates, Pericles, Sophocles and Chumpocles (!) – to provide added humour.

The songs are pretty self-explanatory: Dorothy sings that she's 'An Innocent Kansas Girl'; the Scarecrow is 'A Man of Straw'; the Tin Woodman sings, 'Oh, Love's the Thing'; the Wizard's song is simply entitled 'The Wonderful Wizard of Oz'. As for the Forest Witch, she tells the Tin Woodman 'I'm Freakishly Wicked' while the Tin Woodman advises the Scarecrow to 'Think It Over Carefully' when he's offered the chance to rule the Emerald City.

This wasn't what Mitchell thought would bring audiences in – and the incredible longevity of the show which he put together proved that he was right. He jettisoned anything more than lip service to the plot of the novel, and created a framework that would allow for plenty of comedy, vaudeville routines and chorus girls. He magnified the role of the Scarecrow and the Tin Woodman to such an extent that they became the real focus of proceedings, and the two actors who played them, Fred Stone and Dave Montgomery, achieved fame. Stone created a boneless dance that became the template for all other Scarecrows who followed him – notably both Buddy Ebsen, the original casting for the 1939 film, and Ray Bolger who took on the part were keen to duplicate his unusual gait for their performance.

Neither Baum nor Tietjens was impressed with the wholesale changes that Mitchell was making to their finely crafted work. Out went the majority of the songs which they had written – only eight remained in the final show, along with twenty or so others which Mitchell sourced to fit in with the spectacle that he was devising. Dorothy ceased to be a young girl who needed protecting from the perils that she faced on the Yellow Brick Road; the stage Dorothy, who for the first time gained the surname Gale, is a young woman, who could be placed in romantic situations. Her faithful canine companion was ditched; in Toto's place came Imogen the Cow, whose disappearance from Dorothy's family farm (Uncle Henry and Aunt Em were no longer the owners) meant that her father no longer had 'the only thing to prove he ran a dairy'.

The tornado bringing Dorothy and Imogen from Kansas is retained but they're not the only ones who are transported across. With them are Pastoria II, the rightful king of Oz, who was tricked by the Wizard into travelling to Kansas, and his fiancée Tryxie Tryfle, a Kansas waitress. Pastoria wants to get his throne back from the Wizard, with the help of the one-man army General Riskitt. When they arrive in Munchkinland, they are greeted by Locasta, the Good Witch of the North; Cynthia Cynch, a 'Lady Lunatic' whose piccolo-playing fiancé Niccolo Chopper has been transformed into someone else by a Wicked Witch; and Sir Dashemoff Daily, Oz's poet laureate, who promptly falls in love with Dorothy.

Locasta gives Dorothy a wishing ring, and she uses one to learn a song, and another to bring a Scarecrow to life. Dorothy and the Scarecrow head for the Emerald City, meeting the Tin Woodman on the way – allowing plenty of time for the two experienced vaudevillians to incorporate their standard routines. Pastoria, Tryxie and Imogen also set off for the City, and meet the Cowardly Lion. The quartet pose as a circus to put the Wizard's police off their trail. Both parties are caught by a field of deadly poppies, but Locasta comes to the rescue, and kills them with snow. They continue on their journey.

In the Emerald City, the Wizard is trying to fool everyone that he can do magic, but inventor Sir Wiley Gyle isn't taken in, and wants to oust the Wizard. When Dorothy's group arrives, the Wizard provides brains and a heart for her two companions, and decides that there'll be a party – and asks Pastoria's 'Circus' to provide entertainment. Gyle has just managed to persuade some of the Emerald City dwellers that the Wizard is a phony when Pastoria announces his true identity. Gyle is thwarted, and the Wizard is denounced.

Pastoria isn't necessarily a benevolent king, though: his soldiers arrest the Scarecrow and Tin Woodman, accusing them of rebellion, and they are hoisted up in a cage. Dorothy gets the Tin Woodman to cut the Scarecrow up and pass the pieces out to her, which she then puts together on stage to bring him back to life. When the Tin Woodman starts to play the piccolo, Cynthia realizes that he is her fiancé, and in the end it's down to Glinda to sort it all out.

Despite Baum's initial reservations, *The Wizard of Oz* was a major success, running for over eight years around the country. As he admitted in a letter to the *Chicago Tribune* in June 1904, he did protest about several of the innovations in the show, but now '[t]he people will have what pleases them, and not what the author happens to favour . . . Should I ever attempt another extravaganza, or dramatize one of my books, I mean to profit by the lesson Mr Mitchell has taught me, and sacrifice personal preference to the demands of those I shall expect to purchase admission tickets.'

Baum wasn't above borrowing from the changes Mitchell made either. As well as continuing the use of Gale as Dorothy's surname, he includes the character of Pastoria, the deposed king of Oz, in his books, as well as the Tin Woodman's real name, Nick Chopper. The 1939 film also appropriated some of the innovations: in the book the sleepers are rescued from the poppy field by mice, but the movie follows the stage show in using snow. Ironically, this idea was dropped from later adaptations of the film to the stage because it was too difficult to achieve!

* * *

Baum had high hopes that the next stage show he mounted, *The Woggle-Bug*, would emulate, or even exceed, the achievements of *The Wizard of Oz*. He may have expected people to buy tickets for his shows, but even when he gave them what he thought they wanted, they didn't flock to the theatres.

The Woggle-Bug was a version of Baum's second Oz novel, *The Marvelous Land of Oz*, which introduced the titular character to readers, as well as plenty of other new faces. Baum felt that Dorothy's story was told, and since she had been sidelined in the stage show to a large extent without a lot of negative feedback, it was clear to him that audiences weren't as interested in her as they were in the other characters. The Cowardly Lion was also missing from the book.

However, despite Baum including their pictures in the original endpapers of *The Marvelous Land of Oz*, neither Fred Stone nor Dave Montgomery was keen on tying themselves to another stage show – they were trying to get clear of *The Wizard of Oz*, which they finally achieved in 1906 – so Baum had to rework the storyline to bring Jack Pumpkinhead and the Woggle-Bug to the fore. He also introduced characters similar to Mitchell's additions to *The Wizard*, including Prissy Pring, one of General Jinjur's soldiers, whose plaid skirt becomes the focus of the Woggle-Bug's attentions throughout the play – it's not the person wearing it but the skirt that fascinates him!

The Prologue features Tip and Mombi creating Jack Pumpkinhead and animating him with the Powder of Life, before the play properly begins with the introduction of the Woggle-Bug. A professor is showing his students the magnified image of a bug when the image itself walks off the screen and starts to cause consternation. After the Woggle-Bug and the Professor have exchanged some pun-filled gags, Prissy Pring arrives, looking for General Jinjur and her all-girl army. The Woggle-Bug wants to 'cash the checks' of Prissy's skirt, and follows her when she joins up with Jinjur.

Tip and Jack head to the City of Jewels, and Tip dreams of being Princess Ozma; they also animate a Sawhorse. Tip goes into the city with the Regent, Sir Richard Spud, while Jack remains outside and meets the Woggle-Bug. When Mombi turns up wearing Prissy's skirt, the Woggle-Bug transfers his affections to her, which is handy, since Jack falls in love with Prissy when he meets her. The Regent wants Mombi to restore Tip to his true self – Ozma – but she refuses and unleashes the Army of Revolt (who want victory or fudge). They take the city.

The second act features a bored Jinjur who wants the Regent to fancy her; the Woggle-Bug falling for a black cook, Dinah, since she's wearing the skirt; and then Tip, Jack and the Woggle-Bug escaping from the city to the palace of Maetta, the Good Sorceress. Their flying machine is brought down by Mombi's coven of witches, and their rabbit-drawn chariot also crashes. The trio are faced with a horde of chrysanthemums that is repelled by a spell of rain (originally a literal rain of cats and dogs, although the gag was quickly dropped). They finally reach Maetta who resolves everything: Prissy becomes a housemaid, Mombi loses her power, Jinjur is demoted back to being a milk-maid (and the Regent then asks her to marry him), and, most importantly, Tip is turned back into Ozma. Prissy removes the skirt, which the Woggle-Bug wears as a shirt.

Baum's script hit many of the same high points as Mitchell's earlier text, and perhaps that was its biggest problem: there wasn't anything original in this new show, which opened on 18 June 1905, that audiences hadn't seen done (and often done better) in *The Wizard of Oz*. Hal Godfrey as Jack and Fred Mace as the Woggle-Bug didn't have the repartee and years of experience of working together that Stone and Montgomery brought to the earlier show. The press reviews were uniformly negative, focusing more on

Baum's book than Frederic Chapin's music: 'The book is the weakest portion of the new offering,' stated the Chicago *Tribune*. 'It contains virtually no story whatever and witty lines are almost totally lacking.'

Fred Mace was replaced as the Woggle-Bug after a few days, and assorted changes were made to the storyline, but the damage was done. Word of mouth kept people away, and the producer, Henry Raeder, found himself unable to pay for the electric lights from The Garden City Calcium Light Company; they withdrew their products on 12 July, although the performance that evening still went ahead. The show closed on 13 July.

It took another three years before Frank Baum brought another Oz production to theatres, but this time he believed that he had a show which was sure to attract audiences – it was a true multimedia experience, combining still images, live actors and the still-novel attraction of moving pictures (and colour ones at that). What could possibly go wrong?

The script and the still slides from the 1908 show *Fairylogue and Radio-Plays* still survive, and it certainly seems far more worthy of success than *The Woggle-Bug*. Baum wisely didn't try to match the spectacle of *The Wizard of Oz* beat for beat as he had with the previous play; this time, he came up with a way of bringing the audience into Oz in a way that even the play couldn't.

Baum narrated the show himself, and began by explaining how he had become the Royal Historian of Oz. A fairy visited him and told him the story of Oz, which he then recounted. The first film sees him introducing Dorothy, the Tin Woodman, the Cowardly Lion and others – although there's no mention of the witches at all in the show – who all take a bow to the audience. A slideshow illustrates Dorothy and Toto arriving in Oz, getting the silver slippers and heading down the yellow brick road; on film, Dorothy sees the Scarecrow moving, and they set off for the Emerald City. From there on, the story alternates between slides and moving pictures to show them meeting the Tin Woodman and the Cowardly Lion, arriving in the Emerald City, gaining their desires from the Wizard, then heading off to find Glinda after the Wizard's ballooning accident, and using the slippers to get home. This was followed by similar renditions of the next two Oz books, *The Marvelous Land of Oz*, and *Ozma of Oz* (with some minor changes to the plots of both to fit them within the time). An interval followed the seventy-minute first half, during which slides depicted scenes from the most recent book, *Dorothy and the Wizard in Oz*. In a shrewd move, Baum had copies waiting for patrons to buy in the lobby!

Oz wasn't the only string to Baum's bow, and he was keen to use some of his other material in the show. The forty-minute second act featured his story *John Dough and the Cherub*, about a gingerbread man brought to life, and his adventures alongside Chick the Cherub (a hyperactive child) and Para Bruin, a rubber bear.

Since movies were still silent, Baum provided a running narration throughout the stills and the films, and was accompanied by the Theodore Thomas Orchestra, a twenty-seven-piece band, playing specially composed music by Nathaniel D. Mann. The movies were hand-tinted in France by the Duval Frères (although Baum, ever the showman, claimed that the process was by a 'Michel Radio', hence the name of the show).

Frank Joselyn Baum acted as projectionist during the *Fairylogue and Radio-Plays*' short life. They tried it out in Grand Rapids, Michigan, between 24–26 September 1908, before taking it for three-night runs in Chicago, Saint Louis, Milwaukee, Saint Paul and Minneapolis. They then returned to Chicago for two weeks, before spending the rest of 1908 touring Illinois, Iowa and New York state. They ended in New York City on 14 December, but by New Year's Eve, the Baums had to conclude reluctantly that no matter how enthusiastic the audience might be, the show was losing money hand over fist. Not only were the initial costs high, but the transport for all the equipment coupled with the costs of the actors, the orchestra and the stagehands at each venue, not to mention the hire of the theatres, meant that the show simply couldn't make money. Baum did think about reworking the material – it's one of the projects he mentions in an interview in September 1909 that he is considering – but by that point he was dealing with the financial fall-out from their failure.

As a direct result of the *Fairylogue and Radio-Plays*, L. Frank Baum lost control of his most important asset – *The Wonderful Wizard of Oz*. His debts were so high that eventually he had no option but to declare bankruptcy.

In the years following the *Fairylogue* disaster, Baum came up with many different ideas for musical comedies, both involving Oz and other lands, but the next one to come to fruition was *The Tik-Tok Man of Oz*, which opened at the Majestic Theatre in Los Angeles on 31 March 1913. This had a long road to the stage, originally envisaged by Baum as an adaptation of *Ozma of Oz*, under the title *The Rainbow's Daughter*, with the Shaggy Man trying to rescue his wife and ten children. Unfortunately, the various characters in the story were tied up with the other stage shows – *The Wizard of Oz* and *The Woggle-Bug* – so he reworked the story for a new character in place of Dorothy, and a replacement Ozma, a Rose Princess this time around.

Although the final script for this is lost, earlier drafts suggest that instead of Billina the chicken, Dorothy substitute Betsy Bobbin is accompanied by her mule, Hank, when she drifts to land after being shipwrecked. She meets the Shaggy Man who's determined to rescue his brother Wiggy from the land of the Nome King, Ruggedo. Shaggy has a Love Magnet, which makes those around him love him, and which he uses to get them out of trouble with the gardener of the Rose Kingdom, whose monarchs grow on the royal rose bush. The only one ripe is Princess Ozma, but the roses refuse to have her as monarch, so she joins Shaggy and Betsy as they make new friends, the mechanical Tik-Tok, Polychrome the Rainbow Fairy, and Ann of Oogaboo, who wants to conquer the world.

When they reach the Nome Kingdom, Shaggy and Tik-Tok fall out, and Betsy and Ruggedo have to reassemble Tik-Tok, leaving Shaggy convinced he's seen a ghost. Ruggedo tries to persuade Polychrome to become his mistress, and admires her power of turning rocks to gold (although they change back to rock when he touches them). In the end, they are all rescued by the arrival of a rainbow sent by Polychrome's father.

As Chicago reviewer Amy Leslie pointed out, *The Tik-Tok Man of Oz* was 'almost letter for letter, scene for scene, spectacle for spectacle and chorus girl for chorus girl' a reworking of *The Wizard of Oz*. Once again, Baum had taken to heart the lessons from Mitchell's revision of his script for the first show, but failed to capture the elusive spark that would allow it to enjoy an extended run. The music, by Louis Gottschalk to lyrics by Baum and producer Oliver Morosco, was well received and the show's runs in Los Angeles and San Francisco encouraged Morosco to take it on tour, but eventually he decided against trying to open it on Broadway.

For L. Frank Baum, who had dreamed of creating and producing a successful play throughout his life, it was the end of the road. He turned his attention to movies, with equal lack of success, but died prematurely before he could come up with anything to match the durability of Mitchell's version of *The Wizard of Oz*.

To promote the new books that Ruth Plumly Thompson was adding to the Royal Histories of Oz, publishers Reilly

& Lee came up with various gimmicks. These included a short skit by Eleanor T. MacMillan entitled *Schooldays in the Land of Oz*, as well as another short play by Thompson, *A Day in Oz* (also known as *Scraps in Oz*) with music by Norman Sherrerd that could be put on in department stores by local child actors when the new books arrived. In the version to promote *Jack Pumpkinhead of Oz*, the Scarecrow, the Patchwork Girl, Dorothy, the Tin Woodman, the Cowardly Lion and Ozma are all seen, as Jack explains that his latest adventures are enough to fill a book!

The Larry Semon *Wizard of Oz* movie (see p 229) was promoted as part of a roadshow, created, directed and written by Norman K. Whistler, in which characters from Semon's version were seen alongside the originals in a dozen scenes. This played during the film's engagement at the Forum Theatre in Los Angeles from 7 February 1925. Chances are that this confused the audience even more than the Semon film, which had its own eclectic take on Baum's story.

There were various 'Junior League' plays published by Samuel French, which adapted the Oz stories for younger actors: Elizabeth Chapman (also credited as Elizabeth Fuller Goodspeed) produced versions of *The Wizard of Oz* and *The [Marvelous] Land of Oz* in the late 1920s while March Buchanan adapted *Ozma of Oz* around 1935.

Puppet productions were also common: the Royal Management of Oz presented Jean Gros' French Marionettes in *The Magical Land of Oz* from a script by Ruth Plumly Thompson 'founded on the famous stories by L. Frank Baum'. This opened in 1928, and it was performed at the Chicago World's Fair in 1933. This included a fourteen-piece marionette orchestra formed of the Nomes, as depicted by John R. Neill in the illustrations for the original books.

Another version, directed by Irene Phillips and staged by Ellen Van Volkenburg, was recommended by the

Ellensburg *Daily Record* when it arrived there in November 1934: '[S]o real are the characters and scenes and so true to the story is the play that you will think you are the one who was whirled through the air on that cyclone that picked little Dorothy and her dog, Lots [*sic*], up from their home in Kansas and dropped them in the land of Oz'. Another review from the same tour noted that 'the story was clever and the dialogue light and simple' although the reviewer wasn't as impressed with the music which was 'of the trashy parlour variety hardly better than jazz.' (By an odd coincidence, Volkenburg's offices were in the same building, the Studebaker in Chicago, as the original illustrator of Oz, William Wallace Denslow.)

There wasn't much impetus for new Oz material, until the idea was kick-started by the success of a certain movie starring Judy Garland . . .

2

FROM SCREEN TO STAGE AND
BACK AGAIN

The MGM musical version of *The Wizard of Oz* may not have been the most profitable movie that the studio made, but it certainly was extremely popular, and it wasn't too long before Dorothy and her friends danced back onto theatre stages. Three years after the movie's premiere, audiences in St Louis were able to travel down the Yellow Brick Road, and sing along with many of the songs from the film, even if the story that surrounded them presented a few surprises.

The adaptation was commissioned by the St Louis Municipal Opera (known as the MUNY). Frank Gabrielson, who would later create a television version of the Oz sequel *The Marvelous Land of Oz* for Shirley Temple, adapted the script for the stage. Far from feeling an obligation to follow the beats of the movie, he created a new version of the Oz story that incorporated the songs in relevant places. Characters were added to and subtracted from the story: Miss Gulch, Professor Marvel, the Wink- ies, the Flying Monkeys, the farmhands, and even Toto were notably absent. In their stead came Gabrielson's own creations: a new farmhand, Joe; a skeletal butler, Tibia, for the Wicked Witch; the Queen of the Butterflies; the Wizard's 'daughter' Gloria; and Lord Growlie. There aren't any magic shoes – the Wizard takes Dorothy home with him at the end of the play.

Extra music was added: Dorothy gained a new number, 'Evening Star', with words by Mitchell Parish and music by Peter DeRose; and two dance numbers enlivened proceed- ings – 'Song Macabre' and 'Ghost Dance'. The Jitterbug song, cut from the film, was used here in place of the poppy field sequence.

According to the copyright holders, Tams Witmark, 'The MUNY version is the more theatrically conservative and employs its stage, actors, singers, dancers and musicians in traditional ways to tell Mr Baum's story. The story and the music are treated by the adapters as elements of a classic stage musical without reference to their use in the film.' This is something of an understatement: the end result is some- thing that is neither Baum's story of Oz, nor MGM's.

Dorothy is still a Kansas farm girl who's transported to Oz in a tornado, but when she arrives, there's a delay before she comes out of the house, allowing the Munchkins to put on a short show. As in the film, Glinda sets Dorothy on her way, but the Wicked Witch doesn't arrive until after the Good Witch has departed. The obstacles she encounters on the Yellow Brick Road include a rainbow bridge that revolves to stop forward movement, but not the orchard with the trees pelting Dorothy with apples. Dorothy's extra song, 'Evening Star', comes after they've arrived in the Emerald City, straight after the song 'Merry Ol' Land of Oz'. The trade-off for the extra song is the loss of the Lion's showcase number, 'If I Were King of the Forest'.

The Wizard isn't presented as a giant head, as in the movie, but as a ten-foot-tall monster, and after he's sent Dorothy and the trio to capture the broom, they encounter the Witch's slave Tibia, who catches them with the aid of some ghosts. At this point, an extra scene is added, featuring the Witch, and her 'Witch Buddies' called Mombi (a name familiar to Oz readers), and, rather less traditionally, Sarah. It's a comedy routine that only serves to lessen the tension. The showdown between the Witch and Dorothy is altered as well: the Witch brews up a cauldron of 'magic water' which will shrink Dorothy out of the shoes, but she ends up dumped in the boiling hot water by the Scarecrow, the Lion and the Tin Man, shrinking her to the size of a puppet. Interestingly, Dorothy takes no part in her destruction. The final alteration is perhaps the biggest. The Wizard doesn't have a balloon; in the MUNY script he has a rocket ship – and he takes Dorothy with him back to Kansas in it!

The MUNY production has been presented many times over the last seven decades, with the company nowadays often amalgamating their own script with the later version, which hews closer to the movie. Margaret Hamilton, the original Wicked Witch, reprised her role in the 1950s and 1975, sharing the stage for the latter with the comedy team the Hudson Brothers – Bill played the Tin Man, Brett was the Scarecrow and Mark played the Cowardly Lion – although she wasn't very happy with this performance, pointing out that the trio had added 'smidgens of bathroom humour not appropriate for a children's story'. The brothers had taken the roles in the outdoor show to gain the experience of professional theatre: 'We could have made $15,000 to $20,000 a night in fair dates and concerts,' Bill explained the following year. 'For Oz we made $12,500 a week.' Other important guest stars in the MUNY's home production include burlesque star Phyllis Diller, Cass Daley and Mary Wickes as the Witch, with Olympic gymnast Cathy Rigby one of the many to play Dorothy. Away from St Louis, the show has been mounted around America, with Connie Stevens headlining as Dorothy in a 1963 production in Kansas City, Missouri.

The story continued to lend itself to adaptation for marionettes. The Suzari Marionettes created a version in 1948, and mounted a production at the New York City Center Theater in 1950, accompanying it with music from American folk tunes. Their script, with various alterations, continues to be performed today. Nicolas Coppola joined the Suzari Marionettes in 1954 and when the company disbanded in 1962, founded his own troupe, the Nicolo Marionettes. The Suzari score was reworked by composer Bruce Haack into a more bluegrass country and western sound, and when the Nicolo Marionettes became Puppetworks in 1980, the show continued to be performed at their New York base.

Robin Reed spent ten years preparing his puppet production of *The Wizard of Oz*, before premiering it in 1950. It deviated in places from the exact story, but endeavoured to stick to the spirit of Baum's creation. He and his wife Edith performed it for over forty years around the Midwest, with their son Tim assisting in later years; their story required fifteen scene changes and over thirty characters, with up to five of them on stage at any one time – operated by only two people.

The Oz theme was borrowed briefly for a *Holiday On Ice* production in 1959 in the United States, alongside *The Lady and the Tramp*, *An Adult Western*, *Ten Cents a Dance* and *Holiday in the Stars*. The show starred Tony LeMac, Jinx Clark, Paul Andre and Erika Kraft. Ice Capades in New York presented a thirteen-minute adaptation the following year which featured a poodle as Toto, while the Scarecrow, the Tin Man and the Lion each performed an ice dance. In the UK, *The Wizard of Oz on Ice* also featured the MGM score backing a recreation of the movie.

There were also underwater versions by groups as diverse as the Brooklyn College Women's Synchronized Swimming Group, the Swarthmore Swim Club and even the Weeki Wachee mermaids, who produced a short souvenir film of their performance that can be viewed on YouTube. Ringling Brothers and Barnum & Bailey Circus returned to the Baum story – with field mice rescuing the travellers from the poppies, and silver slippers – for their 1961 spectacle.

Unusually, the Eaglet Civic Theatre in Sacramento, California, adapted one of Ruth Plumly Thompson's stories in 1963 rather than one of Baum's own sequels to *The Wizard of Oz*, which they had already performed. *The Yellow Knight of Oz*, Thompson's tenth book, was rewritten and directed by Richard Fuller after he negotiated the rights with Thompson and publishers Reilly & Lee. The story is pretty faithful to Thompson's tale of Speedy, Sir Hokus Pokus, the Comfortable Camel (played by a puppet) and the living statue Marygolden as they travel across Oz, and learn that Sir Hokus is really the enchanted Prince Corum of Corumbia. Fuller's production has subsequently been revised by Christopher Sterling and often performed at the annual convention of the International Wizard of Oz Club. The only other known arrangement of a non-Baum story came the following year when *Merry Go Round in Oz* was performed by Kent School third grade in Denver, although according to reports of the production, the roundabout horse in question didn't appear!

Throughout the 1960s, various groups adapted the early Oz stories for their productions – a cast of 1,700 performed *The Wizard of Oz* at a Tupperware convention at the Northern Illinois University Stadium in Dekhalb, Illinois on 14 August 1964; the Moppet Players managed to reproduce Princess Langwidere's changing heads on stage with a clever use of wigs and high collars in their April 1964 play *Ozma, Ruler of Oz*. Toby Nicholson combined elements of *Dorothy and the Wizard in Oz* (notably the earthquake that sends Dorothy to Oz) and *Ozma of Oz* for his School of Dance and Musical Theatre's May 1965 production *Dorothy in the Mysterious Land of Oz* – they cast different people as Langwidere to get round the head-changing problem. Dulce Odriozola created three separate musical shows for her Youth Theatre Workshop in Alhambra, California, based on *The Marvelous Land of Oz*, *Ozma in Oz* and *Dorothy and the Wizard in Oz*.

There were plenty more puppet tales: Bill Eubank created marionettes based on the Denslow drawings for *The Wonderful Wizard of Oz* and Neill's illustrations for *The Marvelous Land of Oz*, and presented his own version of the stories to the International Wizard of Oz Club, starting in 1965. The renowned Stevens Puppets theatre began presenting their version the same year. The Royal European Marionette Theatre, also known as the Chicago National Marionette Company, presented *The Wizard of Oz* in 1966 with fifty-five puppets on a huge set that took two years to build. The Smithsonian Puppet Theatre used three-foot-tall marionettes for their tale of *The Marvelous Land of Oz* that toured college campuses in the early 1970s.

One of the most spectacular versions was produced by Bil and Cora Baird over the winter of 1968–1969. In this Dorothy is accompanied by a goat named Tanglefoot rather than Toto – perhaps not surprisingly, since Baird was best known for being the puppeteer of the 'lonely goatherd' puppet show in *The Sound of Music*. The voices were performed live along with a live orchestra. The Baird show was the basis of the promotional events held at Macy's for the fiftieth anniversary of *The Wizard of Oz* in 1989.

The small-scale shows and puppet versions rarely surprised their audiences, but the production that opened in October 1974 at the Morris A. Mechanic Theatre in Baltimore upended the story and reworked it for a 1970s audience.

The Wiz: The Super Soul Musical Wonderful Wizard of Oz (or *The Wiz*, for short), was described as 'a musical featuring an all-black cast, based on "The Wonderful Wizard Of Oz" by L. Frank Baum', and legendary critic Frank Rich summed up its appeal: 'What made *The Wiz* surprisingly moving the first time around was that its creators found a connection between Baum's Kansas fantasy and the pride of urban black Americans. When Glinda, the good witch, musically instructed Dorothy to "believe in herself," she seemed to be delivering a broader inspirational message. *The Wiz* was hardly a great musical in 1975, but it had something to say, and it said it with verve and integrity.'

Its first Broadway run, starting in 1975, extended to 1,672 performances, and received eight Tony Award nominations: Best Musical; Best Original Score; Best Featured Actor in a Musical: Ted Ross; Best Featured Actress in a Musical: Dee Dee Bridgewater; Best Costume Design; Best Choreography; Best Direction of a Musical; and Best Book of a Musical, only failing to triumph in the latter. It also won five Drama Desk awards for Outstanding Musical; Outstanding Music and Lyrics; Outstanding Featured Actor in a Musical: Ted Ross; Outstanding Choreography; and Outstanding Costume Design. Previews began on Christmas Eve 1974, and *The Wiz* opened officially at the Majestic Theatre on 5 January 1975. It moved to the Broadway Theatre on 25 May 1977, where it played until 28 January 1979.

While it was playing in New York, a national tour began, initially in Los Angeles in June 1976; a second tour ran between June 1978 and July 1979, starting in Wilmington, Delaware, and closing in Portland, Oregon. The Starlight Theatre in Kansas City opened a production in 1979, incorporating cast from both the touring and Broadway versions, as did MUNY in St Louis in 1982. It even made a brief trip across the Atlantic to play at the Crucible Theatre in Sheffield, England in September 1980.

A second Broadway run in 1984 didn't fare as well as its predecessor: Rich wrote in the *New York Times* that it was 'depressing to watch a once-fervent expression of black self-respect and talent be spilled on the stage as if it were a trunkload of marked-down, damaged goods'. The show closed after thirteen performances.

The Wiz was the brainchild of actor and director Ken Harper, who came up with the idea of 'a black *Wizard of Oz*' as an abridged TV special while working as program affairs director at WPIX Radio in the early 1970s. He was able to interest executives at 20th Century Fox to finance the idea to the tune of $650,000 in return for the film rights. The storyline and book were provided by William F. Brown, who had previously penned the Broadway show *The Girl in the Freudian Slip* in 1967 (which only lasted three days on the Great White Way); the music came from musical prodigy Charlie Smalls, who had toured with Harry Belafonte and Hugh Masekela as a pianist. The pair came up with a show that 'probably reaches deeper into black consciousness than has been generally recognized', according to Bryant Rollins in the *New York Times* in 1975. 'The score by Charlie Smalls intersperses songs of fantasy and humour with songs of protest. Innovation in black music follows a tradition of protest against oppression.'

Harper tried out the show in various locations, including Detroit and Baltimore before it arrived on Broadway, bringing in renowned choreographer and actor Geoffrey Holder (Baron Samedi from the 007 film *Live and Let Die*) to direct, whose contributions notably included the Tornado Ballet at the start of the show. It nearly opened and closed the same night, but, as William F. Brown recalled a couple of decades later, '20th Century-Fox, the show's major investor, put in another $100,000 to keep it going and everyone agreed to royalty cuts until the production's cost – about $1.1 million – was recouped. By the eighth week, we were selling out.' Many of the songs in the show became hits, in particular 'Ease On Down the Road' (*The Wiz*'s equivalent of 'We're Off to See the Wizard'); and 'Brand New Day', which was written by Luther Vandross rather than Charlie Smalls.

The Wiz is very much a stage version of L. Frank Baum's original story, rather than looking to the Judy Garland film for inspiration. It starts in Kansas with Dorothy's uncle and aunt telling her that everything she needs is at home, before she is blown away in a tornado that delivers her to Oz. Addaperle the Feelgood Girl, aka the Good Witch of the North, gives her the silver slippers belonging to Evvamene, the Wicked Witch of the East, and sends her off to see the Wiz(ard) of Oz. (Addaperle's own magic is a bit lacking; she has to take the bus because her transport spells tend to fail.) Dorothy meets the Scarecrow, the Tin Man and the Cowardly Lion, and together they battle the Kalidah, creatures with 'long noses' and 'grotesque long fingernails'. The Lion gets high and is nearly overcome in the poppy field before being rescued by rodents belonging to the Mice Squad. Arriving at the Emerald City, the four friends are given green glasses (a touch from the book that is frequently missed in the translation to other media), and taken to the Wizard. He appears in several forms before telling them they must kill Evillene, the Wicked Witch of the West, if they want to achieve their desires.

A few days later, Evillene's Funky Monkeys disable the Tin Man and the Scarecrow and then capture the Lion and Dorothy, taking them to Evillene's castle. There they discover that water is lethal to her, and kill her. The Winkies who have been under her control then help them to restore their friends. Returning to the Emerald City, the Wizard tries to go back on his promises, and the Lion (not Toto as is normally shown) reveals the real Wizard. He tells them they already have what they're after (although he gives them some tokens) and promises to take Dorothy back in his balloon – but it slips its moorings before she can join him. Addaperle arrives and suggests she asks Glinda, the Good Witch of the South, for help, and transports her to Glinda's castle. Glinda explains that Dorothy has always been able to get back, and Dorothy heads off to Kansas, where Toto races to greet her.

The show underwent two major makeovers over the next fifteen years, firstly during its transition to the big screen in 1978, and then again for the 1995 revival on tour. Although Ken Harper tried to gain independent interest in a movie version, it ended up as a Universal production, with Harper gaining an executive producer credit. The screenplay, by Joel Schumacher, considerably altered the book by William F. Brown, and the music was reworked by Quincy Jones, with new songs added by Nickolas Ashford & Valerie Simpson.

The film was produced by Motown Productions, with its head, Berry Gordy, keen for Stephanie Mills to reprise her role of Dorothy from the Broadway version for the film. A national talent show to seek the right actress for the part was also considered. However, Motown star Diana Ross was extremely keen to play the part, and begged to be cast; Gordy refused, saying she was too old. Ross therefore went to Rob Cohen at Universal Pictures and persuaded him to back a deal, which would see her play the part and bring Michael Jackson on board as the Scarecrow.

Gordy had hired *Saturday Night Fever* director John Badham to helm the film, but he withdrew, since he felt that Ross was 'a wonderful singer . . . a terrific actress and a great dancer, but she's not this character. She's not the little six-year-old Dorothy in *The Wizard of Oz*.' Academy Award winner Sidney Lumet was therefore brought onto the project in his place, and according to him, Universal were so confident that the combination of Ross, Jackson, and Lena Horne (then Lumet's mother-in-law) would be box-office gold that 'the picture never had any kind of budget tag to begin with'. This was a bad mistake: the film cost $24 million, but only recouped $13.6 million at the box office.

Joel Schumacher's script may have had a lot to do with the negative reaction to the movie, compared with the stage show. In a reverse mirroring of the way Frank Gabrielson had turned the 1939 movie into a stage show, Schumacher retained the songs and core beats from the stage show, but reworked the story and dialogue considerably. He was influenced by the writings of Werner Erhard, who had created a lifestyle training scheme, 'est Training' (later also known as the Forum) which was designed to help people to handle situations better. Diana Ross was a keen proponent of est, and ensured that its precepts formed the core of the script.

Rob Cohen wasn't impressed with this. 'Before I knew it, the movie was becoming an est-ian fable full of est buzz-words about knowing who you are and sharing and all that. I hated the script a lot. But it was hard to argue with [Ross] because she was recognizing in this script all of this stuff that she had worked out in est seminars.' Certainly Glinda's speech to Dorothy at the end of the film mirrors much of the est teaching.

Under the deal Universal reached for the rights, principal photography on the film had to begin by 1 October 1977, leaving Lumet less time in pre-production than he would have preferred. The availability of the stars also tightened the production parameters. The budget began to mount during the production, and Lumet recalled Universal boss Ned Tanen approaching him. ' "Sidney, it looks like at least $18 million at this point; what can you do?" Even at that point, I honestly couldn't answer him. I had no idea what three weeks of engineering work on masks would cost, or how much Albert Whitlock's mattes would come to. And they accepted that, saying, "Spend what you have to to make it right." '

Lumet believed that there was little in common between *The Wiz* and its 1939 predecessor. 'They made a brilliant movie, and even though our concept is different – they're Kansas, we're New York; they're white, we're black; and the score and the books are totally different – we wanted to make sure that we never overlapped in any area,' he explained shortly before the film opened, and later noted that it had been 'one of the most positive movie-making experiences ever. Universal wanted this picture badly, and they were willing to spend anything necessary to get it on the screen.'

The film was very firmly set in New York – at the start, Dorothy (now a twenty-four-year-old schoolteacher – Ross herself was a decade older) is having Thanksgiving dinner with her uncle and aunt at her Harlem apartment. Chasing after her dog into a snowstorm, she finds herself in the Kingdom of Oz – a warped version of New York City. Miss One, the Good Witch of the North, sends her to the Emerald City (the World Trade Center) to find the Wizard. Along the way she meets a man made of rubbish, the Scarecrow; a turn-of-the-century mechanical man; and a vain dandy of a lion who is hiding inside the stone lions outside the New York Public Library. They encounter a crazy homeless man and his puppets; and poppy girls – whores who try to entrance the quartet.

The silver shoes Miss One gave her help Dorothy and friends enter the Emerald City where they meet the Wizard; he will help if they kill Evillene, who runs a sweatshop in the sewers, helped by her motorcycle gang, the Flying Monkeys. The group are captured by the Monkeys and brought to Evillene. The Lion is tortured, the Tin Man is flattened, and the Witch threatens to throw Toto into a boiling cauldron – but the Scarecrow hints to Dorothy to activate the fire sprinklers, and Evillene is flushed down the toilet.

When they return to the Wizard, they learn that he is a

failed politician from Atlantic City who arrived in Oz in the balloon he was flying for his election campaign as dog-catcher. Dorothy persuades her friends that they really do have everything they need and then Glinda tells her to look within herself to find her way home. Clicking her shoes together, Dorothy transports herself back to Harlem.

Even a stellar cast including Nipsey Russell as the Tin Man and Richard Pryor as the Wizard couldn't save *The Wiz* from meltdown at the box office – something that trade paper *Variety* hinted that Universal believed was possible. 'The filmization of the Broadway tuner, based on L. Frank Baum's book (the source, of course, for the 1939 Metro classic with Judy Garland) is considered perhaps the biggest film musical gamble in screen history,' Frank Segers noted in October, shortly before the film opened. '*The Wiz* is the most expensive film tuner. Depending on who you listen to, the pic cost before ad-pub outlays from $30 million to $35 million, with many informed sources putting the total figure at the upper end of that range.' A month after the movie opened, Lumet challenged that figure and stated the final spend (bar studio costs) was $23.4 million.

Universal was hopeful after initial word seemed good, and the film performed well in its first week. Roger Ebert praised its 'great moments and a lot of life, sensational special effects and costumes, and Ross, Jackson, and Russell' but noted that the film 'hedges its bets by wanting to be sophisticated and universal, childlike and knowing, appealing to both a mass audience and to media insiders. *The Wizard of Oz* went flat-out for the heart of its story; there are times when *The Wiz* has just a touch too much calculation.' Pauline Kael was one of many who criticized the casting of Diana Ross in her review in the *New Yorker* magazine, but who also praised Michael Jackson's performance, for which he had extensively researched the movement.

The sets and dressing also gained praise; when Universal was submitting the film for consideration by the Academy in December 1978, they quoted Rex Reed's review: 'Visually *The Wiz* outdoes everything I've seen on the screen in decades. The idea of having New York itself as Oz is truly inspired, and it gives genius designer Tony Walton a chance to pull out the stops. The results are spectacular, kids from eight to eighty will marvel at the ingenuousness of the sets and costumes.'

But despite its stage show roots, this *Wiz* didn't have staying power. It received four Academy Award nominations – Best Art Direction; Best Costume Design; Best Original Music Score; and Best Cinematography – but lost out in all categories. It was to be Diana Ross's last big-screen role.

The original writer of *The Wiz* wasn't impressed by the cinematic version. 'Imagine Emerald City in the World Trade Center. It doesn't work. No matter how you update it, Oz is Oz,' William F. Brown said when promoting the reinvented version of the stage show in February 1993.

'We've sharpened the focus, dropped the frills and emphasized the themes of empowerment and self-esteem – without sacrificing flash, splash and glitter,' George Faison, the original choreographer, explained. 'We couldn't give up the Judy Garland myth in the '70s. Now the lion no longer says, "I almost found that rainbow." The line is out. The story is not about finding the rainbow; it's about finding yourself.'

The show was updated musically to include 'today's new toys', according to Faison: street sounds, rap and hip-hop, and synthesizers and electronic drums. Other changes included removing the idea of giving the Lion a bottle of 'O & Z' whiskey to drown his cowardice, or the Scarecrow receiving a box of 'All Brain' cereal.

This version only lasted twenty-eight performances on Broadway after a short tour. Another short tour followed in June/July 1996 in America, and a decade later, La Jolla Playhouse in San Diego put on a version that ran for six weeks. Overseas, Joop Van den Ende's Stage Entertainment mounted a Dutch version in Utretcht in 2006, and Birmingham Rep and the West Yorkshire Playhouse reworked the story to set *The Wiz* in a Midlands metropolis in 2011.

Like *The Wizard of Oz*, *The Wiz* has become a staple of schools and colleges, although one production in 2013 did raise some eyebrows. Cicero-North Syracuse High School's spring play did not include any African-Americans in the lead roles. 'They have black talented kids at the school, but they chose to put them at the ensemble because they're not theatre kids,' parent Letrice Titus commented. 'They should have made a collaborative effort based on diversity, cultural awareness, [and] sensitivity. How are the black kids going to feel when they see a play?' The school explained that 'only seven African-Americans tried out for the musical and none were selected as leading or supporting roles in the play.' The school had only ninety-three black students out of the total student body of 2,200.

The local chapter president for the NAACP pointed out: 'Why was the version of *The Wiz* picked over *The Wizard of Oz* if you have no intent to bring out the African-American culture as *The Wiz* was made out to be?' And Letrice Titus added, 'When a white school chooses to do a black play, they need to utilize the black students, not just throw them in the background. How are three white women going to produce [*The Wiz*]? I don't know how they're going to convey a play based on black culture.'

Musical director Caryn Patterson noted that 'it has a positive message, it's easy for the students to understand, it has great music and the choreography and script are easy to perform'. After various discussions with the school's principal, North Syracuse School District board of education superintendent Kim Dyce-Faucett and associate superintendent Dan Bowles, the production went ahead.

*   *   *

Most stage versions of the Oz stories restrict themselves to simply retelling the tales that L. Frank Baum (or the MGM screenwriters) created. Just occasionally, though, over the years, some adapters have looked to add something extra to the tales. One such was the version of *Ozma of Oz* written by Susan Zeder for the Poncho Theatre of Seattle in 1979. As Jack Helbig wrote in the *Chicago Reader* of the 1989 revival: 'Susan Zeder's noisy, ill-conceived adaptation, performed by Chicago Children's Theatre, couldn't be less in the spirit of L. Frank Baum's charming, whimsical, and witty original. Zeder takes such silly liberties with the text that her play should begin with a disclaimer: "Any resemblance between this play and any of L. Frank Baum's characters or stories is strictly coincidental." '

Zeder sends both Dorothy and Uncle Henry into Oz at the start of the show, which alters the dynamic of the entire story. Tic Toc [*sic*] is now a time machine: when he was activated, Time began to pass in Oz. Ozma had thrown his key away, freezing Time, but Dorothy finds it, winds him up and thus Time begins to pass again. Various elements are retained from the Baum story – the Kingdom of the Nomes, the Wheelers and the transmutation of people into objects – but Dorothy's friends are not present. According to Helbig, it seems that Zeder's message is that 'growing old and getting wrinkles is natural and nothing to be ashamed of' which he felt 'seems far more relevant to the parents' than the younger audience (who, he reported, kept asking if the show was finished yet).

By the time the show was being revived by the Oklahoma Christian University in February 2012, it was perhaps wisely advertised as 'A play for young audiences by Susan Zeder loosely based upon characters from L. Frank Baum's "Ozma of Oz".' Anchorage Press published Zeder's script as *Ozma of Oz: A Tale of Time* in 1981.

Zeder later reworked her script into the 1999 musical

production *Time Again in Oz*, working with composer Richard Grey. This wasn't simply a question of adding some songs to the existing script. 'There was a lot of stuff in the play that would lend itself to that,' she explained in an interview for the *Austin Chronicle* in 2000. 'But even more importantly, it wasn't just a matter of taking the flashy characters and giving them production "numbahs". Dramaturgically, it looked like music would help us track the primary relationship between Dorothy and her aging Uncle Henry. We found it enormously challenging and a different kind of project.' The musical is a period piece – the original was contemporary – and, like the 1939 film, the characters met in Oz are reflections of those that Dorothy encounters before she's sent there. However, it retained its central theme of time and growth, with Dorothy and Uncle Henry having the choice of remaining in Oz, where Henry will be young and strong but Dorothy will be a child, or returning home, which means Henry is once again confined to a wheelchair.

Others chose to remain faithful to Baum in their adaptations. Thomas W. Olson (book), Gary Briggle (lyrics), and Richard Dworsky (music) created a version of *The Marvelous Land of Oz* for The Children's Theatre Company and School in Minneapolis in 1981, which stayed very faithful to Baum's story. Minor details were changed for stageability – such as adding the character of Colonel Cardamom as a second-in-command for General Jinjur to give her someone to interact with – and there is a little tip of the head to Ruth Plumly Thompson's book *The Lost King of Oz*, when Ozma's father King Pastoria is mentioned. Nine songs were composed for the play, which has occasionally been put on by other theatres.

The 1983 production of *The Wizard of Oz*, adapted by Tom McCabe, was such a success that the Mount Holyoke College Summer Theatre in South Hadley, Massachusetts produced Oz stage plays for over a decade, including *Journey Back to Oz* (based on *The Marvelous Land/The Road to Oz*); and *The Patchwork Girl of Oz*, which added in a romance between Scraps and the Scarecrow, which led to *The Royal Wedding Of Oz*.

The Theatre of the Young at Eastern Michigan University in Ypsilanti, Michigan mounted *Scraps! The Ragtime Girl of Oz* by V. Glasgow Koste in 1986, which kept pretty faithfully to the Baum original. The sixty-minute play is set in 'Oz and anywhere . . . now and then' according to the published script, which begins with Scraps and the author (Baum) arguing about whether they should start the story in the 'magnificent, muddy middle' or at the beginning.

The Patchwork Girl also formed the basis of a Christmas 1988 show at the Palace Theatre, Watford in the UK, written by Adrian Mitchell (who would go on to write a well-received version of C.S. Lewis's *The Lion, the Witch and the Wardrobe* a few years later), with music by Andy Roberts. Mitchell's version starts with Ozma, the Tin Man and the Scarecrow remembering Oz, a land where 'the animals talked/and the furniture walked/and the sky was full of popcorn snow' before starting off Baum's tale. Mitchell creates some characters of his own (Johann Sebastian Box, for example), and also includes a scene with plants that grow humans for food – part of the original version of the book that Baum dropped at the suggestion of his publishers.

In 1986, British actor and writer John Kane was called upon to pen an adaptation of *The Wizard of Oz* for the Royal Shakespeare Company (RSC) that was to be closer to the script for the 1939 movie than the MUNY version had been. Terry Hands, the artistic director for the RSC, wanted to add another show to the company's repertoire for Christmas 1987 that could be revived annually in the holiday season. A version of J.M. Barrie's *Peter Pan* had been a hit for the company previously so RSC director Ian Judge negotiated the rights to the actual screenplay of the 1939 film and then passed that to Kane with instructions to 'fatten it out . . . because you need a few more words in the theatre than you need in the movies.'

According to Tams Witmark, who also control stage performances of this adaptation, 'The RSC version is a more technically complex production [than the MUNY script] and uses as much of the aura of the film as is possible to create in a modern theatre. It is an adaption for live stage performance, even while it strives to look and sound just like the famous film, in telling the story. There is more work for the SATB [soprano, alto, tenor, bass] chorus and small vocal ensembles in the music material for the RSC version.'

In 2007, Mitchell Sommers, the Executive Director for the Community Theatre Of Greensboro, North Carolina, summed up the appeal of the RSC's show: 'It is so universal. It is appealing to all because it is not related to a religious holiday or created for only a certain sect of our community. We all grew up on this story and the RSC version is like watching the movie live on stage!'

Sommers is right. Unlike previous versions, to all intents and purposes this is the MGM musical brought to life on stage, with a couple of additions – an extra verse for 'Somewhere Over the Rainbow', and the reincorporation of the 'Jitterbug' song. It premiered at London's Barbican Theatre on 17 December 1987 with Imelda Staunton as Dorothy, Paul Greenwood as the Scarecrow, Jim Carter as the Cowardly Lion, John Bowe as the Tin Man, Billie Brown as the Wicked Witch of the West, Dilys Laye as Glinda and Aunt Em (a joint casting that was controversial with some fans), David Glover as Uncle Henry, and Tony Church as the Wizard. A revival the following year saw Gillian Bevan as Dorothy and the original Anakin Skywalker, Sebastian Shaw, as the Wizard; this production moved to the RSC's Stratford-upon-Avon theatre in February 1989.

The new version was an immediate success, with Jeremy Kingston writing in *The Times*, 'This is, to come out with it immediately, the most marvellous show'. It quickly transferred across the Atlantic, running in Long Beach, California in the latter part of July 1988 with Cathy Rigby returning to the role of Dorothy. A live arena tour of the production in 1989 didn't go down so well: changes had to be made for the new venues so Glinda had gigantic butterfly wings; the Witch had a huge Pilgrim Fathers-style hat, and a red feather costume; and the Munchkins were considerably taller than Dorothy. With slow scene changes, and frequent errors in the synchronization between the actors and the pre-recorded dialogue and songs, it was slated by critics, and the tour finished prematurely.

The RSC production has been regularly produced on both sides of the Atlantic. Robin Cousins choreographed a version on ice that toured between 1995 and 1999, while a concert performance, featuring Jewel, Joel Gray, Jackson Browne, Roger Daltrey, Nathan Lane and Debra Winger was filmed and broadcast by TNT. A shorter adaptation, suitable for younger audiences, premiered at Madison Square Garden in New York in May 1997 with Roseanne Barr as the Wicked Witch; the following year Mickey Rooney – who had joined Judy Garland for concerts after the initial run of the film in New York nearly sixty years earlier – played the Wizard, with Eartha Kitt as the Wicked Witch. A further tour ran from 2008 to January 2012.

An interesting adaptation, simply entitled *The Wonderful Wizard of Oz*, was premiered in Toronto in 2000. Advertised as being 'in the tradition of the classic MGM movie, the legendary Broadway musical and even more modern hits like *The Wiz* and *Wicked* . . . [a] musical staging of everyone's favourite classic!' the book was by Joe Cascone, with music and lyrics by James P. Doyle. As Claire Martin wrote in the *North York Mirror* when reviewing the 2002 revival, 'Cascone has been loyal to Baum in writing the script for this production, and Doyle has been wonderfully disloyal to the MGM movie musical . . . in composing a collection of very different songs. The sentiments, however, remain the same: a young girl, tossed about by the elements, takes the yellow brick road to wisdom – mind, body and soul.'

Cascone took an unusual approach to his script, incorporating Baum himself as a character and narrator (who also doubles as the Wizard), who is presenting the familiar tale of the Wizard of Oz with his performing troupe (mirroring Baum's own ideas in the *Fairylogue and Radio-Plays* nearly a century earlier). Much of it is faithful to the 1900 book, with the odd addition from later sources – the Good Witch of the North gains the name Locasta, which she first acquired for the 1902 extravaganza; the Wicked Witches are sisters, as in the 1939 film; and the Tin Woodman's backstory is the later one developed for *The Tin Woodman of Oz*. The removal of Toto from the Oz scenes, gives Dorothy another reason to want to get home.

Doyle was a long-time Oz fan, who had compiled a CD of arrangements of music from the earliest Oz adaptations including Paul Tietjens' score for *The Wizard of Oz* stage show; Frederic Chapin's music for *The Woggle-Bug*; Louis F. Gottschalk's scores for *The Tik-Tok Man of Oz* and *The Patchwork Girl of Oz*; as well as six songs that Baum had written for his earliest play, *The Maid of Arran*. His music honoured that legacy, although Claire Martin did think that the songs 'don't seem to be as memorable or hummable, but that may possibly be because they are unfamiliar in the Land of Oz'. Equally, Mark Andrew Lawrence's review of the 2010 revival noted that the 'tuneful score . . . combines a variety of musical styles all of which are appropriate for the book. In addition, his clever wordplay constantly tickles the ears with bright insights.'

A rather less traditional musical could be seen in North

Bergen, New Jersey in April 2001 and then at the Producer's Club II Theatre in New York in the summer of 2003. *Oz: A Twisted Musical* began life as an off-off Broadway workshop in summer 1995, and although it updates the story, it follows Baum's tale – by way of *The Wiz*. In Tim Kelly's script with music and lyrics by Bill Francoeur, Dorothy is now a streetwise Kansas teenager who finds herself, via tornado, in Oz. The Munchkins eat at Dunkin' Donuts; Toto becomes a more human canine; the Scarecrow, the Tin Woodman and the Cowardly Lion bicker with each other incessantly, and the Wicked Witch lives in an S&M dungeon. Choreographer and director Alex Perez had faith in the production, and took his young cast to the off-Broadway theatre, where they attracted attention from the *New York Times*. Each production added different pop-culture references: Gary Coleman's line 'What you talkin' about, Willis?' from *Diff'rent Strokes*; the *Mission: Impossible* theme; and a homage to the slow-motion fight sequences from *The Matrix* characterized the 2003 run.

While the RSC script and, to a lesser extent, the MUNY version continue to bring in audiences to *The Wizard of Oz*, yet another adaptation attracted large crowds to performances in London and Toronto. Like the RSC version, it was based closely on the 1939 film, but it now incorporated four new songs, created by the *Jesus Christ Superstar/Evita* writing team of Sir Tim Rice and Lord Andrew Lloyd Webber.

The new production had its roots in the various 'reality' television shows that had run successfully in the United Kingdom, seeking stars for musicals. Lloyd Webber had been involved with the casting of a new staging of his first musical, *Joseph and the Amazing Technicolor Dreamcoat*, as well as revivals of Lionel Bart's *Oliver!* and the Rodgers and Hammerstein musical *The Sound of Music*. In April 2009, Lloyd Webber approached the rights holders of *The*

Wizard of Oz for permission to stage a musical based on the film, with 'five or six' new songs added to the score. At the time, Lloyd Webber was working on the production of *Love Never Dies*, his sequel to his hit version of *The Phantom of the Opera*, and Glenn Slater, the lyricist on that project, was expected to work with Lloyd Webber on the new additions. Jeremy Sams, the director of *The Sound of Music* revival, was writing the book, based on the MGM script, and would be at the helm of the production.

During the summer of 2009, there was considerable uncertainty over how the show would be cast. There were concerns over the licence-payer-funded BBC promoting a reality series that saw Lloyd Webber casting people for one of his own productions – the composer himself had apparently raised the same objection eighteen months earlier, although he later clarified that he meant that he had scheduling problems at that time, not that he had an objection to the process. In September 2009, the BBC announced that a new reality show *Over the Rainbow* would follow the process for casting not just Dorothy for the new *Wizard of Oz*, but also Toto (the latter something that Lloyd Webber noted was a BBC requirement, not his choice).

The show began broadcasting on Friday 26 March 2010, after the prospective Dorothys had been whittled down from the 9,000 who initially auditioned to twenty, who were sent to a 'Dorothy Farm' for intensive preparation. This number was quickly reduced to eleven, and one Dorothy was eliminated weekly by a public phone-in vote. A different judging panel from previous shows was compiled, featuring dancer, singer and actor John Partridge; actress Sheila Hancock; and singer Charlotte Church. It was decided that the dog cast as Toto would only appear for one special gala night rather than throughout the run of the show. The casting was by a pair of dog-training experts, Gerry Cott and Sarah Fisher.

Over the Rainbow ended on 22 May with Danielle

Hope cast as Dorothy, and miniature schnauzer Danger-
ous Dave as the gala Toto; runner-up Sophie Evans was
later announced as the alternate Dorothy, understudy-
ing for Hope. Shortly afterwards, Sir Tim Rice began
discussions with Lloyd Webber about reviving their part-
nership to create the new songs – the first time the men
had properly worked together since writing *Evita* nearly
thirty years earlier. In July Rice's involvement was officially confirmed. Musical star Michael Crawford was cast as
the Wizard for the show's initial run – popular personality
Russell Grant took over for three months in 2012, and
veteran entertainer Des O'Connor completed the show's
final four months. Sophie Evans played Dorothy opposite
Grant and O'Connor.

Hope and Crawford performed at the Royal Variety
Performance, held on 9 December 2010 at the London Pal-
ladium, which had undergone a refit in preparation for
the run of *The Wizard of Oz*. Four days later rehearsals
for the show began, with previews beginning on 7 February 2011, and a gala performance on 15 February before it
officially opened on 1 March. The new songs written by
Rice and Lloyd Webber underwent considerable changes
during the preview process – 'Red Shoes Waltz', sung by
the Wicked Witch, became 'Red Shoes Blues'; Glinda's
song 'Already Home' was rewritten as a duet ('As Good
As Home') before being removed entirely and replaced by
'You Went to See the Wizard' and a revised 'Farewell to
Oz', itself a late addition to the score, as was 'Bring Me the
Broomstick', which gave a rousing finale to the first act.
Dorothy's opening song, 'Nobody Understands Me', had
some verses replaced with dialogue. Only 'Wonders of the
World', as sung by Professor Marvel, remained virtually
untouched. From the original movie songs, 'If I Were King
of the Forest' was dropped, and unlike some film-based
productions, the 'Jitterbug' song was not reincorporated.

Critics and audiences mostly enjoyed the show. 'This

is a 10-star production if ever there was one,' wrote Tim Walker in the *Sunday Telegraph*, although his colleague Charles Spencer, who admitted that he was not a fan of the original film, noted, 'Dorothy's flight to the enchanted land is thrillingly caught with the help of film effects that wouldn't look out of place on *Dr Who* and the story is told with clarity and pace . . . This finally strikes me as a soullessly efficient production rather than an inspired re-invention of *The Wizard of Oz*.' It won Best Musical Revival and Best Supporting Actress for Hannah Wadding-ham at the Whatsonstage.com 2012 Theatre Awards, and was nominated for Best Musical Revival at the Olivier Awards.

The London production ended on 2 September 2012, but by that time, preparations were already underway for a Canadian version, with Dorothy once again chosen by popular acclaim. Canadian broadcaster CBC's *Over the Rainbow* show began on 16 September and followed the same pattern as the BBC series; Danielle Wade was elected Dorothy. (A Toto was chosen at the Canadian Woofstock dog festival, but the prize was only a ruby collar, rather than a chance to perform on stage.) The stage show opened at the Ed Mirvish Theatre in Toronto on 13 January 2013, and closed on 18 August before embarking on a tour of North America that began at the Smith Center in Las Vegas on 10 September.

Less than two weeks after *The Wizard of Oz* opened officially in London in the spring of 2011, a very differ-ent interpretation of L. Frank Baum's story premiered in Berlin. This was *Oz – The Wonderful Wizard*, a ballet, choreographed and staged by Italian choreographer Gior-gio Madia for the Staatsballet, a new independent ballet group founded in 2004. The music was taken from the soundtracks, suites and overtures by Russian composer Dmitri Shostakovich.

The ninety-minute ballet was advertised a few days

before the opening on 12 March with a 'flash mob' from the corps de ballet descending on the main train station at Berlin and more than 200 people starting to pirouette. At the end the station announcer declared, 'The train to Oz is due to arrive on 12 March 2011 at 7 p.m. at the Komische Oper Berlin . . . You're travelling with the Staatsballet Berlin.' Those who did visit the show were greeted with a multimedia experience, which the reviewer for *Der Taggesspiegel* described as 'theatre magic: aesthetic, witty, never cheesy'. It ended with a wave of balloons descending on the audience – they could choose to push them away or clap! The ballet has been added to the Staatsballet's regular repertoire, and both the flash mob and excerpts from the production can be viewed on YouTube.

With the books now firmly in the public domain, new stage versions of *The Wizard of Oz* that adhere to L. Frank Baum's original text are bound to continue. It's only if directors and producers wish to use some of the aspects that are the intellectual property of MGM – i.e. those that were created for the 1939 film – that there are restrictions. Baum would no doubt be delighted at how many different variants there have been.

3

WICKED

While the MUNY, RSC and Rice/Lloyd Webber versions of *The Wizard of Oz* continue to attract audiences, one stage show based on adventures in Oz has gone from strength to strength, opening in theatres around the world. In this incarnation, it is far closer to the 1939 movie than it is to L. Frank Baum's books, whereas the books upon which it's based are very much a reaction and counter to the world of Oz as presented in those. (The books by Gregory Mitchell are therefore dealt with in detail in part four.)

Wicked: The Untold Story of the Witches of Oz is the *Rosencrantz & Guildenstern Are Dead* of *The Wizard of Oz* – a comparison composer Stephen Schwartz drew right from the start of production. Schwartz's music and lyrics and Winnie Holzman's book combine to show us what was apparently really going on prior to and during the events of the 1939 film from the perspective of the 'Wicked' Witch.

The detailed genesis of the *Wicked* stage show is given

in Schwartz's authorized biography, *Defying Gravity*, which is recommended to anyone interested in learning how a show develops from first ideas to final realization on stage. The theatrical version developed from plans to turn Gregory Mitchell's book *Wicked* into a movie; the rights had been optioned by Demi Moore's production company, but the draft screenplays weren't working for new president of production at Universal Pictures, Marc Platt. Stephen Schwartz had heard about the book in December 1996 from singer Holly Near, and when he started to read it himself, he realized it was exactly the sort of project he would enjoy working on, so started to ask about the rights. Around the same time, screenwriter Winnie Holzman, who had won an Emmy Award nomination for her work on *My So-Called Life*, the ABC TV series she had created, also found a copy of the book, and enquired about the rights. Both Schwartz and Holzman were informed that the rights lay with Moore and Platt.

When Schwartz finally met with Platt, he tried to persuade the producer that *Wicked* was better suited to the stage than the screen, and counted himself lucky that Platt had a background in musical theatre. Platt immediately saw the potential in the idea, but for a time progressed both projects – an all-dancing, all-singing musical on stage, and a non-musical movie. Schwartz met with creator Mitchell, and won him round to his approach – as far as Mitchell was concerned, as long as the stage show maintained the book's examination of fundamental questions about behaviour and acceptance and honesty, then he was in favour of it proceeding, even if many other things changed.

And change it did. Some of the key elements of the *Wicked* stage show that audiences remember are the genesis of the characters from *The Wizard of Oz* (the Cowardly Lion, the Tin Man, and the Scarecrow), and the surprise at the end of the show (which would be unfair to reveal here). None of these is in Mitchell's book. The book is about Elphaba (the name Mitchell gives to the Wicked Witch of the West); the stage show is about the friendship between Elphaba and Galinda/Glinda – her name changes partway through – which crystallized for the writers during the development process when Kristin Chenoweth joined the cast.

Platt, Holzman and Schwartz worked together creating the 'stage story' for the show, before the two writers went off to create their sections of the musical. Unusually for him, Schwartz often ended up writing the lyrics for the songs before the music; this he felt was necessary since each song had to tell exactly the right story to fit its place in the musical. The production was workshopped through 2000 and 2001 with both first and second acts undergoing major changes during the process, particularly between the readings on 23 February and 2 March 2001. David Stone joined the team as producer following the latter reading, and he recommended Joe Mantello should be appointed as director. Mantello had acted in *Angels in America*, and switched to directing plays such as *The Vagina Monologues*, but he had never dealt with a project of this size before.

Mantello brought an outside perspective to the table, and suggested changing the opening – which originally featured the Scarecrow, the Cowardly Lion, the Tin Man, and even Dorothy. This was altered to Glinda in her bubble coming to address the crowds after the death of the Wicked Witch. Preparations continued for a new read-through in December 2001, with some of the cast who would go on to the Broadway production. Yet further revisions were made as a result of this, and continued for the next eighteen months, as the show was honed. Official previews began in San Francisco on 28 May 2003, during which the show evolved further – Galinda's name change came at a different moment, for example – but the producers knew from the very first performance that they had a musical that fundamentally worked. It was now a matter of fine-tuning the emotional arcs and the songs.

* * *

Schwartz and Holman's *Wicked* deals with the use and abuse of power, although the plotline in the book about the treatment of the talking Animals (the A is deliberately upper-cased to differentiate those creatures from the run-of-the-mill beasts) is changed considerably. It's a key element of Mitchell's tale, but, as Joe Mantello pointed out, it is more of a MacGuffin in the stage show – a term created by Alfred Hitchcock to denote an item or goal that is vital to the characters within the story, but not to the audience (such as the Force in the *Star Wars* films, or the eponymous bird in *The Maltese Falcon*). Scenes featuring Dr Dillamond trying to prove that animals had souls were taken out, with the Goat becoming Elphaba and Galinda's teacher. The links to *The Wizard of Oz* are much stronger: we learn the origin of the Tin Man, the Scarecrow and the Cowardly Lion.

The show starts with the people of Oz outside the Wizard's palace, asking if it's true that the Wicked Witch is dead. Glinda descends and confirms it, and tries to answer the question that someone in the crowd poses: 'Why does Wickedness happen?' She explains the Witch's background – an unloved child, rejected by her father, and forced to look after her disabled sister, Nessarose. Glinda recalls their first meeting at Shiz University: known then as Galinda, the future Good Witch is a vapid, dizzy blonde; Elphaba is a powerful social outcast. The pair are put together as room-mates and it's loathing at first sight.

Elphaba is horrified when she learns about the way that a movement suggesting animals should be seen and not heard is spreading across Oz. The apparently shallow Prince Fiyero arrives at Shiz, and he and Galinda realize they deserve each other. Galinda fobs off the Munchkin Boq, one of her admirers, onto Nessarose, and offers Elphaba a pointed black hat. Elphaba thinks it means she's being accepted, but is humiliated at the local ballroom. When

Galinda learns that Elphaba has helped her gain entry to a class she didn't expect to be able to attend, they become friends. Shortly after, Dr Dillamond, their Goat teacher, is prevented from lecturing, and Elphaba and Fiyero help to free a petrified lion cub. Thereafter, Fiyero seems more interested in Elphaba than Galinda, although Elphaba fails to notice this.

Elphaba gains her own heart's desire, when Madam Morrible, the head of Shiz, tells her that the Wizard has sent for her, and she and Glinda (who has changed her name in solidarity with Dr Dillamond, in a vain attempt to get Fiyero to notice her again) go to the Emerald City. When the Wizard sees that Elphaba can read the Grimmerie (an ancient book of spells), he tricks her into creating winged monkeys to use as spies. Angrily, Elphaba grabs the book and runs off, eventually flying off on her broomstick, determined not to play by the rules of the Wizard's game. Glinda doesn't join her.

From here on, everyone believes the Wizard and Madam Morrible's propaganda about Elphaba, even her sister Nessarose. However, Elphaba casts a spell on Nessarose allowing her to walk, and she then learns that Boq never loved her. Nessarose uses the Grimmerie to make him lose his heart, and Elphaba ensures he has a chance to live without a heart.

Elphaba confronts the Wizard and is nearly taken in by him but when she sees what has become of Dr Dillamond, she realizes there is no chance they can ever work together. She and Fiyero run off together, and Glinda, devastated that her fiancé has abandoned her, suggests to the Wizard and Morrible that they can get to Elphaba through her sister. As Elphaba and Fiyero embrace, she sees a house flying through the storm that Morrible has created. It lands on Nessarose, and Glinda and Elphaba face off against each other, destroyed by their losses. Fiyero is captured, and taken to a field to be beaten.

Glinda is the only one who sees that things have gone too far, as everyone is set on Elphaba's path. The two friends have one last meeting with Elphaba insisting that Glinda must not try to clear her name. After Elphaba has been melted by the captured Dorothy (who we only ever see in silhouette), Glinda forces Morrible and the Wizard to face what they've done and the latter elects to leave Oz. But there are a few more twists before the final curtain falls.

Wicked opened in San Francisco on 10 June 2003, staying there until 29 June, when the production moved to New York for further rehearsals and minor alterations. It opened in the George Gershwin Theatre on Broadway on 30 October 2003; two separate North American tours currently operate, one that began on 31 March 2005, the other opening on 12 March 2009. A British production officially started at the Apollo Victoria Theatre on 27 September 2006. All these are still playing to packed houses, and a touring production started travelling around Britain and Ireland from September 2013. Productions were mounted in Chicago and Los Angeles (the latter moving to San Francisco for the last two years of its run). A Japanese translation could be seen in four separate cities in Japan between June 2007 and September 2012; a German edition was put on in Stuttgart and then Oberhausen between November 2007 and September 2011. The Australian production began in Melbourne in July 2008 before transferring to Sydney and then going on tour around Australia and Asia. A Dutch version could be seen at Scheveningen between November 2011 and January 2013; Willemijn Verkaik, its Elphaba, then joined the Broadway show. She had already appeared in the German show. A shortened thirty-minute edition could be seen at Universal Studios, Japan, between July 2006 and January 2011.

The recipient of over ninety awards, *Wicked* has yet to see the drop in ticket sales that was originally claimed would be the justification for committing it to film. Although there were reports over the years that a movie was under consideration, it was only in July 2012 that plans started to firm up, with trade news service Deadline suggesting that *Billy Elliot* director Stephen Daldry was under consideration to helm the film, based on a revised screenplay by Winnie Holzman. In December that year, Marc Platt told *Entertainment Weekly*, 'It's still a ways away. I would expect in the near future to begin the process of development. There will be a movie.' The success of the film version of the musical *Les Miserables* heightened interest in transferring *Wicked* to the big screen, but in February 2013 Universal chief Adam Fogelson told the *Hollywood Reporter*: '*Wicked* has been an enormous win for this company. The way it works, we should be in agreement together on when the right time to do this is. But I will tell you I believe that we are collectively moving toward *Wicked* coming to the screen sooner rather than later.'

Wicked has also spawned an unusual 'spin-off' – or at least, unusual in theatrical terms. The interest in behind-the-scenes footage on DVD and Blu-ray discs of movies, and the growth of TV shows that follow productions, led to the creation of *Behind the Emerald Curtain*. This is a ninety-minute 'exclusive behind-the-scenes look at *Wicked* run by *Wicked* cast-members', according to its website, which shows the audience what goes into the making of the production and gives them access to models and props from the set. It concludes with a question and answer session with members of the cast. It accompanied the Chicago and West Coast productions, and continues to play alongside the Broadway show.

The show occupies that hinterland somewhere between the Judy Garland movie and L. Frank Baum's book series. The former is so engrained now in the public zeitgeist that audience members pick up on the clues to events in the film (such as who is going to turn out to be the Scarecrow or the Tin Man) but there are more than a few nods to Baum, particularly in the look of the show. While there are some elements that may infuriate lovers of the marvellous land of Oz that Baum created, *Wicked* has certainly shown audiences worldwide that there is more to Oz than just Dorothy singing 'Somewhere Over the Rainbow'.

4. OZ REIMAGINED

I

NEW ADVENTURES IN PRINT

Ever since the Oz books entered the public domain – and even before – there have been new adventures set within the kingdoms of Oz. These have ranged in length, fidelity to the originals and quality; suffice it to say that if there is an element of the Royal Histories that the reader thinks might need expansion, then there will already be a story written about it. For those who want more adventures for Dorothy or the Hungry Tiger, Tik-Tok or Ozma, then the website The Royal Timeline of Oz provides details of these stories in chronological order. This section deals with those tales which alter Baum's creation to a greater or lesser extent.

Although it was by no means the first, nor arguably the best of these re-envisionings of Oz, Gregory Maguire's quartet of novels beginning with *Wicked* is probably the most famous attempt to make readers look at Oz in a new way. Much of its notoriety has stemmed from Stephen Schwartz's staging, which is very different in lots of respects from the original book.

Maguire was already a successful author of children's novels when he came up with the idea for *Wicked*, querying some of the decisions that were made within L. Frank Baum's beloved tale. Why did the Wizard insist on Dorothy and her friends killing the Witch – was it simply because she was Wicked? Why didn't Glinda tell Dorothy that the silver slippers would send her home earlier, rather than waiting until she had gone through death-defying adventures in Oz? Was the Witch born Wicked, or was she turned that way through events?

The initial idea sprang to mind in 1988, but Maguire's thoughts were crystallized by the demonization he saw of Saddam Hussein by the British press in the run-up to the First Gulf War in 1990, in particular a headline in *The Times* calling him 'The New Hitler'. A few months later came the kidnapping and murder of toddler Jamie Bulger by two young boys in Liverpool. Maguire understood that Hussein was a 'villain', but what of the boys? Were they born that way – was there something essentially evil about them that was allowed to grow into what they became? That was the focus of his thoughts about the Wicked Witch: he would write about someone who was totally bad. However, during the writing he realized that he couldn't be so one-dimensional: she was no saint, given the actions she performs during the story, but by the end she's sleep-deprived and thus acting irrationally.

Maguire named the Witch Elphaba – derived from the initials of her creator, L.F.B. – and began work on the story in June 1993. Talking about the book in 2008, he revealed that he had three women in mind as he wrote the character: American pop singer Laura Nyro, who had long black hair and 'a powerhouse voice'; poet Emily Dickinson 'for her ability to retire from the world but observe it with uncanny accuracy'; and British writer Virginia Woolf 'for her supreme intelligence and capacity to see the larger picture'. He also consciously didn't give her one single reason for becoming wicked – if indeed that's what the reader decides she is, having heard her whole story. 'Let's, for instance, say you have a terrible sorrow in your life,' he noted. 'I don't believe it's because your mother dropped a frying pan on your toe when you were four, you know? That may have hurt, you may remember it but I don't believe that our fates are determined by a single condition. Therefore, what I tried to do with Elphaba was give her lots of potential conditions, none of which could be, alone, the single reason for why she was the way she was.'

The biggest surprise that readers coming to the book will find is that the original novel is nowhere near as connected to the MGM movie as it is in the stage show. In Maguire's book, according to Madame Morrible, 'Oz is a seething volcano threatening to erupt and burn us in its own poisonous pus.' The description of Elphaba does hew closely to Margaret Hamilton's portrayal in the film, but there are no secret origins for the characters that Dorothy meets once she arrives. The plight of the talking Animals, and their subjugation by the Gale Force – the Wizard's equivalent of the SS dealing with the Jews in Nazi Germany – are far more important, and there is a lot of debate about the actions and consequences of terrorists. Sex and religion also play an important part in the formation of Elphaba's character.

'It's an oversimplification to say that I simply retold *The Wizard of Oz* making the witch the good guy,' Maguire pointed out in 2006. 'My Elphaba is not particularly good. She's a very troubled human being who manages to avoid doing the worst things, like murder, only because she is so ineffectual.

'The main theme of the book is that it is hard to be good. It's easier to be bad, it's easier to sell out. It is hard to stick to your convictions. And even good people are sometimes massively wrong.'

Wicked: The Life and Times of the Wicked Witch of

the West was published in 1995, and received a damning
review in the *New York Times*. '[Maguire's] insistence on
politicizing Oz and injecting it with a heavy dose of moral
relativism turns a wonderfully spontaneous world of fantasy
into a lugubrious allegorical realm, in which everything
and everyone is labelled with a topical name tag,' wrote
Michiko Kakutani. However, others saw its potential,
and within ten days he was being approached for the film
rights. Maguire wasn't happy with the various screenplays
he saw, but was attracted by the idea of a musical.

The success both of the book and the stage show led to
what Maguire described as a 'companion novel' to *Wicked*:
'To call *Son of a Witch* a sequel I think might unfairly
raise expectations that the main character of *Wicked* made
another appearance here. Well, she does, after a fashion,
but the book isn't about her. It's about the world she left
behind at the end of the novel, *Wicked*,' he explained in
2005. It follows the story of Liir, Elphaba's 'son', introduced in the first book, as well as Fiyero's daughter Nor,
and was inspired by the infamous pictures of US soldiers
'interrogating' (i.e. torturing) prisoners at Abu Ghraib.

The third story, *A Lion Among Men* (originally entitled
'A Cowardly War'), focused on the leonine character, Brrr
(it was cold when he was born, hence the name). Maguire
later admitted that the 'Wicked Years', as the saga became
known, was envisaged as a trilogy, and *A Lion Among Men*
was going to be 'a slight book', written as a companion
piece. However, it grew in the writing, as Brrr tries to get
answers about both Elphaba and Liir, and the book talks
about DNA versus free will as well as nature versus nur-
ture. 'I wanted to write about the Lion,' Maguire noted in
2008. 'In almost any American society it's all right not to
be terribly smart and we don't rate someone on their capacity to love but we have deep feelings about cowardice.'

The final story, *Out of Oz*, dealt with Elphaba's granddaughter, Rain, who is brought up in Glinda's household.

Maguire admitted that part of the inspiration for the story subconsciously came from the stage version of *Wicked*: in the song 'The Wizard and I', Elphaba sings about the Wizard 'de-greenify'-ing her. The story is also influenced by Baum's second novel, *The Marvelous Land of Oz*, as well as elements from *Dorothy and the Wizard in Oz*, and wraps the series up. As a coda to the series, Maguire produced *Tales Told in Oz*, a collection of four short stories which was published by Madras Press in Massachusetts, in aid of Vermont libraries that had suffered damage in the 2011 hurricane. This had a very small print run, and is very hard to find.

Oz purists have been up in arms about the 'Wicked Years' series but Maguire noticed that even some of the most ardent have come round: 'It took the Oz people a little bit longer to realize, yes, I was playing around with sacred material, but not in any way to disgrace the original material, just actually to make it seem richer and to make its richness make more sense.'

One of the most interesting reworkings of the Oz mythology isn't easily available to most Western fans, as it was written in Russian. Although some of the stories have been translated, and others themselves reworked, Alexander Volkov's tales are by and large unknown in Western countries even though they first appeared in 1939.

Alexander Melentyevich Volkov was a Soviet mathematician who wrote a loose translation of *The Wonderful Wizard of Oz*, which was published as *The Wizard of the Emerald City*. In his epilogue (which wasn't always reprinted in later editions), Volkov credited L. Frank Baum, but otherwise the book does not acknowledge the heavy debt it owes to the original story.

Volkov's heroine is Ellie Smith, who travels with her dog Totoshka to the Magic Land, where her arrival kills Gingema, the Wicked Witch of the East. She has to travel to the Emerald City to find Goodwin the Great and Terrible, with help from the Scarecrow, the Iron Lumberjack, and the Cowardly Lion. The Wizard sends them to deal with Bastinda, the Wicked Witch of the West, and events play out similarly to the original book.

There are some key differences, notably that as soon as he arrives in the Magic Land, Totoshka can speak. Although Baum established quite late in the Royal Histories that Toto always had that power but chose not to use it, Totoshka is a talking animal throughout. There are some additions to events: Ellie is kidnapped by an ogre and has to be rescued by the Lumberjack and the Scarecrow; she is also aware of Bastinda's severe allergy to water long before she arrives in her castle. The replacement of kalidahs with sabre-toothed tigers, and Hammer-Heads with Leapers demonstrate Volkov's willingness to depart from the original text.

Volkov wrote various other historical novels following the Second World War, but was encouraged to return to writing about the Magic Land. He revised the text for *The Wizard of the Emerald City* in 1959, when he was aged 68, and started to write further stories. These moved progressively further away from Baum's vision of Oz, although Volkov quite cheerfully appropriated elements that fitted his stories.

Urfin Jus and his Wooden Soldiers appeared in 1963, and featured a powder of life that is used to animate an army of wooden soldiers. They capture the Emerald City, and Kaggi-Karr the crow is sent to Kansas to collect Ellie. She, Totoshka, and her uncle Charlie Black (a one-legged sailor who is highly reminiscent of Cap'n Bill from the later Oz tales) return to the Magic Land and free their friends.

The Seven Underground Kings, published a year later, follows the adventures of Ruf Bilan, who betrayed the Emerald City to Urfin Jus in the previous book. He ends up in the Underground Land ruled by seven kings, six of whom are kept asleep by the Soporific Water at any one time. Ellie, her cousin Alfred, and Totoshka arrive there via a cavern in Iowa, and help to set the situation right.

Four years elapsed before *The Fiery God Of The Marrans* was published, although it is set ten years after *Urfin Jus and his Wooden Soldiers.* The exiled Jus presents himself as a god to the ignorant Leapers. He tries to conquer the Emerald Island (the City now has a canal around it) but is defeated by Ellie's younger sister Annie and her friend Tim, who arrive in the Magic Land on solar-powered mules.

The Yellow Fog arrived in 1970 and filled in some of the backstory for the Magic Land, as wicked giantess-witch Arachna awakes from an eon-long sleep and tries to conquer the land. Annie, Tim, Charlie Black, and Annie's dog Artoshka create an iron giant, Tilly-Willy, to come to the rescue.

Volkov's final book was written in 1975, two years before his death, but only published in 1982. *The Mystery of the Deserted Castle* sees an alien race visit Earth and decide to start conquering the Magic Land. The people from the Outer World – Annie, Tim and Alfred – end up using the Soporific Water to put the alien slave masters to sleep, and allow their slaves to take emeralds from the Magic Land back to their own planet, which will help them free their comrades.

The tales from the Magic Land gained large audiences in Communist countries, and following Volkov's death, there was still an appetite for more stories. Russian writer Sergei Sukhinov took up the mantle of alternate Royal Historian with twenty further adventures.

Goodwin the Great and Terrible, published in 2001 after most of Sukhinov's other stories, comes first chronologically, and tells the story of *The Wizard of the Emerald City* from Goodwin (the Wizard)'s point of view. A failed actor from Kansas is blown to the Magic Land by balloon, and sees an Emerald City from the top of a magic mountain. When he discovers it doesn't exist – yet – he sets out to create it with the help of the locals, while posing as a wizard. After a disastrous campaign against Bastinda, he retreats to his city – until the arrival of Ellie and her friends.

Sukhinov's other books divide into two groups: the 'Emerald City' series, and 'Tales from the Emerald City' series. These maintain a separate continuity, but only treat Volkov's original book as having happened. Sukhinov provides a very different origin for the Magic Land: it was created by Atlantean wizard Torn who was in conflict with an evil warlock named Pakir. The ten stories in the 'Emerald City' series (1997–2004) chart Pakir's attempts to conquer the Magic Land, culminating in a massive battle between good and evil, which fans of the series have compared favourably with Tolkien's *The Lord of the Rings*. Ellie returns, as do most of the key figures from Volkov's first book.

'Tales from the Emerald City' (all first published in 2000) filled in some of the gaps from the Emerald City stories, charting the youth and early exploits of the lead characters. Each was self-contained, but often presented a new viewpoint on events in those books.

Other Russian authors also added to Volkov's saga. Leonid Vladimirsky, who illustrated Volkov's books and contributed to the plotting, penned *Buratino in the Emerald City* in 1996; Buratino was a Russian version of Pinocchio and this effectively is 'Pinocchio in Oz', as James Goodwin helps Buratino's owner find a powder of life which will restore the puppet. Yuri Kuznetsov has written five further sequels to Volkov's stories, which get increasingly into the realms of parallel universes, wormholes and time travel. Nikolai Bachnow also contributed eight stories between 1996 and 2002.

All of Volkov's novels were translated into English by Peter L. Blystone, and published by Red Branch Press between 1991 and 2007. He has recently begun work on translating and publishing Sukhinov's tales.

A stop-motion animated version of *Voshebnik Izrumrudnogo Goroda* (*The Wizard of the Emerald City*) was produced in 1974, directed by Valentin Popov and L. Smironov. The ten twenty-minute episodes were also shown as a (long) TV movie. The opening song can be viewed on YouTube and shows the series' minimal budget. Although the series went by the title of Volkov's original book, it actually adapted the first three novels in the sequence.

The Malaya Bromaya Theatre in Moscow put on a staging of the first book in 1976; an Anglicized version was brought to the UK as *The Scarecrow, the Lion, the Tinman and Me*. A ballet interpretation was mounted by the State Academic Children's Musical Theatre in St Petersburg in 1996.

The first story was also adapted for the cinema in 1994 with a screenplay by Vadim Korostelyev, directed by Pavel Arsenov; this version was nominated in the Nika Awards given by the Russian Academy of Cinema Arts and Sciences for Best Costume Designer and Best Production Designers.

March Laumer reworked some details of Volkov's stories into his own Oz fiction, much of which is pretty much compatible with the Famous Forty – bearing in mind the inconsistencies that are present in those books themselves, it's hard to call something 'wrong' because it clashes with some details. However, his 1978 book *Green Dolphin of Oz* is usually regarded as a different take on the realm (or, as literary critic Frank Kelleter described it, a 'deliberately non-canonical and pornographic' Oz tale).

Laumer wrote and self-published a great many Oz stories, but *Green Dolphin* has been accused of incorporating elements of both bestiality and paedophilia; Laumer called it a 'fairy tale for adults'. The general story is about the hunt for a green dolphin through various times and places, one of which is Oz, and there's a character that turns out to be L. Frank Baum himself. The Ozites resemble their counterparts in the Royal Histories, but seem to be mentally more mature.

The book is, perhaps, of most interest because it incorporates a fragment of a story that some believe was penned by Baum himself, the start of a tale that has subsequently been lost. Otherwise, it's pretty disposable.

That can perhaps equally be said of *The Number of the Beast*, published in 1980. It was written by Robert Heinlein, the first of a number of high-profile science fiction and fantasy writers to incorporate Oz into their texts. It is by no means Heinlein's most highly regarded book ('an embarrassment . . . unremittingly awful', 'the first SF novel you should only read while wearing latex gloves and a condom' is a representative sample of reviews), with jejune writing, and a sophomoric obsession with sex and, particularly, nipples.

The Number of the Beast follows a group of characters as they visit different dimensions (there are six to the sixth power to the sixth power of them – hence the title) in their ship the *Gay Deceiver*. They find themselves on Mars, overflying Lilliput, and in Oz for a short time. Many of Baum's creations make cameo appearances in the Emerald City, and Tik-Tok has a productive chat with the computer on board the *Gay Deceiver*. Taken on its own the Oz section is consciously not controversial – the characters themselves note that they can only use mild swear words, and not make sexual references while they are there – and there's a point made about the lack of births and deaths in Oz.

Two years later, Philip José Farmer wrote *A Barnstormer in Oz*, subtitled 'A Rationalization and Extrapolation of the Split-Level Continuum' which may well have worried Oz fans that their favourite land was about to be subjected to further torments after Heinlein's book. Farmer's story is a sequel to L. Frank Baum's original Oz story set in 1923, nearly a quarter of a century after the events of *The Wonderful Wizard of Oz*. According to Farmer, the events of the first book really happened, but the subsequent tales were created by Baum to feed public interest.

Like Maguire in the *Wicked* novels, Farmer tries to explain a lot of the seemingly contradictory elements of Oz, which effectively is in a parallel universe to the world of his hero Hank Stover, Dorothy Gale's son. A mysterious green cloud transports former air ace Stover to Oz, where he has to help Glinda against a new Red Witch, Erakna the Uneatable, as well as the incursions of the US Army and the corrupt President Warren G. Harding, who have created the cloud as a gateway between the dimensions.

A Barnstormer in Oz fits with Farmer's habit of reworking other authors' creations – he notably 'reinvented' both Tarzan and pulp hero Doc Savage – and tried to fit their worlds into some form of consistent pattern. Here he explains Oz's creation, and its languages, and how birth, death and magic work within the land. For some fans, delving this deep beneath the surface can spoil the magic; for others, Farmer provided an intriguing new look at Baum's creation.

L. Frank Baum's son, Frank Joslyn Baum, tried his hand at penning an Oz tale, which was quickly taken out of print as it contravened Reilly & Lee's copyright. Frank's grandson, Roger Stanton Baum, has had rather more luck with his Oz tales. In common with Philip José Farmer, the younger Baum has used only the original story as the basis for his series of stories, which are aimed at younger readers. 'I'm always using the first book as my launching point,' he told the *Hollywood Reporter* in March 2013. 'Some of the contradictions – Great-granddad never meant for his books to be a series, so he would write one and then another, and there would be a contradiction from the first one to the fourth one. So I just use the first book.'

In an interview in the *Journal Newspapers of South Illinois* in 1992, which he posts on his website, Baum notes, that 'Maintaining the quality of the Oz books is my main concern. I am not trying to follow in Great-granddad's footsteps – they're pretty big. I just want to carry on the love of Oz and add to the legend.' He started writing stories in the 1980s, and was encouraged to pen an Oz tale, *Dorothy of Oz*, which was published by William Morrow & Co. This has been followed by fifteen further tales, which endeavour to maintain the feel of the original stories.

Baum's 1995 story *Lion of Oz and the Badge of Courage* – which suggested that the Lion and the Wizard knew each other prior to the events of *The Wonderful Wizard of Oz* – was turned into the animated movie *Lion of Oz* in 2000, with the voices of Jason Priestley, Jane Horrocks, Tim Curry and Dom DeLuise. *Dorothy of Oz* has also been prepared for the big screen. With an all-star vocal cast including Kelsey Grammer, Dan Aykroyd and Jim Belushi as the Tin Man, Scarecrow and Cowardly Lion respectively, Lea Michele as Dorothy, and Patrick Stewart as new character Tugg, it was aiming at a 9 May 2014 release, now retitled *Legends of Oz: Dorothy's Return*. IDW Comics issued a tie-in comic rather prematurely in spring 2013, which set the scene for the story.

In 1990, L. Sprague de Camp provided an interesting take on Oz in his novella, *Sir Harold and the Gnome King* which was first printed in the 1990 World Fantasy Convention Program Book. It forms part of the Harold Shea series of parallel world stories which de Camp wrote with Fletcher Pratt, and later Christopher Stasheff.

Shea is trying to rescue his colleague Walter Bayard,

and needs the Magic Belt of the Gnome King, which is now in the possession of Ozma of Oz (de Camp used the Thompson spelling of Gnome, rather than Baum's original 'Nome'). Shea travels to Oz but finds it's changed a great deal: Dorothy and Ozma are no longer magically kept young. Each has married and now has children, and Shea becomes embroiled in an attempt to rescue Ozma's son, Prince Oznev, who is being held by Kaliko, the Gnome King. Shea gains help from the original Gnome King, Ruggedo, and Ozma brings Walter to Oz. This provides de Camp with the opportunity to psychoanalyse Ruggedo, one of Baum's more contradictory characters.

Geoff Ryman's *Was*, first published in 1992, has been hailed as one of the greatest pieces of gay and lesbian writing, as well as being a finalist in the 1993 World Fantasy Awards. It's a complex novel which combines the stories of three very different people: Jonathan, an actor in present-day Los Angeles dying of AIDS, who dreams of one day playing the Scarecrow in *The Wizard of Oz*; Frances Gumm, a young girl experiencing a difficult childhood, which gets no better when she changes her name to Judy Garland and becomes a star; and Dorothy Gael [*sic*], a young girl growing up in turn-of-the-twentieth-century Kansas. When she meets a substitute teacher named Frank (Baum), he tries (and fails) to help her escape from the terrible life she is experiencing, but then he writes a story about the sort of life she should have had.

How these three intertwine forms the core of the novel, which is not an Oz story in the traditional sense, but has much to say about reality and fantasy. Like many of the books in this section, it's not aimed at the readership that the real Baum wrote for, but for those who have grown up with *The Wizard of Oz* and wonder if there really is no place like home.

Was has been brought to the stage in two different

versions. Paul Edwards penned a version for Northwestern University in 1994, which he initially intended as a staged reading of various chapters. As he worked on it, he realized the potential for a small chamber-theatre piece, which was subsequently put on, directed by Edwards himself, in Chicago. Given that many authors complain about the liberties that are taken with their text in adaptations for other media, Ryman found that this version was too faithful to his story. In a 2001 interview with the British Science Fiction Association, he explained that it 'was very educational because it was terrible' – not because of the acting, but because they tried to jam four hundred pages of text into two hours on stage. He wouldn't allow further productions, despite the *Chicago Reader* calling Edwards' interpretation 'a jewel on the stage as on the page, a beautifully balanced work of brain, courage, and heart'.

A musical version, with a book by Barry Kleinbort and score by Joseph Thalken, was workshopped at the Lincoln Center Theater in New York, and subsequently mounted at the Human Race Theatre Company in Dayton, Ohio; and then by Northwestern University's American Music Theatre Project in 2005. This eliminated the Judy Garland plotline from the book entirely. Kleinbort and Thalken had both been taken with the book, and wrote twenty minutes of material that they performed for Ryman in 1998. He gave them permission to proceed, and the show received various awards for excellence in music theatre.

The master of horror, Stephen King, is adept at creating many different parallel worlds within his fiction, with his 'Dark Tower' series bringing them all together to create a moderately coherent whole. The fourth book in that saga, 1997's *Wizard and Glass*, sees the gunslinger Roland Deschain and his ka-tet (the group travelling with him) find a set of ruby shoes waiting for them before they enter an Emerald City.

As with Heinlein's *The Number of the Beast*, this is just one of a number of places that the central characters visit which has resonances with fiction in 'our' world, although King parallels the structure of both the Baum book and the MGM musical in his tale. There's an important reveal as well when the ka-tet look 'behind the curtain', and find a Wizard who is much worse than the humbug charlatan of Baum's tale. To say more could spoil things too much for the reader, but fans of the Oz books seeking more adult fantasy are likely to enjoy the depth of King's world-building in the 'Dark Tower' series.

The centenary of publication of *The Wonderful Wizard of Oz* in 2000 saw a number of new stories written which were designed to correlate with the Famous Forty. Some authors saw this as an opportunity to revitalize the Oz saga for the twenty-first century, notably David Hardenbrook, whose *The Unknown Witches of Oz* tried to find a way to attract 'adults and teens who love Harry Potter and other modern fantasy worlds'. Hardenbrook produced 'The Oz 2.0 Mission Statement: A Fairyland for the 21st Century', which suggested that Oz's popularity would be improved by removing 'the mundane and monotonous' repetition of plots, bringing the stories up to date (so including computer programming and fundamental physics), and introducing science fiction and sex to the stories.

Hardenbrook described his own stories as 'an alternate Ozziverse in which the beautiful Queen Ozma is courted by a lovable computer geek from Los Angeles. Also in the cast of non-standard characters are Jellia Jamb the sassy Emerald City palace maid with a magic feather duster, Gyma a teacher of high sorcery, and a lot of dinosaurs.' His Oz 2.0 movement embraced Charles Phipps' stories about Milo Starling, 'a mild-mannered, magic umbrella-bearing Kentucky minister who finds himself living in Oz and courting its lovely ruler, Ozma'; and 'The Changing Beasts of Oz' by Mike Conway, which never appeared under that title, although a Michael J.M. Conway did pen a pornographic Oz story entitled *Passion in Oz* around this time.

The Emerald Burrito of Oz certainly was a different look at Oz. John Skipp and Marc Levinthal's 2000 novel posited that travel between our world and Oz had been possible for some time, although there were no guarantees that it would be safe. This is the cue for a story that's set in an Oz that is initially barely recognizable from the Baum tales, but which, once you get used to the narrative style of the two protagonists, is an affectionate homage, told in a very different way. The book was initially published by Babbage Press but was then picked up by cult specialists Eraserhead who emphasize the 'zombie Munchkins, turd-flinging Flatheads, evil corporate conspiracies, [and] delicious Mexican food' to be found within.

Susan Casper's novella *Up the Rainbow* was first published in *Asimov's Science Fiction Magazine* in December 1994, and then printed by Fictionwise in 2001. It's an intriguing tale about Gale Osterman who goes to Oz after the death of her grandmother, Dorothy Gale. Everyone has assumed Dorothy inspired rather than lived the stories Baum told but Gale realizes that they were true. When she travels around Munchkinland, she discovers that the people aren't happy, and they want her to talk to Ozma for them. Gale organizes passive resistance and a protest movement (with signs like 'Ban the Baum' and 'Magic is a Rite') that eventually bring Ozma to the table for discussions. A hard to find story, Casper's tale questions some of the assumptions about Oz while still maintaining the air of magic about it.

Amid the plethora of updates of the Oz saga, the L. Frank Baum Family Trust chose Sherwood Smith to produce official continuations of the books. Although these have the estate's imprimatur, and she is described as the new Royal Historian of Oz, the delays in publication, caused by the death of Byron Preiss who commissioned them, mean that there has not been the continuity of twenty-first-century Oz adventures that had been hoped for.

So far, two stories have appeared: *The Emerald Wand of Oz* and *Trouble Under Oz*. A third, *Sky Pirates of Oz*, was apparently revised and completed for publication in spring 2013. Smith neatly incorporates elements of Alexander Volkov's saga – her updated Witch of the West, the niece of the original, is called Bastinda – as she brings Dorothy Gale's grand-nieces, Em and Dori, back to Oz to help Ozma. Numerous characters from the original series reappear, counterpointed with the very modern Em and Dori.

What if Oz wasn't a dream? That's the question posed on the cover of David Anthony's trilogy of novels that began in 2004 with *In Search of Dorothy*. Based, he claimed, on vivid dreams that he had experienced for many years, the first volume was self-published, and then picked up by Frederick Fell publishing in 2006. They also printed *The Witch's Revenge* the following year, and *Dorothy and the Wizard's Wish* in 2010. The books were well received by their young target audience.

Anthony saw them as linked to the MGM musical, which he admitted he had watched around 5,000 times. 'The whole idea was to continue the movie,' he said in a 2007 interview. 'Dorothy clicks her heels together and – whoosh – it was all just a dream. But what if it wasn't? What would happen next?' However, Anthony had to respect the copyright holders so Dorothy's shoes are still silver, rather than ruby.

A very different audience was envisaged for Christopher Golden and James A. Moore's version of the story, *Bloodstained Oz*, a novella that also came out in 2006. The two veteran horror novelists were attending an event in New York and joking about various ideas, Golden recalled in an interview for this book. 'Somehow we came up with this idea that somebody should do Oz with vampires – they just come and eat everybody. We were just kidding, but then looked at each other, and went, "Oh we've got to do that." It started as a joke but we took it very seriously. I think the finished product is very grim, one of the darkest things I've ever done.'

Set in Hawley, Kansas, part of the Dustbowl, in 1933, the story revolves around three parties: nine-year-old Gayle Franklin and her parents; Elisa, Stefan and her baby son Jeremiah; and a labour party at Guilford Prison. There's a Scarecrow, a Lion and a Tin Man, but this story is quite definitely not the world that Baum (or the makers of the MGM movie) envisaged. For a change, the creatures come to Earth, rather than the other way around . . .

The creators see *Bloodstained* Oz as the start of a trilogy; after various delays, the sequel, *Bloodstained Wonderland*, is finally near completion, with some of the characters from *Oz* returning for that rewrite of Lewis Carroll's fantasy. This is very definitely a story for mature readers, and those who enjoy horror fiction, but it grips from the start, and unlike some new versions of the Oz tales, doesn't outstay its welcome.

2006 was a busy year for anyone wanting a complete set of Oz spin-off books. Like David Anthony, Jon M. Weber was inspired to tell more stories about Oz after enjoying the MGM musical, but his mind went in the opposite direction – what was Oz like before Dorothy arrived? *Beginnings: A New Novel Set in Oz* was the result.

Starting with a birth and a wedding, it's an odd novel: the chapter heads refer to elements we know well (such as the Yellow Brick Road), but render the familiar phrase in Greek lettering – but sometimes using letters that look like the Roman equivalents, such as capital Psi for Y, despite the sounds being wrong – with a more pretentious 'translation' given below. Dorothy's parents are still alive – she is only staying with Uncle Henry and Aunt Em. Oz historian Jared Davis noted that *'Beginnings* sorely lacks character development or well-defined characters'; the self-published book is really one for completists only.

Father and daughter Leo Moser and Carol Nelson's first story, *Halloween in Oz*, which arrived in 2007, received a mixed reception. This is a reworking of *The Marvelous Land of Oz*, although, unlike Baum's second Oz story, it features Dorothy's return, and new origins and names for some of Baum's characters, including Jack Pumpkinhead. Tip becomes Mitt (who also resembles a boy Dorothy knew in Kansas); Jack Pumkpinhead is Punk N. Head; Mombi is Salmanta; Jinjur becomes Ginger (a 'ravishing redhead'); the Sawhorse is Stubs; and Ozma is Esmera. The book was revised and reprinted in 2012 on Smashwords as *The Mysterious Tintype of Oz*, with a follow-up, *Balloon to Oz: Pinhead to Potentate* promised – this will tell the story of '17-year-old Pat McLarkey who sailed off to Oz under unusual circumstances from a circus in Omaha' and became known as the Wizard.

Moser and Nelson also explained the reasoning behind their update on their website, HalloweeninOz.com. The 'Hidden Chronicles of Oz' series 'attempts to retain the spirit of Baum's imagination and the fantasy land revealed in that first Oz book'. They posited that there is 'a mysterious and magic-ridden world called Erdavon of which Oz is a part. In the terms used in fantasy and sci-fi today, Erdavon might be called an "alternative Earth" set in an "alternative dimension", where even the course of time is somewhat askew.' They decided to spell Dorothy's surname 'Gayle' and, consciously following the style of J.K. Rowling's *Harry Potter* series, incorporate a mystery

about Dorothy's parents, and why she is with her uncle
and aunt in Kansas, into the series. Each book has a 'fram-
ing sequence' set in 1973 featuring Dorothy Gayle and her
great-grandson Jeremy; she realizes that he has a magical
link to Oz, as she did, so tells him the 'true' stories of her
time there. While a younger audience has enjoyed these,
older Oz fans have tended to be more critical.

Paul Miles Schneider's reimaginations were better received.
Silver Shoes gained a highly complimentary review from
Marcus Mébès in the *Baum Bugle* ('seldom do I have the
pleasure of reading such a skilfully crafted tale') and gar-
nered a 2010 Kansas Notable Book Award. The sequel,
Powder of Life, was equally praised: 'there are a number
of chapters that are basically a long love letter to the Oz
books,' Jared Davis wrote in his review.

Schneider had been an Oz fan for many years – he was
pen pals with Margaret Hamilton when in the second
grade – and after viewing a genuine pair of ruby slippers
worn by Judy Garland in the movie, he started wonder-
ing what happened to the slippers in the story when
Dorothy returned from Oz. With the Baum books in the
public domain, he decided to use those as the basis for his
adventure, which features Baum himself as a character in a
story about a modern boy, Donald Gardner, who finds one
of the silver slippers that Dorothy brought back. Baum's
story was far from fiction, as Donald finds out, and there
was a government conspiracy to cover it up.

As Schneider himself admits, this feels as if elements
from the TV series *The X-Files* and Dan Brown's *The Da
Vinci Code* have been added into *The Wizard of Oz*, but
the story is well told. Schneider has recently revised the
two books and released them as a single volume.

*The Undead World of Oz: L. Frank Baum's The Wonder-
ful Wizard of Oz Complete with Zombies and Monsters*

also arrived in 2009, as part of the trend for incorporating horror tropes into classic pieces of fiction (known as 'mash-ups'). In these, the original text was retained for the most part, although new portions were added to provide some horror content. The highest-profile versions of these were *Pride and Prejudice and Zombies* and its spin-offs.

For his contribution to the genre, Ryan C. Thomas used Baum's first Oz novel and pasted in pieces of extra text, often with jarring effect. When Dorothy arrives in Oz, the Munchkins greet her, explaining that the Wicked Witch of the East set a plague on them, which revives the dead. Shortly after Glinda's arrival, the zombie Munchkins attack – seeking 'small braaaiiins' – at which the Witch says, 'Let me handle this' and eliminates the zombies. By the time Dorothy and her friends reach the Emerald City, they have had numerous gory encounters, leading to Dorothy behaving in a considerably less restrained manner than she does in Baum's original.

The Undead World of Oz allowed for the possibility of a sequel; so far, this has yet to appear. Like its fellows, this sort of mash-up is an acquired taste; *Bloodstained Oz* handled the idea of combining the two genres together considerably better.

Another horror-filled take on Oz comes in the unlikely form of a tale that was printed to accompany Todd McFarlane's *Twisted Land of Oz* figurines. Each of the grotesque figures (a bondaged Dorothy being branded by mannequins, or a Lion whose bones can be seen through the savage wounds) was boxed with a chapter of the story, which has been compiled and can be read online. Twisted is the appropriate adjective for the storyline ('Dorothy had never felt a pain so intense, so liberating, so sensual'), which at one stage was considered as the basis for a *Dark Oz* movie.

*   *   *

'Oz is not one singular vision, it's a wide array of experiences seen through a specific lens,' wrote Michael M. Jones in the preface to his review of *Oz Reimagined: New Stories from the Emerald City and Beyond*. This collection of Oz short stories was published in spring 2013, edited by John Joseph Adams and Douglas Cohen with a foreword by *Wicked*'s Gregory Maguire. It covered the gamut of differing versions of Oz and was published to coincide with the release of Disney's prequel movie, *Oz the Great and Powerful*.

As with all the books discussed in this chapter, not all of the short stories will be to everyone's taste. Some delve beneath the surface of Oz – Theodora Goss's 'Lost Girls of Oz'; Seanan McGuire's 'Emeralds to Emeralds, Dust to Dust'; Dale Bailey's bleak 'City So Bright'; or Jeffrey Ford's 'A Meeting In Oz' – while others reinvent it completely: Ken Liu's 'The Veiled Shanghai' is set in 1919 Shanghai; Rachel Swirsky's 'Beyond the Naked Eye' updates it as a reality show. There are science-fiction trappings to Tad Williams's 'The Boy Detective of Oz: An Otherland Story' (picking up on elements from his Otherland stories which include a virtual version of Oz), and David Farland's 'Dead Blue'. Some could fit with the saga as written: 'The Great Zeppelin Heist' is yet another look at the Wizard's adventures before the first Baum Story, and Jonathan Maberry eschews his usual zombie and action stories to introduce 'The Cobbler of Oz'.

What *Oz Reimagined* proves beyond doubt is that the characters and situations created by L. Frank Baum continue to inspire writers, who will use the power of their words to bring readers into Oz.

2

OZ REIMAGINED ON SCREEN

Although it could be argued that some of the early versions of *The Wizard of Oz* deviated so far from L. Frank Baum's original stories that they could fairly be described as 'reimaginings', lip service was paid in these to the format of the classic book – even if, as in the Larry Semon 1925 film, nearly everything that made *The Wizard of Oz* work for a literary audience was removed from the end product.

The Wizard of Mars, released in 1965 and also known as *Horrors of the Red Planet* or *Alien Massacre*, was the first of many movies either to extrapolate from Baum's fantasy world, or to take some of its characters and situations and dump them into a new format. Some hid their debt to Baum and only a closer examination of their plotlines or themes reveal their links; others were upfront about it.

Stage magician David L. Hewitt was the writer, director, producer and co-creator of the story (with Armando Busick) for this mid-1960s offering, which is set a decade in its future. *Mars Probe I* crashes on the Red Planet, and the four crew – Dorothy, Steve, Charlie and Doc – follow a golden road to an alien city. There they meet the disembodied head of a Wizard, played by John Carradine, who explains that the Martians have frozen time, but now need someone with a corporeal body to fix their time controller.

The film was promoted as 'the fantastic space-age shock show', projected in 'ultra-depth', and its poster dared, double-dared, and triple-dared audiences to experience its thrills. Contrary to the claim on some video releases, it didn't star Lon Chaney Jnr – although he would certainly have enlivened what is mostly a very dull movie!

One of Sean Connery's most infamous screen appearances was in *Zardoz*, another science-fiction reworking of *The Wizard of Oz*. Zardoz is a god-like gigantic flying stone head on the post-apocalyptic Earth of 2293 AD. Its teachings are simple: 'The gun is good. The penis is evil. The penis shoots seeds, and makes new life to poison the Earth with a plague of men, as once it was, but the gun shoots death, and purifies the Earth of the filth of brutals. Go forth . . . and kill!' Connery's character, an Exterminator (one of those who worship Zardoz) called Zed, hides inside the head and finds the 300-year-old Arthur Frayn. Zed kills Frayn and we later learn that Frayn had earlier taught him to read, giving him a copy of Baum's book. Zardoz derives from the name the **Wiz**ard of **Oz**. Zed wanted to see 'behind the curtain' and in the end learns the truth about his world.

The film was promoted with the tagline 'Beyond 1984. Beyond 2001. Beyond Love. Beyond Death.' With a time-lapsed ending showing Connery and co-star Charlotte Rampling aging to death, it proved to be beyond most of the audiences as well, and is probably best known now for the highly unusual costume that Connery sports during the film. Describing it as a red leather posing pouch with a few additions hardly does it justice.

* * *

A rather more down to earth – although equally adult – version was produced in Australia in 1976, written and directed by Chris Lofven. *Oz* (known as *20th Century Oz* for its US release) updates the story effectively, setting it in contemporary Australia, where small-town girl Dorothy wants to find something more exciting. She wakes up in an odd place, where she discovers that there's been a motor accident in which the town bully has been killed, and everyone assumes Dorothy was driving. She is given a pair of red-sequinned platform shoes by Glynn, an effeminate man in the Good Fairy clothing store, and heads off to see rock star the Wizard giving his last concert. With the help of dumb surfer Blondie, surly (and heartless) mechanic Greaseball, and outwardly tough biker Killer, she manages to evade the attentions of the bully's brother.

The film includes a strong rock soundtrack, but the combination of modernization, adult language and violence (Dorothy evades the trucker at one point by kicking him in the genitals with the 'ruby slippers') meant it didn't find an audience. However, as a rock-and-roll version of the story, it perhaps works better than the Motown-inspired *The Wiz* which followed it into cinemas two years later.

Under the Rainbow was a comedy vehicle for Chevy Chase and Carrie Fisher which also failed to ignite the box office. It was set in 1938 and includes the supposedly hilarious antics of the actors who played the Munchkins during the filming of the MGM musical of *The Wizard of Oz*. At the time *Under the Rainbow* was made in 1981, the legends of misbehaviour were more commonplace than they are now – many of the memoirs detailing what really happened had yet to be written – and this movie dramatizes them. There's a spy plot involving one of the small people, Adolf Hitler and the Japanese secret service, with Chase playing a bodyguard who is trying to prevent American secrets from being handed over.

Even setting aside the amount this film plays fast and loose with history, its biggest failing is that it simply isn't funny. Ruth Duccini, one of the original Munchkins, admitted later she appeared in *Under the Rainbow* because 'they paid us good money' but summed up the movie simply: 'They were trying to make fun of *The Wizard of Oz*, but they didn't succeed.'

A Brazilian film *Os Trapalhões E O Magico De Oroz* ('The Tramps and the Wizard of Oz') from 1984 was one of a series of slapstick films starring Dedé Santana, Zacarias, Mussum and Renato Aragão, stars of a successful TV show that ran for sixteen years from 1977. The ninety-three-minute film (which can be seen on YouTube) follows Didi (Aragão) as he tries desperately to look for water – Brazil was genuinely suffering from a drought at this time. His search is helped by the other Trapalhões, playing a 'Man of Can', 'Clownbrush', and Sheriff Lion respectively. Although the story deviates quite considerably from the beats of Baum's tale, the core message – that the Trapalhões already have the brains, heart and courage that they believe they lack – is maintained. Slapstick, as ever, requires no translation, although the intricacies of the villainous Ferreira's plans may be lost to an audience who don't speak Portuguese.

References to *The Wizard of Oz* are rife in David Lynch's 1990 thriller *Wild at Heart*, starring Nicolas Cage and Laura Dern, based on Barry Gifford's novel. These are made clear in the short behind-the-scenes documentary *Love, Death, Elvis & Oz: The Making of Wild at Heart* released in 2004. Dern's Lula (wearing ruby slippers) and Cage's Sailor are on a road trip pursued by Diane Ladd's 'Wicked Witch of the West', and towards the end of the film Glinda the Good Fairy makes an appearance. *Wild at Heart* was often described as Lynch's 'psychotic take' on *The Wizard of Oz*; Pete Travers summed it up in *Rolling*

Stone magazine: 'Imagine The Wizard Of Oz with an oversexed witch, gun-toting Munchkins and love ballads from Elvis Presley, and you'll get some idea of this erotic hellzapoppin' from writer-director David Lynch.'

Frequently violent, *Wild at Heart* is a very different interpretation of the themes, owing more to the 1939 film than it does to Baum's innocent adventure.

A year later came another darkened vision of Oz, in Mark Manos' *Liquid Dreams*, starring Candice Daly as Eve, a Kansas woman who is searching for the killer of her sister Tina in a sleazy town of the near future. She poses as 'Dorothy' and works firstly as a 'taxi dancer' (a hostess in a strip club who will dance with any man for money) wearing red stilettos, then as a stripper. Finally she becomes a porn actress for a mysterious film production company, Neurovid, as she seeks the truth – including making a scene where she's dressed as Judy Garland in the film, and is seduced by a scarecrow for a porn version of the film. It turns out that drugs are being siphoned out of sexually excited women's brains at the point of death. Unlike *Wild at Heart*, though, this does not have pretensions to art.

Two movies tried to combine *The Wizard of Oz* with the surprise hit from 1999, *The Blair Witch Project*, one of the first – and certainly the best – of the crop of 'found footage' movies from that period. The conceit is that the ease of use of video cameras has allowed someone to record unlikely (and usually horrific) events as they happen; after they disappear, the camera and the footage is found.

Michael Rotman's nine-minute-long *The Oz Witch Project* is a comedy parody of the two movies, promoted with a tagline borrowed from Ridley Scott's *Alien*: 'In the woods no one can hear you sing.' 'In October of 1994, four friends disappeared in the woods near Emerald City while shooting a documentary called "The Oz Witch Project". A year later their footage was found.' Dorothy and her friends (resembling their MGM counterparts) set off to explore the legend of the Wicked Witch of the West. But they find themselves under attack.

The Oz Witch Project neatly spears both the 1999 horror movie and the 1939 MGM musical – at one point the chirpy Dorothy is told in no uncertain terms to stop singing 'Over the Rainbow'. Available on YouTube, it's an enjoyable diversion.

The Wicked Witch Project, which was released at Halloween 1999, runs for nearly half an hour in its special-edition extended cut. This suggests that Dorothy and her friends are trying to make a documentary about the Wicked Witch and run into some unexpected trouble.

This was a larger-scale spoof than *The Oz Witch Project*. An accompanying website (http://www.darbro creative.com/wickedwitchproject/) parodies the very serious *Blair Witch* tie-in site, with spoof biographies for all the 'characters', mocked-up photos such as the Scarecrow testing flame-retardant chemicals, a new timeline for Oz ('November 1940–May 1941: Seven Munchkin children are abducted from the town. Fortunately no one cares, as they were all spoiled little bastards anyway') and much more (Toto's Journal is well worth a read). The film lives up to the humour of the site.

Twenty-first-century reimaginings of *The Wizard of Oz* have been mainly created for the small screen, even if some of them (such as *Dorothy and the Witches in Oz*) have received theatrical presentations. Barring *Oz the Great and Powerful*, discussed earlier, only one notable short film has appeared: *Apocalypse Oz*, released in 2006. This combined *The Wizard of Oz* with Francis Ford Coppola's Vietnam War epic *Apocalypse Now* (itself a reworking of Joseph Conrad's novel *Heart of Darkness*).

Marketed with the tagline 'Terminate the Wizard', *Apocalypse Oz* follows Dorothy, an angst-ridden Asian girl who sets out to hunt down an insane renegade psychotic military leader, code-named the Wizard. The half-hour film throws in all the expected references from both films (in a way that makes David Lynch's *Wild at Heart* seem ponderous) and only uses dialogue that featured in one or other movie – often combining the two to darkly humorous effect.

Creator Ewan Telford won an Audience Award from the Filmstock International Film Festival for *Apocalypse Oz*, which played at numerous film festivals. Unfortunately, the full-length version that was being planned has yet to materialize.

3

SMALL-SCREEN ODYSSEYS

It's sometimes difficult to assess when a film or TV show moves so far from the source material that it ceases to be an adaptation, and instead becomes a reimagining, or simply uses the original as an inspiration. You could argue that the 1960s *Wizard of Oz* cartoon series simply continued the work of some of the Royal Historians of Oz, bringing the saga kicking and screaming into post-Second World War culture. However, the majority of users of the Oz characters and situations reworked them to fit within their own shows' structures.

Three years before he went to see the Wiz, an instalment of *The Jackson Five* cartoon show, 'The Wizard of Soul', first broadcast on 20 November 1971, saw Michael Jackson's animated form whizzed by tornado out into the desert, along with his pet snake Rosey. He finds himself in the Land of Soul, and meets a Tin Man, a Straw Man and a Lion, all of whom used to be instrumentalists, but have been cursed by the Witch of the East so they can't play any more. Michael and his friends go to see the Wizard of Soul, who lifts the curse, but tells Michael that only the Witch is able to get him home. Michael is kidnapped, but the Witch unwisely also kidnaps his friends; they play a rock song which shatters the castle – and Michael wakes up. As the Witch flies overhead . . .

Six years later, on 23 January 1977, Marcia Brady – one of the oh-so-perfect Brady Bunch – imagined that she was Dorothy in the first episode of *The Brady Bunch Hour*. The other members of the extended family played the friends she meets in Oz – or rather at the Emerald City Carwash.

At Christmas that year, British early-evening magazine programme *Nationwide*, which usually combined news stories of local and national interest, ran a special edition featuring a pantomime version of *The Wizard of Oz*. Chancellor of the Exchequer Denis Healey, Liberal MP Cyril Smith and Post Office Union leader Tom Jackson starred. It prompted a cartoon by Mac in the *Daily Mail* showing Conservative Party leader Margaret Thatcher juggling (and dropping) a large number of items in front of the *Nationwide* producers and being told, 'Thank you, Maggie –we'll let you know.'

Yogi Bear came to Oz on 28 October 1978 in the 'Race Through Oz' episode of *Yogi's Space Race*, and faced off against the Wicked Witch of the Spaceways who was after one of the other racers' ruby-red slippers. A month later *The World's Greatest Superfriends* – DC heroes Superman, Aquaman and Wonder Woman – were sent to 'The Planet of Oz', and were turned into the Tin Woodman, Scarecrow and the Cowardly Lion in a fiendish plot by their old enemy, Mxylplk [*sic*]. Interestingly, there's no Dorothy in their reworking of the story.

In 1981 the mystery-seeking Great Dane Scooby Doo had a hallucinatory 'Trip to Ahz' as part of the *Richie Rich/ Scooby Doo Hour*. When he hits his head before watching

The Wizard of Oz on TV, Scooby and friends are transported by cyclone to Oz. Scooby becomes a Lion, Shaggy is the Scarecrow and, unfortunately, his nephew Scrappy Doo is with them and becomes a Tin Dog. A Yellow Brick Toad says he can take them to the Wizard, but vanishes when the Witch appears. Various elements of the story appear, including the poppy field and the winged monkeys.

February 1983 saw the kids from *Fame* finding themselves 'Not in Kansas Anymore' late in their second season. Highly rated by viewers, this episode, written by *Starsky & Hutch* creator William Blinn, featured Doris Schwartz hallucinating after being told she can't be in the school production. The teachers become the Witch and Wizard, comedian Danny is the Scarecrow, pianist Bruno is the Tin Man, and the funky Leroy is the Cowardly Lion. *Fame* was the prototype for the current TV hit *Glee*, and this episode featured arrangements of songs from the MGM movie. A neat recreation of the monochrome to colour switch was rather ruined by a voiceover explaining that 'The opening portion of tonight's episode will be brought to you in black and white'.

The following January, Ricardo Montalbán's Mr Roarke welcomed three friends to *Fantasy Island* who were looking for brains, courage and a heart. Unfortunately, they weren't heralded by Hervé Villechaize's cry of 'The plane! The plane!' in this episode – the former Bond actor's services were no longer required by this point in the series.

Episode 9,413 of very long-running soap opera *The Guiding Light*, first broadcast in May 1984, saw Lisa Brown's character Nola Reardon as Dorothy looking for the Wizard so he can help her name her unborn baby. Anyone with a burning desire to see how Oz and 1980s big hairstyles merge should look for photos from this episode!

The Muppets went to Oz twenty years earlier than most people remember – the TV movie from 2005 was preceded by an episode of the animated series *Muppet Babies*, which first aired in November 1985. When the babies fantasize about being characters in various books, Piggy becomes Pig-orothy, with Ralph-Ralph as her little dog, who find themselves in Oz. The Silly Sorcerer of the South (Scooter) sends them to find the Wizard – aka Bunsen Honeydew. Kermit is the Scarecrow, Fozzie is the Cowardly Comic, and Gonzo is the Tin Weirdo, looking for a job, courage, and a new nose. Bunsen and assistant Beaker create a 'New-Job-New-Courage-New-Nose-Going-Home' machine.

African-American comedy series *What's Happening Now!!* was centred around the grown-up adventures of the teen leads from the ABC 1970s series *What's Happening!!* (an idea mined in the UK with *The Likely Lads* and its sequel). Regular characters from the series were fitted into the plotlines as Reina King's character Caroline knocks her head and dreams she's no longer in the local diner.

The same year writer Morrie Rubinsky incorporated Oz into superhero show *Misfits of Science*, which featured *Friends* star Courtney Cox in one of her first major roles. The episode was a money-saving clip show, featuring excerpts from earlier episodes, as leader Billy Hayes tries to persuade alternate versions of his colleagues that they are really superheroes. The Oz connection comes when he wakes and realizes they were all there in his dreams.

Two years later, Vietnam War-based drama series *China Beach* used some of the themes in the episode 'Somewhere Over the Radio', written by Ann Donahue. Two of the characters head into the jungle but their helicopter crashes, and they encounter a platoon apparently run by Captain Osborne. They realize that Osborne's second in command is preventing his troops from finding out their captain is dead by using misdirection and an animal skull wearing the captain's head.

The short-lived Hanna-Barbera cartoon series *The Completely Mental Misadventures of Ed Grimley* also travelled to Oz in November 1988 – or rather, in this case, to Kansas in the aftermath of Dorothy's adventures in Oz. In 'Blowin' in the Wind', Grimley, voiced by Martin Short who created the character for Toronto's Second City troupe's show *SCTV*, tries to help Dorothy's aunt and uncle who are contending with Miss Gulch pulling the plug on their mortgage, and Dorothy hallucinating about yellow brick roads after being injured in a tornado.

September 1989 saw Lee Horsley as gunslinger Ethan Cord in the Western series *Paradise*. The two-part season opener 'A Gathering of Guns'/'Home Again' featured familiar Western figures such as Wyatt Earp, the Clantons and Pat Garrett, as well as a scarecrow, a tin man, and a balloon ride. The pieces come together when young journalist Frank admits he's been inspired to write a story of 'courage, heart and wisdom' which leads to a short montage ending in the cover of *The Wizard of Oz*.

ALF – an Alien Life Form from the planet Melmac, or (in the live-action version) a small actor running around in a not very convincing furry suit – was the star of a series of animated tales, *Alf Tales*, whose second season began at the same time. 'The Wizard of Oz' saw Gordon Shumway (ALF's real name) sent to Oz, and pointed towards Cubic Zirconium City. He recruits the usual friends – Tin, Straw and Fur – and finds the Wizard, who's an off-stage Bill Cosby. He tells them to get the Witch, who forces them to play a game of basketball during which she is killed. The Wizard promises to make Gordon a sitcom star.

Although that may not have been the funniest episode of *Alf Tales*, it was considerably better than the episode 'Surfside Over the Rainbow' in the Hasbro toy-based series *Maxie's World*, which aired at the end of October 1989. The thirty-minute episode may follow the beats of the MGM story more closely (albeit with the slow-witted Lifeguard, heartless Beach Bully and a Cowardly Shark in place of the usual trio), but it's one of those shows whose characters' vapid outlook was pilloried so well in the movie *Legally Blonde*.

A rather better account appeared in 1991 during the final season of the animated *Beetlejuice* series, loosely based on the 1988 Tim Burton movie about the 'ghostest with the mostest'. As with a lot of this series, the jokes in 'The Wizard of Ooze' were often aimed at the adults watching with their children – the Munchkins here come from the Land of Public Domain; to get home Dorothy stand-in Lydia has to say 'Ripple dissolve to scene 328!' 'The Wizard of Ooze' was also the title of an episode of *Earthworm Jim* from 1996 in which the eponymous vermicular hero becomes the Wizard of Ooze in his ongoing battle with Queen Slug-for-a-Butt.

The Wonderful Galaxy of Oz was a Japanese anime series that arrived in the US in 1992. The twenty-six-part adventure features eight-year-old Dorothy Gale who is sent by a storm to the far galaxy of Oz with her genetically enhanced dog Talk-Talk. She helps Dr Oz, Mosey, android Chopper, Lionman and Plantman battle against witch Gloomhilda to get the crystals of Wisdom, Love and Courage. TV Tokyo's series tried to capitalize on the fad for space-based cartoons, but this wasn't one of the more successful efforts.

From all accounts, the Fox series *Townsend Television*, featuring comedian Robert Townsend as himself, didn't show itself at its best in the 14 November 1993 edition that used *The Wizard of Oz* as its basis. Townsend finds himself in Oz, and helps a Scarecrow who has a brain but no job, a Lion looking for a weapon, and a Tin Woman who wants a date. The Wizard provides them with a job, a self-defence course and some self-esteem for the Tin Woman.

The Oz Kids was the next series to come from the Japanese market trying to use the Baum story as the basis for a show. This 1996 programme followed the adventures of the next generation of Ozites: Dorothy's children Neddy and Dot; the Scarecrow's clever-dick son Scarecrow junior;

the Wizard's computer-whiz son Frank; Tin Boy; Pumpkinhead junior; the Lion's cubs Bela and Boris; Glinda's daughter Andrea; Toto 2; and Nome Prince Otto, who can't decide which side he's on. Baum characters featured included Mombi, the Patchwork Girl and Santa Claus. *The Oz Kids* was an attempt to return to Baum's version of Oz, even if by a roundabout route, and avoid comparisons with the MGM movie. Writer Willard Carroll, who was a massive fan of Baum's work, even included stories from Baum's non-Oz tales in the series. (Carroll later wrote *I, Toto*, the supposed biography of Judy Garland's canine co-star from the MGM movie.) Twenty-six episodes were produced, which were later re-edited into nine compilation stories of varying lengths for issue on VHS.

Veteran scribe Tracy Tormé was the creator of parallel-world television series *Sliders*, and the writer of its trip 'Into the Mystic' in March 1996. The quartet of Sliders are desperate to escape from the world of magic and superstition in which they find themselves, and need help from a Sorcerer who can open gates to other worlds. When they find him, he seems to be a huge image, but they see through the disguise and are able to get back on their travels. With quotes from the movie, and the Sorcerer acting like the Wizard in his disguise, this pays homage without feeling beholden to the letter of the MGM movie.

Russian television combined elements of the original L. Frank Baum story with portions of Alexander Volkov's *Wizard of the Emerald City* to create a one-hour animated tale, divided into two episodes first broadcast on NTV in 1999. Yevgeni Markov's *Adventures in the Emerald City: Silver Shoes* is a weird hybrid that cherry-picks elements from both stories. The Witch of the East summons Dorothy from Russia to Oz, but the farmhouse lands on her. The adventures of Dorothy, Toto and their three friends combine menaces from both books before they reach the Emerald City, where they meet the Wizard. The Witch is dispatched per Baum and Glinda shows Dorothy how to use the silver shoes to get home.

A sequel followed a year later. *Adventures in the Emerald City: Princess Ozma* is a pretty close adaptation of *The Marvelous Land of Oz*. Like many others who have used this as the source text, Mikhail Bartenev and Andrei Usachev couldn't resist bringing Dorothy into the mix, but they give her little to do, since they retain Tip as the hero.

Weird Canadian science-fiction series *Lexx* wandered into Baum territory with their March 1999 episode 'Woz'. Very much an acquired taste, Lexx was a huge organic spaceship, shaped like a giant insect, crewed by an unlikely combination, including Xev, a former housewife who's now a sex slave. She's the focus of this episode, since her body needs recharging in a Lustacon. With lines like 'Ding, dong the bitch will be dead!', 'Woz' is open about its reworking of the MGM movie, even concluding with Xev saying that there's no place like home.

The Rugrats visited Lots O'Tots Land in their seventh-season episode entitled 'No Place Like Home' in 1999. In Barbara Hendon and Jill Gorey's script, Susie is in hospital having her tonsils removed and while under anaesthetic, she dreams of her friends as she tries to find the Magic Lizard who lives in a castle at the other end of the playground while wearing pink bunny slippers. On Hopscotch Road, she encounters a Scarecrow with straw in his nappy, Tin Woodsmen (twins inside a garbage can), and a Cowardly Lion before finally waking up.

The twenty-first century was meant to start off with a major new reinvention of the Oz mythos on television, courtesy of *Batman* director Tim Burton. According to a contemporary report at website Ain't It Cool News, the pilot for *Lost in Oz* was set in modern times, starting at the Emerald City Gas & Oil gas station in Kansas. A group of disparate characters, including seventeen-year-old Kimber Denslow, described in the script as an 'anti-Dorothy', all end up there just before a tornado sends the gas-station owner's Winnebago, in which they're all hiding, into Oz. Although they are sent to find the Wizard, there's a snag: he's vanished, and no one knows either where he is, or indeed what he looks like. The pilot was written by Trey Callaway from a story by Callaway, Michael Katleman, Burton and Joel T. Smith and featured characters such as Scoodlers (updated Wheelers), described as 'two-sided and two-toned black & white' with 'round heads, skinny bodies, each one uglier than the rest'. Some preliminary footage may have been shot for this project in 2000, and a binder of visual-effects designs by Steve Johnson was auctioned by Elemental Auctions some years later.

Although the idea didn't progress with Burton involved, an alternate pilot, also entitled *Lost in Oz* was completed two years later. It was directed by Mick Garris, who had brought a number of Stephen King stories to the small screen, and starred Melissa George and Colin Egglesfield as two people from different times who find themselves stranded in Oz. In David Hayter's script, the land has changed since Dorothy's visit, and the two visitors are forced to try to rescue the captured Princess Ozma. Egglesfield's Caleb Jansen is a 1943 pilot, call sign 'Scarecrow', who doesn't realize it's now 2002; George's Alex Wilder (originally named Tina Vittori) has to make a decision that traps them both there. At times the pilot feels like a remake of the 1970s series *The Fantastic Journey* combined with elements of *Star Trek* and the Disney *Return to Oz* – the Munchkins have met a terrible fate, and darkness stalks the land. However, it would have been interesting to see a series featuring the revised version of the Patchwork Girl. There was a lot of interest in the project – the WB network gave it a pilot commitment in August 2001, but they failed to take up the option on a series.

The Simpsons creator Matt Groening's sci-fi series

Futurama tackled Oz in 'Anthology of Interest 2: Wizzin''. This smart parody of the MGM movie, by Jason Corbett and Scott Kirby, works both as a homage to the 1939 film and as an episode of the show (something that is occasionally overlooked when characters are shoehorned into the archetypes of *The Wizard of Oz*). Central character one-eyed alien Leela is knocked out and finds herself in Oz, killing the Man-Witch on her arrival. The Cute Witch of the North sends her to find the Professor in the Emerald Laboratory on Martin Luther King Boulevard (the council apparently renamed the Yellow Brick Road in 1975). Aided by human Fry (as the Scarecrow), robot Bender (the Tin Man), and Zoidberg as an incontinent 'other guy', she decides she wants to be a replacement Wicked Witch, but is doused with water from a leaking toilet. When she wakes, she says she was having a wonderful dream – *except* that the others were there.

That '70s Show made a point of emphasizing how much the characters didn't really fit the parts they were given in the dream sequence – one of the boys is imagined as the Scarecrow because he loves chasing birds (i.e. girls). It's only a small part of an episode that focuses on who's going to be Snow King and Queen at the prom, but assumes more import in Oz history, as it was the first time that Mila Kunis, who played Jackie on the show and later starred as Theodora in *Oz the Great and Powerful*, visited the magic land.

Episodes of the unusual soap opera *Passions* also sported an Oz theme, using situations from both the 1939 movie for a set of episodes in 2002, and *Wicked* in June 2007, the latter complete with two songs which composer/lyricist John Henry Kreitler quite rightly called 'a beautifully done tribute to the style and substance of *Wicked*, but done in our own way and completely original'. 'Perfectly Frightful' blends 'What is This Feeling?' and 'Popular' while 'Spellbinding' is a flip side of 'Defying Gravity' – either song would fit in the original stage show as Esmeralda and Tabitha recall their school days.

Five years earlier characters Julian and Timmy found themselves in the Rainbow Hotel, which was filled with Munchkins, as they tried to find a Wizard to help cure another character who had been magically cursed. With an evil scarecrow, a chainsaw-wielding Tin Man, and Julian and Timmy dressed as the Cowardly Lion and Dorothy, it was the usual *Passions* mix of soap opera complications and fantasy elements.

The Muppets reunited with the Wizard of Oz for their May 2005 TV spectacular, which was extended for its US DVD release later in the year. Jim Henson's creatures were now part of the Walt Disney organization, and Disney wanted to revive the franchise's fortunes. Debra Frank, Steve L. Hayes, Tom Martin and Adam F. Goldberg's script for *The Muppets' Wizard of Oz* was closer to L. Frank Baum's original novel, although suitably updated for the twenty-first century, than the MGM film. There was a musical element to the movie: composer Michael Giacchino worked with Jeannie Lurie, Adam Cohen, Debra Frank, and Steve Hayes on five new songs for the film.

Pop star Ashanti plays Dorothy Gale, who's living in a trailer park in Kansas with her uncle and aunt and wants to become a famous singer. She hears the Muppets are looking for a female singer, but on the way back from giving them a demo CD, she and her pet prawn Toto are caught in a tornado and find themselves in Oz. There the story unfolds as expected – all the Witches are played by Miss Piggy; Kermit is the Scarecrow; Gonzo is a Tin Thing; Fozzie Bear is the Cowardly Lion. The Wizard sends them to fetch the Witch's magic eye before Glinda sends Dorothy home, where she learns that Kermit has been looking for her to join the tour.

While not as much fun as some of the Muppets' other

mash-ups, there are plenty of enjoyable moments. Quentin Tarantino and Kelly Osbourne both make cameos in the extended version, although their involvement, and some of the sexual innuendo in the piece, did raise some eyebrows.

Medical comedy *Scrubs* celebrated its hundredth episode with 'My Way Home', which first aired on 24 January 2006. The 'sly, circuitous homage' won the prestigious Peabody Award, which honours excellence in radio and television, for 'fearlessly smashing traditional comic formulas, all the while respecting the deepest emotional and moral issues of its life-and-death setting'. The series followed a group of medical students as they became experienced doctors, and in this episode, J.D. simply wants to go home; Turk needs a heart – or, rather, needs a heart to be donated by the family of a coma patient; Elliot has been bluffing that she has more brains about her specialty than she believes she has; and nurse Carla believes she lacks the courage to be a good parent. Guest character names include Fleming (director Victor Fleming); Baum; Ray Bolger; and Burke (the actress who played Glinda). With direct quotes from the screenplay, and performances of some of the songs, this was the smart comedy firing on all cylinders.

US comedy *That's So Raven* also tried their hand at an Oz episode, with 'Soup to Nuts' in August 2006, during which central character Raven hallucinates about the showdown with the Wizard in the movie. The school principal, with whom she's had yet another falling out, is the Witch; however he refuses to die, and instead melts Raven's Dorothy.

The following January, *SpongeBob SquarePants* encountered some 'Hocus Pocus' when he tried to find a cure for Squidward, who SpongeBob believes he has turned into an ice-cream cone. SpongeBob and Patrick visit Mister Magic, who invented the Magical Magic Kit that SpongeBob used to cast the spell. Mister Magic appears as a giant floating hat, but Patrick discovers the fish behind the curtain – who then refuses to help. (Squidward really just caught a bus to get away from SpongeBob!)

A considerably more serious version, which acted both as an update and a sequel to *The Wizard of Oz*, was co-produced by Robert Halmi International Entertainment and the Sci-Fi (now Syfy) Channel in the US in 2007. *Tin Man* was a $20 million major production, running over three nights, starring Zoey Deschanel as D.G. (whose ancestor was one Dorothy Gale); Alan Cumming as Glitch (the Scarecrow equivalent); Neal McDonough as Wyatt Cain who is the titular Tin Man, the Oz nickname for a cop; and Raoul Trujillo as Raw, a part-man, part-lion telepath.

Sci-Fi president Dave Howe explained that 'We feel collectively these classics deserve to be re-imagined for a new generation', with Robert Halmi noting that the story is a 'bit darker' than Baum's original. 'To make a classic understood by young people today, you have to talk an entirely different language,' he explained. Nor was this going to be a remake of the MGM film. Director Nick Willing was clear that this 'wasn't *The Wizard of Oz* we all know and love; we couldn't possibly do that. It's like trying to improve Mona Lisa's smile.'

The show originally began as a series about a police officer in Oz but developed in a reworking of Baum's first story, with D.G. brought from Kansas to the Outer Zone (the O.Z.), and seeking the Emerald of the Eclipse that is also being sought by sorceress Azkadellia. Steven Long Mitchell and Craig Van Sickle's script plays with audience expectations throughout and, as *Entertainment Weekly* pointed out, their innovations tend to work better than their attempts to tie the story back to Baum's text. (Syfy's website accompanying the show still includes comparisons between the book and the series, as well as a short web-comic setting the scene.)

Tin Man was the channel's highest-rated series up to

that point, and the top-rated miniseries of 2007. It received multiple Emmy nominations, although only won one, for non-prosthetic make-up.

Various further comedic takes on *The Wizard of Oz* followed over the next few years. *Phineas and Ferb* met 'The Wizard of Odd' in the second season of their animated adventures in 2010. Seven new songs were written for the episode, which again didn't always follow the template of the MGM musical which it was using.

Comedy *The Suite Life on Deck* wandered into Oz for a brief dream sequence in the second instalment of the three-episode story 'Twister', which was broadcast in January 2011. When some of the main characters are trapped in a cellar during a tornado, Bailey finds herself imagining her friends as some of the Ozites to help her decide who she wants to be with. The sequence includes one of them complaining about being the Cowardly Lion – he wanted to be the Wookiee Chewbacca from the *Star Wars* films.

The episode 'Bro-gurt' from *Raising Hope* ended, according to the AV Club reviewer, with 'the strangest and most elaborately drawn-out tribute to *The Wizard Of Oz* that I've seen since *Wild At Heart*'. The series follows Jimmy Chance, who is bringing up the daughter he gained in a one-night stand with a serial killer, who has since been executed. In this episode, seen in November 2011, baby Hope reveals the truth behind a conman using a videoconferencing illusion, and tells characters that they have the various attributes they think they need – a brain, a heart, and courage.

'April Fools Blank' was an episode of the teen sitcom *VicTorious* (the odd spelling was used to indicate that it was centred on singer Tori Vega). The episode parodied a number of different shows, with the actors breaking the fourth wall, production assistants appearing in shot, and various hallucinatory devices. One such moment is called 'The Wizard of Wazz' which sees the characters dressed as the various roles, but which finishes in a very *Monty Python* style with a director calling one of the actors off to appear in another scene.

The Witches of Oz was designed as a miniseries, but then re-edited into a shorter feature film and released in 2012 as *Dorothy and the Witches of Oz*. The longer version has subsequently been issued on DVD and aired on the Syfy Channel. It's an updating of four of L. Frank Baum's novels: *The Wonderful Wizard of Oz, Ozma of Oz, The Road to Oz*, and *The Magic of Oz*. A grown-up Dorothy is a successful children's author who discovers that her stories are based on repressed childhood memories – and the Ozites have come to New York. With the help of her friends she has to stop the Wicked Witch, Princess Langwidere (who can change heads) and the Nome King from trying to take over Manhattan. The shortened version received considerably more praise than the miniseries, and there are places where the low budget doesn't allow director Leigh Scott to develop his ideas fully. However, it makes for an entertaining rethink of the Oz story, which unusually looks to more than just the standard tropes for its tale.

4

REIMAGININGS IN OTHER MEDIA

Reimaginings of the Oz stories haven't been confined to literary and screen stories. The Focus on the Family Christian group gave a quite severe twist to L. Frank Baum's story for their two-part audio tale *Adventures in Odyssey: The Great Wishy Woz*. This was first broadcast in October 2000, and subsequently released on CD.

It's midway between a reimagining of the MGM musical and a parody: the four songs especially composed by John Beebee definitely lean towards the latter: 'Follow the Big Fat Road' features those five words repeated plus the line 'That's the way that everyone goes'. And at the end Dotty says, 'So you think I should follow the big fat road?' However, according to the group's website there was a serious purpose: this was designed to illustrate the verse from St John's Gospel: 'I am the way and the truth and the life. No one comes to the Father except through me,' and in their catalogue *The Great Wishy Woz* is listed under 'the perils of humanism.'

In John Fornof's script Dotty and her dog Nono end up in Littleland, where they encounter Manny Kin, Metal Guy and Mystical Mountain Lion on their way to the Really, Really Green and Environmentally Correct City. The Great Wishy Woz believes he can help them by getting to realize they can achieve their goals through their own efforts. He sends them to collect four items – a book of philosophy; a Valentine's Day card; a candle from the Temple of Eternal Truth; and a compass – while the Wicked and Mean and Generally Not Very Nice Woman tries to stop them. In the end Dotty understands she has to take the Wee Skinny Road and trust a fisherman, Mr I Am, to get home: she can't get there through her own efforts.

Oz has been reinvented on stage too. The most famous of these are *The Wiz* (see p 178) and *Wicked* (see p 196); Geoff Ryman's *Was* has also been adapted into two separate productions, as noted on p 220.

Not long before *The Wiz* burst onto the stage, Willard Simms came up with a novel epilogue to the movie of *The Wizard of Oz*, entitled *The Wizard of Oz in the Wild West*. This 1973 play sees the characters from the film sent by a curse from the Wicked Witch back to Kansas in the 1880s. Trying to escape from local inhabitant Miss Grimshaw, who wants the slippers for herself, Dorothy and her friends end up in the Wild West. They meet Wild Bill Hickock, Buffalo Bill, Annie Oakley and Billy the Kid, and in the end, the Scarecrow, the Tin Man and the Lion elect to stay in the frontier town while Dorothy goes home. The actors are encouraged to involve the audience in the decision-making during the play.

Ruth Perry penned a short play, *Christmas in the Land of Oz*, which was first performed in 1977. The sixty-five-minute production is a direct sequel to Baum's novel, with

Dorothy desperate to find a way to relieve her uncle Henry's broken heart when everything is going wrong at the farm – she even considers going to Omaha to find the Wizard – so she gets Toto to find the silver slippers and heads back to Oz. It's a very Christmassy story (the Tin Woodman wants to have Christmas all the time; the Scarecrow can't get into the seasonal spirit), but respects Baum's characters.

A tribute to the MGM movie came from Fred Barton in 1983 in his one-man show *Miss Gulch Lives!* (later known as *Miss Gulch Returns!* following Margaret Hamilton's death). The idea behind it was that Miss Gulch was a genuine actress who played herself in the 1939 film but couldn't get much work subsequently. She's still bitter that her big song 'I'm a Bitch' was cut from the movie. Barton calls the show 'my musical comedy valentine to the romantically disenfranchised, who can find a new metaphorical spokesperson in Miss Gulch, the ultimate "spinster" (as they used to be known)'. One of the most unusual – and funniest – stage versions of Oz, this has continued to be performed for three decades and is well worth seeking out.

Eldridge Press published Michelle Wan Loon's short play *A Recall to Oz* in 1984, in which Dorothy returned to Oz as an old woman. Four years later Virginia Koste incorporated characters from Baum's work into her play *On the Road to Oz*, which is described as a 'jokey, jubilant journey through the American dream of Oz [which] recreates the cheerful, vaudeville-and-magic brand of fantasy with which Frank Baum charmed America's Great Plains from the Mississippi River to the Rockies'.

It had more serious intent than Joseph Robinette's *Dorothy Meets Alice, or The Wizard of Wonderland*, which came out the same year, in which characters from Baum's books meet Lewis Carroll's creations. Given the tagline 'Wiz you were hare' by Dramatic Publishing, it's a chaotic mix of the two mythologies that won't really please fans of either.

Ken Kesey's *Twister! A Musical Catastrophe for the*

Millennium's End (or *Twister: A Ritual Reality*) first appeared in 1994, and is a very twisted sequel to the MGM film, as one might expect from the creator of *One Flew Over the Cuckoo's Nest*. According to Kesey's own notes, his plan was to 'people it with a cast of archetypes ranging from the clearly obvious characters, like the Tinman and the Scarecrow, to the murky and mysterious, like Elvis and Frankenstein . . . scramble them all together in ever-bickering banter until they're all crazy at each other's throats, then snap them into sanity with a last-minute tear-jerker twist guaranteed to touch everybody's heart.' The play is as torturous as that description would suggest.

Uri Paster's *Hakosem!* (*Wizard!*) was rather more trad-itional: a Hebrew reworking of *The Wizard of Oz* with original songs (as well as 'Over the Rainbow'), it sees young Dorothy set off from the land of the Green People to find Great Wizard Sam in the City of Fire. Meeting the usual friends in unusual places – the scarecrow is the only one who doesn't head back to Scarecrowland when Dorothy frees his comrades; the metal man is attached to a wrecked car; and the lion is part of a circus act – she reaches the city and is sent to catch three witches. They use butterfly nets to trap them while they're stealing strawberry tarts, and are given gifts by the Wizard.

The 1994 show was a success, entering the *Guinness Book of Records* for most shows of a production in a given time frame. Paster updated it as *The Wizard 2000* for the mil-lennium, giving it a science-fiction spin, but this wasn't as well received. It was returned to its roots for a 2006 revival.

1997's *The Wizard of Clods* (subtitled 'A Big Wind Brings a Lot of Hot Air) was an updating and parody by R. Eugene Jackson transplanting the action into Emerald City High School. A group of oddball students find themselves in the middle of an odd quest when Dorothy suddenly arrives in their school. Various tropes from the story are reworked as the students and the staff try to outdo each other.

* * *

Many comic-book and graphic-novel creators have re-interpreted the land of Oz over the past few decades with varying degrees of success and acceptance from fans. Some – like Steve Ahlquist's *Oz Squad* comics or Alan Moore's *Lost Girls* – have been highly controversial either for their content or their treatment of the subject matter. Others have simply found new ways to tell stories about Baum's creations – Eric Shanower, currently working on the Marvel adaptations of the original stories, wrote five highly regarded additions to the saga. *The Enchanted Apples of Oz*, *The Secret Island of Oz*, *The Ice King of Oz*, and *The Forgotten Forest of Oz* were published between 1986 and 1988 by First Comics. Dark Horse printed *The Blue Witch of Oz* in 1992, and the entire collection has been reprinted by IDW Publishing in various formats, with assorted extras including alternate endings. Although the series fits within the Royal Histories continuity, Shanower's stories have consequences for the land, which qualify them in some eyes as a new take on the mythos.

One of the earliest complete reimaginings was *The Oz – Wonderland War*, a three-issue miniseries from DC Comics written by Joey Cavalieri and E. Nelson Bridwell that appeared between January and March 1986. Captain Carrot and His Amazing Zoo Crew (superhero animals) help a group of heroes from both Wonderland and Oz battle against the Nome King Ruggedo, who has kidnapped Ozma and others and threatens the future of both lands. The art by Carol Lay is worth finding: the Oz characters resemble John R. Neill's versions; Wonderland creations are in the John Tenniel style; while the Zoo Crew retain their own distinctive look.

Perhaps the most controversial of all the Oz-related spin-offs in any format was Alan Moore and Melinda Grebbie's *Lost Girls*, which began life as a strip in *Taboo* magazine in 1991, and was eventually published by Top

Cow in 2006. The three Lost Girls are Dorothy Gale, Alice Fairchild and Wendy Durling – the latter two from *Alice in Wonderland* and *Peter Pan* respectively. The three meet in a hotel in Austria on the eve of the First World War and exchange stories of their lives – but not the tales that we know from the works of Baum, Carroll or Barrie. Moore and Grebbie were quite open about the fact they were writing pornography, and all manner of sexual couplings are depicted graphically in the book. Moore's reinterpretation of the stories is well thought through, although it will not be to many people's tastes – for example, Dorothy's friends are three farmhands with whom she has different sorts of sexual experiences.

Oz Squad earned the distinction of being called 'the most repellent published work with the name Oz in the title I have ever seen' by Oz historian Steve Teller. The ten issues updated the concepts behind Oz so that an adult Dorothy, the Scarecrow, the Tin Woodman and the Cowardly Lion become part of 'Gale Force', whose mission is to protect Oz from various threats, starting with Tik-Tok who comes through to Earth from Oz and sets himself up as a crime lord. Time travel, Leonardo da Vinci, flying monkeys, the assassination of JFK, and Rebecca Eastwitch (aka the Wicked Witch of the East) are all encountered in what one reviewer called 'one part modern fairy tale, one part black comedy, one part psychological thriller'. It's not suitable for children – the first issue includes Tik-Tok throwing babies from a roof and 'Ozchwtiz', a counterpart to the Nazi concentration camp. The series started at Brave New World press in 1991 with creator Steve Ahlquist then setting up Patchwork Press to complete the run, after an unsuccessful dalliance with Millennium Publications for one issue. *Little Oz Squad* – a junior and child-friendly version – made brief appearances, and Ahlquist revived the Oz Squad in a novel, *March of the Tin Soldiers*, in 2010, fourteen years after the last comic-book adventure for the team.

Another equally dark vision of Oz ran concurrently with *Oz Squad*, with forty issues appearing from Caliber and Arrow presses between 1994 and 1999. The title changed from *Oz* to *Dark Oz* with the move between publishers, and then became *The Land of Oz* following the cataclysmic events of the final issue of *Dark Oz* (everything is quite literally wiped out, leaving Oz as a blank white space). Three contemporary teenagers and their dog are drawn from Earth to Oz by a magic book, to discover a world in danger. Dorothy has vanished; Ozma has been captured by Mombi and the Nome King. The Scarecrow, Tin Man and the Lion are now evil – prequel stories explain how this happened – and a group of freedom fighters, including Jack Pumpkinhead and Tik-Tok, are trying to set things right. The twenty issues of *Oz*, six specials, and the five instalments of *Dark Oz* dealt with this battle; the nine issues of *The Land of Oz* tried to reboot the story nearer to L. Frank Baum's original vision.

The rights to *Dark Oz* were optioned in 2008 with a view to creating a trilogy of movies. In what seems an odd way to garner interest, a novelization of the script by Aaron Deneberg appeared in 2009 entitled *Dark Oz: Book One: Of Courage And Witchcraft*. Credited as an adaptation of the comic book, it reworks the plot so it's a modern-day adult Dorothy who comes back to Oz, rather than the new characters from the comic. Despite some inaccurate listings online, the movie has yet to materialize.

Four issues of a black and white comic entitled *Peter Pan and the Warlords of Oz* appeared in 1998, written and drawn by Rob Hand. Like many before him, Hand brought together characters from the Peter Pan, Alice and Oz stories, and added Norse mythology, Nazi scientist Josef Mengele, the Scooby gang and even Jesus Christ into the mix. Barrie's Tick-Tock the crocodile and Baum's Tik-Tok the mechanical man both feature but when a

Lovecraftian monster, the servant of Yogsoggoth, is summoned, it becomes totally incoherent.

Although many people believe that Alan Moore's *The
League of Extraordinary Gentlemen* is unusual in combining characters from different parts of literature together,
Bill Willingham's *Fables* comic book for DC's adult
imprint Vertigo has been doing this consistently since
2002. The premise is that the characters have been forced
from their worlds, and have ended up living in Fabletown,
in our New York. Bufkin, a winged monkey from Oz, is
a regular character, and many of Baum's creations have
also appeared. Dorothy is an assassin for hire in the spin-
off book *Cinderella: Fables are Forever*; Toto is eaten by
a tiger in one of the Jack of Fables stories; Ozma seems
to have learned rather more about diplomacy and cunning
than Baum permitted her. In the 2012 storylines, Bufkin
led a revolution in Oz, partly, Willingham admitted, so
that he could rework elements of the Oz story to fit in with
his ongoing saga.

An Eastern vision of Oz can be found in *Toto! The Wonderful Adventure*, a parody of *The Wizard of Oz*, which
appeared between 2003–2005 in Japan, and from 2008–
2009 in an English edition. Kakashi (the Japanese for Scarecrow) is the hero of the story who is off on an adventure
along with a little dog he adopts and names Toto. On their
way they meet Dorothy, a young girl heading for a place
called Emerald. Although the elements may be similar,
author and artist Yuko Osada juggles the various ideas and
provides what reviewer Deb Aoki called 'cleverly pay[ing]
tribute to the spirit of the Oz adventures without allowing
readers the luxury of predicting what comes next.'

An equally unusual comic book began in 2004, written
by Mark Masterson with digital art by Greg Mannino.
The artist, also credited as director and producer, described the end result as 'a motion picture put to paper',
since he was using real actors to play the parts, including

sixteen-year-old Catie Fisher as the heroine. *Dorothy* is
an updating of the story with the characters reworked for
a modern audience. 'I always thought the Dorothy from
the books and from the movie wasn't troubled enough,'
Mannino said in an interview to coincide with the launch.
'I wanted to add some real resentment and hate for this
world. We all know that being a teenager in this world
isn't easy and generates a boatload of disturbed feelings.
These feelings often lead to bad decisions, sex, drugs and
God knows what. I wanted to portray that in Dorothy and
have her really represent teenagers of today.' Mannino had
grand plans for a twenty-issue series, appearing quarterly,
which would totally reinvent the story; in the end, only
seven issues were produced.

A three-issue black and white miniseries was created
by Scott Oliver and Corey Bechelli. *No Place Like Home*
tells the tale of the Scarecrow's descent into madness in the
period after the events of *The Wizard of Oz* – in a neat
touch, he speaks in rhyme – and the attempts of his friends
Glinda, the Tin Man and the Lion to save him.

This 2004 series shouldn't be confused with Angelo
Tirotto and Richard Jordan's similarly titled comic from
Image, which began in February 2012. This is a contemporary take on the story (whose website is cheekily named
noonemournsthewicked.com) with Dorothy returning to
Emeraldsville after the death of her parents. The Oz connection becomes increasingly apparent as the tale unfolds.

Dorothy Gale: Journey to Oz was a five-issue miniseries by Shane Kirshenblatt that began in 2005, although to
date only three issues have appeared. Covers for the final
two can be seen on Freefall Comics' website, although this
has not been updated since 2006. It's another contemporary reworking, with Dorothy, her friend Thomas (aka
Toto) and a peddler named Edward crossing to Oz and
discovering that Dorothy is the double of the world's ruler,
Ozma. The Tin Man and the Scarecrow make appearances

in altered forms, and much of the plot is centred around a stolen map of Oz.

OzF5 features another 'Gale Force' but this is not connected to the Oz Squad continuity. 'Dorothy's back in Oz and this time she's brought a water gun,' runs the tagline. 'Rocket-packed Flying Monkeys prowl the skies, Winkie Warmachines roam the lands, and two Witches join in unholy alliance to subjugate the people.' The first issue arrived in 2005 and reworked the story as a blockbuster action/adventure tale. A second issue was threatened but has yet to arrive.

The Oz/Wonderland Chronicles, which also started in 2005, is set in modern-day Chicago with both Alice and Dorothy as students who realize that their childhood fantasies of Wonderland and Oz were actually real. Their room-mates include Susan (Pevensie – the girl left behind when her siblings entered Narnia in C.S. Lewis' tales), and Dee (Wendy Darling from *Peter Pan*), as they battle their enemies Jabberwocky, the Wicked Witch and the Nome King. A sequel series *Jack and Cat* featured Jack Pumpkinhead and the Cheshire Cat's adventures on the road together, while a prequel, *Prelude to Evil*, was released in trade paperback in spring 2013.

A Korean manhwa, *Dorothy of Oz*, follows the adventures of a schoolgirl from Seoul. When her little dog Toto steals her 'lucky' glove and heads into an alleyway, Mara Shin follows and finds herself on a yellow brick road in Oz. There she meets Serruliah, a scientist referred to as the Witch of the East, who believes Mara is the legendary saviour known as Dorothy who can find the fabled Yellow Brick Road (no one else can see it). Everyone she meets calls her Dorothy – to her intense annoyance – and she becomes embroiled in local politics as the Witches, and their clones, try to capture her. Four volumes have so far been translated into English, introducing new variants of the Scarecrow, the Tin Man, and the Lion; a fifth has been published in Korea but no English translation has yet been scheduled.

A short foray into Oz faced the World's Mightiest Heroes in the Marvel spin-off comic *Avengers Fairy Tales*. In C.B. Cebulski's script for issue 4, published in December 2008, with art by Ricardio Tercio, Jennifer Walters (aka the She-Hulk) is the Dorothy stand-in, with the Mighty Thor as the Scarecrow, Iron Man as the Tin Man, and Captain America as the Cowardly Lion. Magneto was the Wizard, and the Scarlet Witch played the Wicked Witch of the West.

Another offbeat take on the saga can be found in Tom Hutchison's *Legend of Oz: The Wicked West* series, which began as a six-part miniseries with a two-part spin-off *The Scarecrow*, but has become an ongoing story. The opening issue of this Western-inspired version throws the reader straight into the tale: Dorothy Gale has been searching for the Emerald City for three years. The Yellow Brick Road has been torn apart, so it's hard to follow. Her horse Toto and her ruby-handled revolvers are her only allies. Hutchison draws inspiration from all of Baum's Oz stories, and provides some very interesting takes on the characters.

Between Vertigo's *Fables* and its multiple spin-offs, Eric Shanower's ongoing adaptations of the Baum stories for Marvel, and Tom Hutchison's *The Wicked West*, Oz continues to be well represented on comic racks each month.

AFTERWORD

'True wizardry, whether in books or on the screen, is age-less. In the magical land of Oz, nothing changes.' That was *Time* magazine's opinion in 1949 when reviewing the re-issue of *The Wizard of Oz*. And certainly that is true for the many millions of people who have been delighted by the adventures of Dorothy and her friends on the Yellow Brick Road as encapsulated in that 1939 film.

But Oz does change. Writer L. Frank Baum and artists William Wallace Denslow, who shared the copyright, so could both justly claim to be Oz's creators, had vastly dif-fering ideas about the direction in which the stories should go. Ruth Plumly Thompson and her successors as official Royal Historians of Oz introduced concepts that were alien to the ideas that Baum wrote. Come to that, the Oz that Judy Garland skipped through wasn't precisely the same one that children had read about for four decades.

In his introduction to *The Wonderful Wizard of Oz*, Baum wrote, 'Folklore, legends, myths and fairy tales have followed childhood through the ages, for every healthy youngster has a wholesome and instinctive love for stories fantastic, marvellous and manifestly unreal.' Oz has now become an inextricable part of that tapestry, and each new story – whether designed to fit with what came before or its own retelling – is just that bit richer. Long may it continue.

ACKNOWLEDGEMENTS

As ever, I am very grateful to various people for their assistance in the research and writing of this guide to Oz.

Brian J. Robb, for once again looking over the manuscript and pointing out where things could be clearer.

Duncan Proudfoot and Becca Allen at Constable & Robinson for commissioning this second book in what is becoming a fantasy trilogy for 2013/2014 – we've travelled through Narnia and Oz . . . Next stop, the Dark Tower.

Gabriella Nemeth, my copy editor, for ensuring a few idiocies avoid seeing print; any that remain are strictly my own.

Paula M. Block, Kate Doyle at AudioGO, Christopher Golden, Rich Handley, Andy Mangels and Lance Parkin for pointing me in the right direction on certain aspects of the topic (and particularly thanks, Andy, for the help with the *Variety* Archives, an incredibly useful source of information about the world of Hollywood in the twentieth century); Adam Walker for sterling translation of the German station announcements; and to Patricia Hyde and Adina Mihaela Roman for their time helping with the fine detail.

Iain Coupar, Lee Harris, Amanda Rutter, Emlyn Rees, Caitlin Fultz, Jeannine Dillon, Clare Hey and Emma Capron for keeping the wheels of commerce going.

Carol Matthews and Alan Smith for helping me to fulfil other commitments, as well as the choir of ASCAT parish and All the Right Notes singers for providing the musical outlets.

The staff at the Hassocks branch of the West Sussex public library for their help tracking down items that I needed and for providing such a good, efficient service. Support your public library – or it won't be there next time you need it.

All those anonymous people who have posted snippets of Oz-related material to YouTube – it's so much easier to cut through the inaccurate descriptions that populate the internet when you can just watch the item in question!

Fred Barton for providing some laughs at just the right time during the writing of this book: check out the album of *Miss Gulch Returns!* on iTunes.

My daughter Sophie and my partner Barbara for their love, support, and allowing me the time to work on this, and my terriers Rani and Rodo for not being too demanding about walks and playtime.

BIBLIOGRAPHY

Rogers, Katharine M.: *L. Frank Baum, Creator of Oz* (Da Capo Press, 2002)

Schwartz, Evan I.: *Finding Oz* (Houghton Miflin Harcourt, 2009)

Baum, Frank Joselyn and Russell P. MacFall: *To Please a Child: A Biography of L. Frank Baum* (Reilly & Lee, 1961) [N.B. Many other contemporary sources contradict this.]

Greene, David L. and Dick Martin, *The Oz Scrapbook* (Random House, 1977)

Daniel P. Mannix, 'To Ruth With Love,' *Baum Bugle* (Autumn 1976)

Dictionary of Literary Biography, volume 22

Billboard 14 Dec 1996: 'Shelf Talk'

Scheimer, Lou with Andy Mangels: *Creating the Filmation Generation* (TwoMorrows Publishing, 2012)

http://www.animenewsnetwork.com/old-school/2003-06-17

Rushdie, Salman: 'Out of Kansas' in *Step Across This Line* (Jonathan Cape, 2002)

McClelland, Doug: *Down the Yellow Brick Road* (Bonanza Books, 1989)

Lahr, John: *Notes on a Cowardly Lion* (Alfred A. Knopf, 1969)

Jablonski, Edward: *Harold Arlen: Happy with the Blues* (Doubleday, 1972)

LeRoy, Mervyn and Dick Kleiner: *Take One* (Hawthorn, 1974)

Raabe, Meinhardt and Daniel Kinske: *Memories of a Munchkin: An Illustrated Walk Down the Yellow Brick Road* (Back Stage Books, 2005)

Scarfone, Jay and William Stillman: *Wizardry of Oz, The: The Artistry And Magic of The 1939 MGM Classic — Revised and Expanded* (Applause Books, 2004)

Fricke, John *The Wizard of Oz: The Official 50th Anniversary Pictorial History* (Warner Books, 1989)

Harmetz, Aljean: *The Making of The Wizard of Oz* (Hyperion, 2004)

New York Times, 18 August 1939: 'Wizard of Oz, Produced by the Wizards of Hollywood, Works Its Magic on the Capitol's Screen'

Variety, 24 August 1981: 'Two "Oz" scribes hired by Disney'

Variety, 26 August 1981: 'Disney preps an Oz screenplay but it's not sequel to Wizard of—'

Variety, 16 July 1982: 'Four New Film Projects For Disney Prods.; More In Hopper, Says Wilhite'

Variety, 28 November 1983: 'Kurtz, Disney Attempting to Solve "Oz" Financing'

Variety, 21 December 1983: 'Disney To Roll "Oz;" Budget Flap's Over'

Calgary Herald, 31 October 1964: 'Films from Canada; New Field Opened'

Los Angeles Times, 7 September 1990: 'A Cartoon "Oz" for Saturday TV: Television: Children's series will be based on the MGM movie. Story lines will be original.'

Sherman, Fraser A.: *The Wizard of Oz Catalog: L. Frank Baum's Novel, Its Sequels and Their Adaptations for Stage, Television, Movies, Radio, Music Videos, Comic Books, Commercials and More* (McFarland, 2005)

Swartz, Mark Evan: *Oz before the Rainbow: L. Frank Baum's The Wonderful Wizard of Oz on Stage and Screen to 1939* (Johns Hopkins University Press, 2002)

Nashua Telegraph, 10 July 1976: 'The Hudson Brothers Are Both Radio And TV Talent'

New York Times, 4 September 1987: 'Charlie Smalls Is Dead; Composer of "The Wiz" '

Variety, 11 October 1978: 'Does "Wiz" have needed B.O. wizardry?'

Variety, 20 December 1978: 'Just how much did "Wiz" cost?'

New York Times, 7 February 1993: 'Dorothy and Wiz Hip-Hop Into the 90's'

The Grio, 28 February 2013: 'Parent upset over high school's all-white cast of "The Wiz" '

Der Taggespiegel, 14 March 2011: 'Das Zauberquartett'

De Giere, Carol: *Defying Gravity: The Creative Career of Stephen Schwartz, from 'Godspell' to 'Wicked'* (Applause Theatre Book Publishers, 2008)

Cote, David: *Wicked: The Grimmerie* (Hyperion, 2005)

Brown, William F. and Charlie Smalls: *The Wiz* (Samuel French, revised & rewritten 1979)

Variety, 14 January 1925: Full page ad for *The Wizard of Oz*

Ellensburg Daily Record, 4 November 1934: 'Wizard of Oz here Thursday'

Austin Chronicle, 21 April 2000: 'Life Again in Oz: Playwright Suzan Zeder Revisits Oz and Finds Part of Herself'

New York Times, 27 July 2003: 'Toto, There's No Place Like Off Off Broadway'

Billboard, 19 August 1967, 'Golden Names London Distrib'

Mancunian Matters, 24 May 2010: 'The Wizard Of Oz – Made In Manchester!'

Newsarama, 28 September 2010: 'Dorothy Returns w/ New Friends For All-Ages OZMA OF OZ'

Theatre of Ideas, 18 September 2008: 'An interview with Eric Shanower'

iVillage 2008: 'An Audience with Gregory Maguire'

New York Times, 24 October 1995: 'BOOKS OF THE TIMES; Let's Get This Straight: Glinda Was the Bad One?'

Tampa Bay Times, 15 January 2006: ' "Wicked" good fortune'

Kelleter F. 'Remakes and Popular Seriality' in *Film Remakes, Adaptations and Fan Productions: Remake/Remodel* (ed. Loock, K. and Constantine Verevis, Palgrave Macmillan 2012)

Hollywood Reporter, 7 March 2013: 'Heir of "Oz": L. Frank Baum's Great-Grandson Weighs in on Disney's 3D Blockbuster, Reveals Family Secrets'

Christopher Golden, interview with the author, 30 April 2013

Vector #218, July/August 2001: 'A Fireside Chat: Geoff Ryman' (reprinted at http://tamaranth.blogspot.co.uk/2011/10/interview-geoff-ryman-march-2001.html – the reference to original appearance in issue #217 is incorrect)

Attention Deficit Delirium, 28 October 2009: 'Journeying Back To Munchkinland'

Ain't it Cool News, 1 November 1999: 'Mysterio gives us a look at Tim Burton's LOST IN OZ'

Comic Fanatic, 25 August 2004: 'A Dialogue With Dorothy's Greg Mannino!'

INDEX